Knowledge, Politics and Policymaking in Indonesia

Arnaldo Pellini • Budiati Prasetiamartati
Kharisma Priyo Nugroho • Elisabeth Jackson
Fred Carden
Editors

Knowledge, Politics and Policymaking in Indonesia

 Springer

Editors
Arnaldo Pellini
Overseas Development Institute
London, UK

Kharisma Priyo Nugroho
Winrock International
Bangkok, Thailand

Fred Carden
Using Evidence Inc.
Ottawa, ON, Canada

Budiati Prasetiamartati
Knowledge Sector Initiative
Jakarta, Indonesia

Elisabeth Jackson
Knowledge Sector Initiative
Jakarta, Indonesia

ISBN 978-981-13-0166-7   ISBN 978-981-13-0167-4   (eBook)
https://doi.org/10.1007/978-981-13-0167-4

Library of Congress Control Number: 2018943295

Printed on acid-free paper

This Springer imprint is published by the registered company Springer Nature Singapore Pte Ltd.
The registered company address is: 152 Beach Road, #21-01/04 Gateway East, Singapore 189721, Singapore

Preface

Knowledge is not power until it is turned into action (Aristotle)

This book has been triggered by a couple of circumstances. The first is the unique opportunity the editors and contributors have had to be involved directly and indirectly in the implementation of the first phase of Australia-Indonesia Partnership for Pro-Poor Policy: The Knowledge Sector Initiative between 2013 and 2017. This programme is now in its second phase and seeks to improve the lives of the Indonesian people through better quality public policies that make better use of research, analysis and evidence. The programme is being led by a consortium of RTI International, the Australian National University, the Nossal Institute for Global Health at the University of Melbourne, and the Overseas Development Institute in the United Kingdom.

The uniqueness of the programme is that it is testing the assumption that in order to strengthen evidence-informed policymaking systems and processes in a country it is necessary to work in an integrated way on the capabilities to produce good quality and timely evidence, the capabilities to demand and make use of the evidence (mainly) within government, the capability to produce synthesis of research results and reach policymakers, and last but not least the capability of a system of rules and regulations that encourage the production, demand and use of evidence.

This book is not about the Knowledge Sector Initiative programme, it is about the Indonesian knowledge sector. The programme has provided a unique view point from which to observe, study and interact with the actors who are contributing to the development of Indonesian knowledge sector to try to better understand where it comes from, where it stands now and (to some extent) where it is going.

As editors of this book we recognise that the main influencing factor in policymaking is politics, but we also believe that policy decisions can greatly benefit from access to and use of different types of evidence. This is particularly important when countries reach a middle-income status and the complexity of policymaking continues to increase.

Being involved in a programme and being able to study and learn from the Indonesian knowledge sector about the complexity of evidence-informed policy-making make us think that we ought to capture that learning by writing this book.

The second circumstance that triggered this book was a conversation that one of the editors had in 2015 with policy researchers and experts on Indonesian politics. As part of its implementation, the Knowledge Sector Initiative has produced a number of working papers reflecting on initiatives and programmes that have helped to strengthen elements of the knowledge sector in other countries. Writing about those experiences was a way to generate ideas and suggestions about what could be tested (not copied) in the Indonesian knowledge sector. Those working paper were informative but did left unanswered the question about what is distinctly Indonesian in the principles, processes and tools that define evidence-informed policymaking in Indonesia.

These two circumstances put together led to the production of this book. It is our way of sharing the knowledge and learning we have acquired in and on the Indonesian knowledge sector with an international audience of researchers, practitioners and civil servants interested in the way the Indonesian knowledge sector is evolving.

The intended audience of this book is policy researchers interested in policymaking processes and the use of research-based evidence in Indonesia; practitioners involved in problem-driven and adaptive development programmes; policymakers and policy analysts interested in exploring evidence-informed policymaking processes in Indonesia; policy researchers in Indonesian think tanks, professors, researchers and students in Indonesian and international universities; and advisors and staff of multilateral and bilateral development agencies.

The book is structured in three parts. The three parts structure the book along elements of the knowledge sector as it relates to public policy: *producing knowledge for policy*; *knowledge and the politics of policymaking*; and *the enabling environment for evidence-informed policymaking*. In addition, a general introductory chapter (Chap. 1) provides the background on the topic of the book, and a concluding chapter (Chap. 9) sums up the main findings of the book. Depending on the reader's needs it is possible to read the book cover to cover, or pick any part or chapter and read it on its own.

We would like to convey our thanks and appreciation to all the authors who contributed to this book. Our special thanks to Ms. Robin Bush, Ms. Derval Usher, Mr. Andrew Thornley, Mr. Nana Widiestu, Ms. Zuhaira and Mr. Hizbullah Arief. We thank the Knowledge Sector Initiative partners and team for sharing their experiences in contributing to the development of the Indonesian knowledge sector. We also thank Bappenas (Ministry for National Development Planning/National Development Planning Agency), and the Australian Department of Foreign Affairs and Trade, the shareholders of the Knowledge Sector Initiative, and RTI International, for their support. In addition, we thank Ms. Ameena Jaafar of Springer Singapore for her kind support, all the reviewers, Ms. Alison Raphael for her assistance in copy editing the book and Mr. Agus Wiyono for the graphic design.

As usual, the views, findings and conclusions expressed in this book are those of the editors and authors alone and do not necessarily reflect the views of the organizations supporting this work.

Tampere, Finland	Arnaldo Pellini
Jakarta, Indonesia	Budiati Prasetiamartati
Bangkok, Thailand	Kharisma Priyo Nugroho
Jakarta, Indonesia	Elisabeth Jackson
Ottawa, Canada	Fred Carden

Contents

About the Editors and Contributors

About the Editors

Arnaldo Pellini is a Senior Research Fellow of the Research and Policy in Development team at the Overseas Development Institute in London. His background is in economic development with a specialisation in education policy reforms in Southeast Asia. He holds a Ph.D. in Education and Development from the University of Tampere (Finland), and has been working for about 15 years on governance reforms and on systems and processes to support the production, demand and use of evidence to inform policy decisions in Cambodia, Vietnam, the Philippines, Thailand, and Indonesia. Arnaldo has been part of the team implementing the Australia-Indonesia Partnership for Pro-Poor Policy: The Knowledge Sector Initiative from 2013 to 2017 when he led the learning and research work of the programme. He has published extensively on the use of evidence in policymaking with the Overseas Development Institute, in addition to academic articles, book chapters, blog posts and opinion pieces. His 2007 Ph.D. thesis (*Decentralisation Policy in Cambodia: Exploring Community Participation in the Education Sector*) was published as a monograph by Tampere University Press. He is also the editor of the 2012 publication *Engaging for the Environment: The Contribution of Social Capital to Community-Based Natural Resource Management in Cambodia*, published by the Learning Institute. He is an Associate Editor with the journal Evidence & Policy.

Budiati Prasetiamartati is a Programme Lead at the Australia-Indonesia Partnership for Pro-Poor Policy: The Knowledge Sector Initiative. She manages the programme's work on the enabling environment, which, through multi-stakeholder working groups, focuses on strengthening evidence-informed policymaking through legislative and regulatory reforms in the Indonesian knowledge sector. Before joining the Knowledge Sector Initiative, she managed programmes in decentralisation and local governance for the United Nations Development Programme in Indonesia. She has worked for over 12 years on governance and governance reform, environmental policy reforms, development planning and programme management with multilateral and bilateral organisations, NGOs, governments and research institutions. She has an undergraduate degree in urban and regional planning from Bandung Institute of Technology, a Master's in Public Policy and Administration from the Institute of Social Studies in the Netherlands and a Ph.D. in Coastal and Marine Resources Management from Bogor Agricultural University.

Kharisma Priyo Nugroho was the Programme Lead at the Australia-Indonesia Partnership for Pro-Poor Policy: The Knowledge Sector Initiative from 2015 to 2017 when he managed the knowledge production and intermediary component, working with 16 key Indonesian policy research institutes to address the problems constraining effective knowledge-to-policy processes. He is now a Research Associate at the Indonesian Alliance for Policy Research. His professional background includes accounting and sociology, with a specialisation in research and evaluation of development programmes in Indonesia in the areas of health sector policy reform, public sector reform and disaster risk reduction. He holds a Ph.D. in Sociology from the University of Indonesia and is a Research Fellow at the Institute of Health Policy and Management at Erasmus University in the Netherlands. In 2016, he co-authored an article on the political economy of Indonesia's universal health coverage programme ("Indonesia's Road to Universal Health Coverage: A Political Journey"), published in the Oxford journal *Health Policy and Planning*. **Through his research and advisory work, Kharisma has promoted and advocated for fair-minded international research collaborations between international and subnational research institutes in Indonesia.**

Elisabeth Jackson is a Programme Lead at the Australia-Indonesia Partnership for Pro-Poor Policy: The Knowledge Sector Initiative. She has lived and worked for over 7 years in Jakarta in various projects and programmes with international NGOs and bilateral donors managing development programmes in education, democratic governance and civil society capacity building. Most recently, she was responsible for overseeing the Knowledge Sector Initiative for the Australian Department of Foreign Affairs and Trade. She has worked in higher education and development for over 12 years and has conducted research and published in academic journals on a range of issues, including state accountability, student politics, civic education and democracy, Islamic education, private schooling, civil society development and approaches to policy reform in Indonesia. She has a Master's degree in Development Studies and a Ph.D. in Southeast Asian Studies, both from the Australian National University.

Fred Carden holds a Ph.D. from the Université de Montréal. He is the Principal at Using Evidence Inc., a research and evaluation consultancy firm that focuses on improving the use of evidence in policymaking. From 2013 to 2016 he was based in Jakarta with the Australia-Indonesia Partnership for Pro-Poor Policy: The Knowledge Sector Initiative. Prior to that, he was director of evaluation at the International Development Research Centre in Canada, where a primary focus of his work was the influence of research on public policy. Among other publications he is the author of *Knowledge to Policy: Making the Most of Development Research* (Sage, 2009) and co-author of *Outcome Mapping: Building Learning and Reflection into Development Programs* (IDRC, 2001) and *Organizational Assessment: A Framework for Improving Performance* (IDB & IDRC, 2002), and *Local Knowledge Matters: Power, Context and Policy Making in Indonesia* (Policy Press, 2018). He serves on the Board of the global Partnership for Economic Policy network.

About the Contributors

Tanty Nurhayati Djafar is a Programme Officer at the Australia-Indonesia Partnership for Pro-Poor Policy: The Knowledge Sector Initiative, focusing on capacity building for leading Indonesian think tanks and universities. Her passion is to advance social issues, especially expanding access to health services and early childhood education for people in developing countries. She previously worked in social service administrative programmes in New York City. Tanty earned her M.Sc. in Social Enterprise Administration from the School of Social Work at Columbia University and a Bachelor of Arts in Psychology at Baruch College of the City University of New York. In 2017 she co-authored a Knowledge Sector Initiative working paper entitled, "Is Measuring Policy Influence Like Measuring Thin Air?".

Iskhak Fatonie is a Senior Programme Officer at the Australia-Indonesia Partnership for Pro-Poor Policy: The Knowledge Sector Initiative. He oversees the programmes's multi-stakeholder working group on bureaucracy and public sector reform (involving policymakers, universities, CSOs, NGOs and local governments). Over the past 8 years he has worked with national and subnational Indonesian government bodies to provide technical support in the area of public administration. He previously worked with the United Nations Development Programme in Indonesia, managing public sector reform, including local governance, regional competitiveness, public service delivery and regulatory frameworks governing decentralisation. He obtained his Ph.D. in Political Science, majoring in public administration, from the University of Vienna. His research interests include public policy, bureaucracy reform, government studies, peace studies and political science.

George Hodge manages Pulse Lab Jakarta's Trade and Economic Competitiveness portfolio, which includes an eclectic mix of projects to develop better evidence for development policy. Over the past 14 years he has worked with governments in the Balkans, the Arab world and Southeast Asia to improve policy and programme design and delivery. George holds a Bachelor's degree in Natural Sciences from the University of Durham, and a Master's degree in Public Policy and Management from the School of Oriental and African Studies of the University of London.

Petrarca Chawaro Karetji joined the Australia-Indonesia Partnership for Pro-Poor Policy: The Knowledge Sector Initiative in August 2016 as the Team Leader. His experience includes bureaucratic reforms, decentralisation, governance and partnership development among organisations, NGOs, government and research institutions. As the senior advisor for development partnerships for the Department of Foreign Affairs and Trade at Jakarta's Australian Embassy, he was responsible for providing advice to senior management and programme teams, ensuring effective partnerships with government, civil society and private sector stakeholders, as well as identifying high-level relationships with the Government of Indonesia. Working for AusAID between 2010 and 2015, he managed a portfolio of over US$500 million in grant funds covering rural development, decentralisation, bureaucratic reform, community development, social protection and women's leadership. Prior to AusAID, Petrarca worked in the World Bank from 2004 to 2008 to establish a multi-donor support office for Eastern Indonesia which has successfully evolved as an independent institution (BaKTI – The Eastern Indonesia Knowledge Exchange). Before the World Bank he directed an international subsidiary delivering a range of private sector, multilateral, bilateral and Government of Indonesia projects (1995–2004). Petrarca's expertise includes programme management, developing and building interpersonal and organisational networks, knowledge exchange, project management troubleshooting, institutional analysis, project design and management. He has a first degree in education and a Master's in Development Studies from Satya Wacana Christian University.

Irene Astuti Kuntjoro was a Programme Officer at the Australia-Indonesia Partnership for Pro-Poor Policy: The Knowledge Sector Initiative between 2015 and 2017 where she worked closely with 16 Indonesian policy research institutes to improve their capacity in the areas of organisational development, knowledge production and communication. Her professional experience over the past 15 years evolved around policy analysis, programme management, organisational development, development issues, political security affairs and business intelligence for development organisations, the private sector and think tanks in Indonesia and abroad. Her first degree was in International Relations from the University of Indonesia. She obtained her Master's in International Security and Terrorism from the University of Nottingham in the United Kingdom under a British Council Chevening and Open Society Foundation scholarship.

Yanuar Nugroho is an academic, researcher and senior policymaker in the field of development. He was appointed in 2015 as deputy chief of staff at the Executive Office of the President, Indonesia, and is currently responsible for analysis and oversight of strategic issues on social, cultural and ecological affairs, after previously managing national priority programmes. Since 2004 he has been a research fellow at the Manchester Institute of Innovation Research, University of Manchester, in the United Kingdom, and a core member of the Centre for Development Informatics. In 2007 he earned a Ph.D. in Innovations and Social Change. Yanuar held the Hallsworth Fellowship in Political Economy of Innovations and Social Change (2010–2012). He trained as an industrial engineer at the Institute of Technology in Bandung, Indonesia, and received a British Council Chevening Award to obtain his M.Sc. in Information Systems Engineering at the University of

Manchester's Institute of Science and Technology (2000–2001). Prior to his doctoral study, Yanuar was active in Indonesian NGOs and was a visiting lecturer at some Indonesian universities. From 2012 to 2014, he was seconded from Manchester to become a special advisor to the President's Delivery Unit for Development Monitoring and Oversight. His academic publications address issues of innovation, development, sustainability and knowledge dynamics. He also contributes to major Indonesian newspapers.

Farini Pane was a Programme Manager at the Australia-Indonesia Partnership for Pro-Poor Policy: The Knowledge Sector Initiative between 2015 and 2017. Her work focused on capacity building for leading think tanks and universities in Indonesia. She previously worked in the electoral reform and democratic governance programme at United Nations Development Programme's Partnership for Governance Reform in Indonesia and several USAID-funded projects in Indonesia. Farini earned her Master of Arts in Women's Studies from Flinders University in South Australia and a Bachelor degree in English Literature at Padjadjaran University, Bandung, Indonesia. Her professional experience over the past 17 years includes civil society strengthening, gender mainstreaming, women's empowerment, project management and policy advocacy.

Agus Pramusinto is a Professor at the Universitas Gadjah Mada, Yogyakarta, Indonesia, currently serving as Head of Department at its Faculty of Social and Political Science, and previously as director of the School of Public Administration. His research interests include public policy, decentralisation and policymaking processes. Among his publications are *Bureaucracy Reform, Leadership, and Public Services* **and** *Evaluation in Public Policy*. **Agus holds a Ph.D. in Policy and Governance from Asia Pacific School of Economics and Government of the Australian National University and obtained his Master's degree in Development Administration from the same university.**

Endah Bayu Purnawati was a Programme Officer at the Australia-Indonesia Partnership for Pro-Poor Policy: The Knowledge Sector Initiative between 2013 and 2017. Since 2015 her portfolio has included managing relationships with government counterparts and some leading civil society organisations, as part of the programme's "knowledge community on village development issues". Prior to joining the Knowledge Sector Initiative, she worked on development issues involving national and subnational governments, universities and civil society organisations for the United Nations Development Programme and the Australian Embassy in Jakarta, Indonesia. She received her undergraduate degree from the International Relations Department of the University of Indonesia, and obtained her Master's degree in International Relations from the Australian National University, under the Australian Development Scholarship programme.

Diastika Rahwidiati is passionate about civic innovation, particularly the thinkers, doers and fixers that create positive change across Indonesia. As Deputy Head of

Office for Pulse Lab Jakarta, she connects ethnographers, social activists and technologists to the Lab's big data research projects to add local context and encourage the diffusion of the technologies they embody. With over 15 years' experience in international development assistance, she has managed projects on topics such as education, policy-relevant research and civil society support. Dias holds a Bachelor's degree in Socio-economic Sciences of Agriculture from Bogor Agricultural University, and a Master's degree in International Development and Environmental Analysis from Monash University.

Inaya Rakhmani is a lecturer in the Department of Communication, Faculty of Social and Political Sciences at the University of Indonesia, and serves as Head of its Communication Research Centre. An associate at the Asia Research Centre, Murdoch University, Australia, and a member of the Indonesian Young Academy of Sciences, she has a particular interest in the cultural political economy of knowledge, information and entertainment, as well as the role of media in democratisation processes. Inaya is also the author of *Mainstreaming Islam in Indonesia: Television, Identity and the Middle Class* (**Palgrave MacMillan, 2016**).

Siti Ruhanawati was a Programme Officer at the Australia-Indonesia Partnership for Pro-Poor Policy: The Knowledge Sector Initiative between 2015 and 2017. She managed the programme's multi-stakeholder sub-working group on research and higher education, with a particular focus on identifying and overcoming barriers to research, including in the area of human resources in higher education. She also managed capacity building for leading think tanks and universities in Indonesia as well as being actively involved in the Knowledge Sector Initiative's gender and social inclusion task force. Prior to joining the Knowledge Sector Initiative, she was the lead researcher for Mercy Corps Indonesia, and also conducted research for the World Bank on community organizations and gender issues. Siti also worked as project coordinator for a peacebuilding programme in Aceh with the United Nations Development Programme and the International Organisation for Migration. She has worked for over 10 years with international non-government organisations and multilateral and bilateral agencies. She received her Master's in Development Management in 2007 from the Asian Institute of Management, in the Philippines; her Bachelor's degree is from the Department of Management, University of Gadjah Mada, Yogyakarta.

Louise Shaxson is a Senior Research Fellow in the Research and Policy in Development Programme at the Overseas Development Institute in London. Her work focuses on improving public sector policy and strategy within the broad framework of evidence-informed policymaking. Over the past 12 years she has worked with government departments in several countries to strengthen the ways they source, handle and use evidence. This has included advising on how to take a more strategic approach to evidence planning, provide scientific advice to ministers and create links between researchers and policymakers. Louise has a M.Sc. in Agricultural Economics from Cornell University and is currently pursuing a Ph.D. in Implementation Science at Kingston University in London.

Ade Soekadis was the Deputy Team Leader for the Australia-Indonesia Partnership for Pro-Poor Policy: The Knowledge Sector Initiative between 2015 and 2017. Prior to joining the programme, he was the head of operations, programme development and learning at The Nature Conservancy Indonesia, a United States-based global environment organisation. Prior to his tenure at The Nature Conservancy, he spent 15 years with various national and multinational corporations in the manufacturing, chemical, consulting, financial services and pharmaceutical sectors, mainly working on project management, operational excellence and commercial excellence. Ade received Master's and Bachelor degrees in Industrial Engineering from the University of Houston (United States). His expertise includes project/programme management, strategic planning, organisational development and operations excellence.

Sugiyanto is a Monitoring and Evaluation Officer at the Australia-Indonesia Partnership for Pro-Poor Policy: The Knowledge Sector Initiative. During his career, he has worked on a range of multilateral and bilateral development programmes in the areas of education, poverty reduction and natural disaster recovery. He has extensive experience with capacity building interventions for civil society organisations and government institutions, including the development of networks and coalitions and implementation of data-driven decision-making processes. During the past 7 years he has been increasingly involved in monitoring and learning activities in development projects. He is particularly interested in innovative approaches to monitoring, evaluation and learning such as social network analysis and multi-stakeholder policy networks monitoring. Sugiyanto has an undergraduate degree in education from Walisongo State Islamic University in Semarang and a Master's degree in Humanities with a specialisation in anthropology from the University of Leiden, the Netherlands.

List of Abbreviations and Other Terms

AAKI	Asosiasi Analis Kebijakan Indonesia (Indonesian Policy Analysts Association)
AIPI	Akademi Ilmu Pengetahuan Indonesia (Indonesian Academy of Sciences)
APBD	Anggaran Pendapatan dan Belanja Daerah (Annual regional budgets)
APBN	Anggaran Pendapatan dan Belanja Negara (Annual state budget)
AusAID	Australian Agency for International Development
Balitbang	Badan penelitian dan pengembagan (Research and development unit)
Bappeda	Badan Perencanaan Pembangunan Daerah (Regional Development Planning Agency)
Bappenas	Kementerian Perencanaan Pembangunan Nasional/Badan Perencanaan Pembangunan Nasional (Ministry for National Development Planning/National Development Planning Agency)
BPS	Badan Pusat Statistik (National Statistics Office)
CSIS	Centre for Strategic and International Studies
CSO(s)	Civil society organisation(s)
DDD	Doing Development Differently
DFAT	Australian Department of Foreign Affairs and Trade
DJPT	Direktorat Jenderal Pendidikan Tinggi (Directorate of General Higher Education)
DIPI	Dana Ilmu Pengetahuan Indonesia (Indonesian Science Fund)
DJPT	Direktorat Jenderal Pendidikan Tinggi (Directorate General Higher Education)
DPME	Department of Planning, Monitoring and Evaluation
DRPM	Direktorat Riset dan Pengabdian Masyarakat (Directorate of Research and Community Service)

ELSAM	Lembaga Studi dan Advokasi Masyarakat (Institute for Policy Research and Advocacy)
KPPOD	Komite Pemantauan Pelaksanaan Otonomi Daerah (Regional Autonomy Watch)
KemRistekDikti	Kementerian Riset, Teknologi dan Pendidikan Tinggi (Ministry of Research, Technology and Higher Education)
Kemdikbud	Kementerian Pendidikan dan Kebudayaan (Ministry of Education and Culture)
KSI	Australia-Indonesia Partnership for Pro-Poor Policy: The Knowledge Sector Initiative
KSP	Executive Office of President (Office of the President's Staff)
LAN	Lembaga Administrasi Negara (National Institute of Public Administration)
LIPI	Lembaga Ilmu Pengetahuan Indonesia (Indonesian Institute of Sciences)
LKPP	Lembaga Kebijakan Pengadaan Barang Jasa Pemerintah (National Goods/Services Public Procurement Agency)
LPDP	Lembaga Pengelola Dana Pendidikan (Ministry of Finance Education Endowment Fund)
LP3ES	Lembaga Penelitian, Pendidikan dan Penerangan Ekonomi dan Sosial (Institute for Social Economic Research Education and Information)
MoF	Ministry of Finance (Kementerian Keuangan)
MoSA	Indonesian Ministry of Social Affairs (Kementerian Sosial Republik Indonesia)
Musrenbang	Musyawarah rencana pembangunan (Consultative development planning forum)
NAS	United States National Academy of Science
NGO(s)	Non-governmental organisation(s)
OECD	Organisation for Economic Co-operation and Development
PAK	Pusat Analisis Kebijakan (Centre for Policy Analysis)
Pappitek LIPI	Pusat Penelitian Perkembangan IPTEK / Lembaga Ilmu Pengetahuan Indonesia (Science and Technology Development Research Centre/ Indonesian Institute of Science)
PDDIKTI	Pangkalan Data Pendidikan Tinggi (Higher education database)
PDIA	Problem-driven iterative adaptation
PISA	Programme for International Student Assessment
PPIM UIN	Pusat Pengkajian Islam dan Masyarakat di Universitas Islam Negeri (Centre for the Study of Islam and Society at the National Islamic University)
PRI(s)	Policy research institute(s)
PSHK	Pusat Studi Hukum & Kebijakan Indonesia (Indonesian Centre for Law and Policy Studies)
R&D	Research and development

RKP	Rencana Kerja Pemerintah (Annual national development plans)
RPJMD	Rencana Pembangunan Jangka Menengah Daerah (Medium-term regional development plan)
RPJPD	Rencana Pembangunan Jangka Panjang Daerah (Long-term regional development plan)
RPJPN	Rencana Pembangunan Jangka Panjang Nasional (Long-term national development plan)
RPJMN	Rencana Pembangunan Jangka Menengah Nasional (Medium-term national development plan)
SDGs	Sustainable Development Goals
SKPD	Satuan Kerja Pemerintah Daerah (Local government unit)
SEKNAS FITRA	Sekretariat Nasional Forum Indonesia Untuk Transparansi Anggaran (The Indonesian Forum for Budget Transparency)
Swakelola	Self-managed contracts
TAK	Tim Analisis Kebijakan (Policy Analysis Team)
UKP4	Unit Kerja Presiden Bidang Pengawasan dan Pengendalian Pembangunan (Presidential Delivery Unit for Development Monitoring and Oversight)
UN	United Nations
UNESCO	United Nations Educational, Scientific and Cultural Organisation
USAID	United States Agency for International Development

Chapter 1
Introduction

Arnaldo Pellini, Budiati Prasetiamartati, Kharisma Priyo Nugroho, Elisabeth Jackson, and Fred Carden

1 Introduction: Knowledge, Politics and Policymaking in Indonesia

Indonesia's growth and prosperity as a democratic, middle-income country hinges on the ability of the country's policymakers to develop effective public policies that increase productivity and competitiveness and ensure that growth benefits all. Governance is too complex to be managed without access to good evidence about the problems and the potential – and actual – impacts of public policy change. Good governance requires access to different types of evidence – including scientific research, administrative data, data analytics, professional knowledge and citizen

A. Pellini (✉)
Overseas Development Institute, London, UK
e-mail: a.pellini@odi.org.uk

B. Prasetiamartati · E. Jackson
Australia-Indonesia Partnership for Pro-Poor Policy: The Knowledge Sector Initiative, Jakarta, Indonesia
e-mail: budiati@ksi-indonesia.org; eljackson@ksi-indonesia.org

K. P. Nugroho
Indonesian Alliance for Policy Research (ARK Indonesia), Jakarta, Indonesia

Winrock International, Bangkok, Thailand

F. Carden
Using Evidence Inc., Ottawa, ON, Canada
e-mail: fred@usingevidence.com

© Springer Nature Singapore Pte Ltd. 2018
A. Pellini et al. (eds.), *Knowledge, Politics and Policymaking in Indonesia*,
https://doi.org/10.1007/978-981-13-0167-4_1

1

knowledge – and policymaking processes that invest in and make effective use of such evidence to inform policy decisions. Of course, evidence is only one of the factors that policymakers need to consider: policy and policymaking are inherently political, and policy decisions are always bound by what is politically feasible. This book draws on experiences derived from efforts to strengthen the potential of evidence-based policymaking in Indonesia. With contributions from academics, policy researchers, policymakers and development practitioners, the book presents practice-based insights that deepen understanding of how knowledge and politics shape Indonesia's policymaking process.

Indonesia's strong economic growth over the last decade has enabled it to regain its lower-middle-income country status, following the Asian financial crisis of 1997–1998. The number of people living in poverty has declined steadily, although inequality has risen and tens of millions live just above the poverty line. Indonesia faces many challenges in both generating and using evidence for the public good. Creating a scientific culture – *Budaya ilmiah* in Indonesian – must build on the country's culture and spirit. Done well it will serve as an engine for enhancing the social and economic potential of this large and diverse country.

How well equipped is Indonesia to address these challenges? Is the country developing the intellectual capital required to transform knowledge into growth? Are universities and think tanks producing research and evidence that is relevant to the needs of policymakers, or is 'post-truth' politics on the rise? What degree of engagement do citizens exercise in policy processes? How do policymakers make use of evidence to inform policy decisions? In what ways are new information and communication technologies changing the way evidence informs policymaking in Indonesia? What rules and regulations are in place to support the production of policy research and its use in policymaking? This book examines these and other key questions through the lens of the Indonesian 'knowledge sector', as Indonesia transitions to a knowledge-based economy. The authors draw their insights and evidence from the experience acquired through the implementation of the Australia-Indonesia Partnership for Pro-Poor Policy: The Knowledge Sector Initiative, a donor funded programme that aims to strengthen the demand for and use of evidence in policymaking in Indonesia.

Indonesia is one of the most populous countries in the world and transitioned to democratic governance less than 20 years ago. It faces many challenges – uneven development, a bureaucracy with a tendency towards centralisation, a weak educational system, much corruption and significant levels of intolerance. But it is also a country rich in resources, cultures and natural beauty with a resilient population. It has the potential to be one of the economic powerhouses of Asia and indeed the world. The knowledge sector is key to realising that potential.

Before exploring the book's contents, two concepts require clarification. First, the knowledge sector has been defined as 'the institutional landscape of government, private sector, and civil society organizations that provide research and analysis to support the development of public policy' (AusAID 2012). The knowledge sector is horizontal in nature; no one ministry or department is focused on ensuring its development, but all sectors of the economy need strong knowledge to grow and develop. The evidence generated can be used not only by governments in policy-making but also by advocacy organisations and policy think tanks to inform their recommendations and proposals to government, as well as to the broader society through the media.

The knowledge sector is weak in Indonesia, as underlined in this book and thoroughly documented in a series of diagnostic studies conducted by AusAID (now Department of Foreign Affairs and Trade, Australian Government) (Karetji 2010; Sherlock 2010; Sumarto 2011; Datta et al. 2011; Suryadarma et al. 2010). It is weak in the areas of producing high-quality evidence and of demand and use of evidence to inform public policy. Indonesia's growth over the past 20 years has relied heavily on the natural resource sector and a consumption-oriented economy (Indonesia Investments 2016). Further growth calls for a shift to a production-oriented economy in which knowledge and innovation play critical roles (Carden 2017).

Klaus Schwab argues that the world is in the early stages of the Fourth Industrial Revolution that will have profound impacts on global society. He believes that 'with effective multi-stakeholder cooperation…the fourth industrial revolution has the potential to address – and possibly solve – the major challenges that the world currently faces' (Schwab 2016, 113). But participating in the new industrial revolution demands a strong knowledge sector: it calls for a government and population that can think critically and in interdisciplinary and cross-disciplinary ways. Traditional sectoral and linear thinking will not help; making the shift to more creative and innovative ways to govern and enhance production requires new thinking and an educational system that builds the capacity of its students to think critically. As demonstrated in this volume, creating an Indonesian knowledge sector that is prepared for the new industrial revolution also calls for changes in the enabling environment, which at present hinders the production of knowledge.

Second, this book focuses on a specific aspect of public policy: the use of evidence to inform and influence policy decisions. Evidence-informed policymaking is about how to 'help policymakers to make better decisions, and achieve better outcomes, by using existing evidence more effectively, and undertaking new research, evaluation and analysis where knowledge about effective policy initiatives and policy implementation is lacking' (Davies 2012, 41). The hypothesis is that when high-quality, timely evidence informs policy decisions, those decisions yield policies capable of improving people's lives.

Using different types of evidence to inform policy decisions is not a new idea. It originated with evidence-based medicine, which is defined as the 'conscientious, explicit, and judicious use of current best evidence in making decisions about the care of individual patients' (Sackett et al. 1996, 71). With respect to public policy, Sutcliffe and Court (2005) argue that the term 'evidence-based policymaking' started to become widely used in international policy debates after the election of Tony Blair as Prime Minister of the United Kingdom in 1997. The United Kingdom government's White Paper on modernising government, published in 1999, stressed that policy decisions should be based on sound evidence and that substantial changes in the relationship between government and the social research community were needed to help determine what works and why and what types of policy initiatives are likely to be most effective (Government of the United Kingdom 1999).[1] Worldwide, a number of leaders continued to stress the importance of using evidence to inform policy decisions.

Policy instruments and decisions can be informed by evidence in several ways. Research-based evidence is only one of the types of evidence that can inform policy decisions. Shaxson (2016) has identified five main types of evidence that policymakers tend to use and access: statistical data from national statistical offices, administrative data from service providers, research-based evidence, evidence from citizens and evidence from formal evaluations. Data analytics presents a new source of evidence that is changing the costs, timeliness and accessibility of data and thus becoming a new way for policymakers to source evidence (Stuart et al. 2015).

Evidence also plays a useful role in policy by informing preliminary steps that may or may not lead to a decision or policy instrument. Weiss (1979) argues that evidence, in the form of research, can help to inform solutions to problems identified by policymakers or enlighten public discourse, all of which can lead to policy decisions. It can also inform and influence the way decisions are made, so-called procedural changes, such as opening new spaces for more evidence or policy dialogue.

Policymaking is a never-ending process. The end of the policy cycle is the beginning of the next policy iteration. Lindblom (1968) referred to the continuity of the policy process, where there is no beginning and no end. Effectively, resolving a policy problem with a policy decision is the start of identifying the next policy problem. Policy problems evolve and change as does the evidence that can help inform policy solutions and responses. Evidence-informed policymaking is about the set of methods that can inform this never-ending process (Sutcliffe and Court 2005). It provides a basis upon which policymakers can form a judgement, which then may or may not result in a change in policy. For Cairney (2016), this is not a limitation. It is reality. Evidence is only one of the many factors that contribute to policy decisions. Others include politics, beliefs, ideology, individual experiences and expertise.

While politics is a necessary part of the policy change process, it will not suffice to ensure the rise of a discourse in favour of the use of evidence in policy and practice. Davies et al. (2000) identify other critical factors: the growth of an increasingly well-educated and well-informed public, the explosion in the availability of data of all types, the growth in size and capabilities of the research community, the importance of productivity growth and international competitiveness and a growing emphasis on scrutiny and accountability of government. These preconditions face what Leicester (1999) has defined as the 'enemies' of evidence-informed policy: *bureaucratic logic* (which argues that processes and procedures are right because they have always been done that way), *consensus* (demanding extensive consultation to find a policy solution that satisfies everyone), *politics* (when defined as the art of

---

[1] Interestingly, Flynn (1999) notes that the White Paper 'Modernising Government' was published a year later than expected, reflecting the difficulties and negotiations resulting from changes and reforms in the civil service required by the new emphasis on gathering evidence to inform policy decisions. https://doi.org/10.1093/pa/52.4.582

the possible, rather than as what is rational or might work best), a *civil service culture* (which tends to show a particularly strong distrust of information generated from outside the system), *cynicism* (the mind-set of agreeing to the institutional view, even though the evidence says otherwise) and, last but not least, *time* – which is always in short supply in policymaking. These preconditions mirror the requirements for successful participation in the Fourth Industrial Revolution.

2 Structure and Content of the Book

The underlying framework for this book is derived from the work of Karetji (2010) who, in his diagnostic study of the Indonesian knowledge sector produced for AusAID during the design phase of the Knowledge Sector Initiative, described the evolution that Indonesia is undergoing from a recent past characterised by the Soeharto regime that ended in 1998 after 31 years of dictatorship to a future scenario characterised by solid democratic rule. During the Soeharto regime, the role of the knowledge sector was to generate evidence that would justify the government's autocratic policies. Critical thinking was perceived as a threat and discouraged. Consequently, the system of higher education remained under developed. Karetji's argument is that Indonesian institutions are moving away from a highly centralised system with little accountability to citizens and economic policy based on revenues from oil and other extractive industries. They are moving towards a more open, democratic system.

Indonesia has a short history as a democracy and remains in transition – the current period is known as the 'reform era'. Karetji argues that Indonesia today is characterised by a government system that, while in the process of democratising, has not fully stabilised. Power and authority are still being reconfigured, with a strengthening of the role of provincial and district governments and of citizens. However, major budget allocations are still determined by the central government. Local government authorities often feel a greater need to be accountable to Jakarta than to their constituents. Patronage systems are still in place, enabling local elites to access state resources and channel them to their clients, based on ethnic, religious or geographic links. Economic growth in the regions is largely dependent on public spending, with limited involvement by the private sector. Although the role of the knowledge sector in influencing decision makers is becoming stronger, it still depends on the extent to which it is perceived as supporting political and bureaucratic leaders to gain and maintain power and access resources.

On the positive side, the increasing authority and power of local authorities has enhanced the demand for more local, context-driven solutions. This has provided greater scope for knowledge to be developed, with a shift from macro-oriented and external concepts to more local concepts and solutions. As well, a more open attitude towards critical thinking is evolving. Knowledge providers must strive to overcome policymakers' suspicions about the intent and purpose of critical perspectives: are they intended to challenge authority and power or to improve governance?

Thus, knowledge suppliers must gain the confidence and trust of authorities. They must get better at building strong relationships with both policymakers and those who influence them, building networks and coalitions to promote evidence and communicating their findings in policy terms. Finally, they must develop deeper understanding of the institutional and organisational systems in which action needs to be taken (Carden 2009). In sum, knowledge suppliers must develop strategic approaches to introducing and presenting new perspectives. The future is about a more ideal and conducive environment for knowledge producers and suppliers (Karetji 2010). Over time, the authors envisage an increasingly democratic Indonesia with a stable, decentralised governance system. As political and bureaucratic leaders become increasingly accountable to their local constituents, more leaders will be in positions based on their performance and capacity, with an emphasis on citizen welfare.

In this scenario, Indonesia's economic growth will be dependent on a strong private sector and local industries, with tax-based revenues and increasing accountability and public service performance. The role of the knowledge sector will shift towards supporting government to improve and assess performance. In turn, this should also increase the need for a knowledge sector able to provide contextual and internal frameworks. In such frameworks, external concepts and experiences are positioned as important comparisons, rather than as the main point of reference. In this environment, independent input and critical thinking would be valued by policymakers as the needed knowledge base to increase or enhance policy performance.

Each chapter of this book applies this framework to put into context the specific components of the knowledge sector. The chapters address the role of universities, think tanks, decision makers and bureaucrats, as well as the role and potential of data to support the transition to a knowledge economy and the underlying constraints.

Chapter 2 focuses on the academy. It explores the challenges faced by Indonesian academics to producing policy-relevant research and using research evidence to inform policymaking. National- and university-level policies and practices discourage academics from undertaking research. These disincentives include lack of funding, an overly strong emphasis on teaching and undervaluing of research, in terms of financial rewards and career paths. The chapter highlights the marked divide between the political world of policymaking and the intellectual world of research: policymakers' needs and priorities are not well communicated, and academic researchers seldom see policymakers or the public as key audiences for their research. The authors reflect on these challenges and provide insights into how the development of a strong research culture in universities could support policymakers to develop appropriate policy responses to the issues confronting Indonesia today and in the future.

As organisations largely independent of government, policy research institutes and think tanks have an important role to play in bringing new issues and alternative viewpoints to the attention of policymakers and the public. In so doing, they help to improve the quality of policymaking, enrich democratic debate over ideas and promote government accountability for policy decisions.

Chapter 3 examines the emergence, evolution and role of think tanks in policymaking in the context of Indonesia's transition to democracy. Drawing on the experiences of some Indonesian policy research institutes, the chapter reflects on the opportunities and challenges for think tanks in regard to informing and influencing public debate and public policy. It explores how and under what circumstances Indonesian think tanks are able to influence policy and how they can improve their impact on policymaking.

Policy analysis is a key capability for modern policymaking bureaucracies. As public policymakers grapple with increasingly complex issues, their need for systematic evaluation of evidence from a range of sources and sound assessment of policy alternatives grows. The authors of Chap. 4 examine the nature of policy analysis within the Indonesian bureaucracy, exploring the role and functions of policy analysis units as knowledge intermediaries in synthesising and translating knowledge. They explore the challenges faced by bureaucrats and policy analysts in producing relevant, quality and timely policy analysis in response to policymakers' information needs. In addition to departmental research and development units (Balitbangs) and internal 'think tanks' – such as the Ministry of National Development Planning's Centre for Policy Analysis – the chapter considers other ways in which policy analysis is undertaken in the public sector. It reflects on the motivations underlying the 2014 decision to create a new functional position in the civil service ('policy analyst') and its implications for evidence-informed policymaking in Indonesia.

Chapter 5 explores how policymakers use evidence. Evidence-based policymaking is both a technical and a political undertaking. Policymakers must have the skills and knowledge to understand and articulate their evidence needs, source and evaluate evidence and apply it to policy problems. Policymaking organisations also need systems and processes that support the use of evidence, including adequate human and financial resources and quality assurance systems. Yet the use of evidence is also determined by policymakers' values, beliefs and motivations, the institutional context within which policy is made and the broader political culture. This chapter examines the use of evidence in national and subnational policymaking in Indonesia from a political economy perspective. It outlines how existing processes and systems for evidence-informed policymaking interact with political and organisational factors to shape policymakers' demand for and use of evidence.

Big data and digital innovation are changing the research and policy landscape in profound ways. Chapter 6 explores this phenomenon and its potential for informing public policy. In Indonesia the near ubiquity of mobile phones, improvements in connectivity and coverage and availability of new and cheaper technologies is providing policy researchers and policymakers with access to new sources of real-time information and new tools for collecting, managing and analysing large volumes of data. These developments have the potential to change the way policymakers source and use evidence to inform policymaking. This chapter examines the implications of new technologies for policymaking. The authors argue that although advanced data analytics and data visualisation help to make sense of new data sources and to attract policymakers to some of these prototypes, actual uptake and adoption are more likely to depend on political factors.

Knowledge sector actors do not exist in a vacuum. They are immersed in a web of rules and regulations that define how they link and interact with each other, the amount of funding available for procuring and generating evidence and the space for evidence to influence plans and policies. The authors of Chap. 7 examine the policies, procedures and practices that govern and shape the production and use of knowledge in policymaking in Indonesia. The chapter begins by examining some of the challenges that inhibit the production and use of research to inform policymaking. It then discusses two examples of reforms in the enabling environment for evidence-informed policymaking: funding for research and regulations for government procurement of research. These reforms have expanded the space for producing high-quality, policy-relevant research, enabling policymakers to commission research from universities and policy research organisations. The authors describe the policy changes that led to the establishment of the Indonesia Science Fund and a change in government procurement regulations. The chapter concludes with suggestions about regulatory changes that may still be required to continue reforming the enabling environment in which Indonesia's knowledge sector operates.

In recent decades recognition that politics and political institutions matter for development has increased, along with interest in contextually grounded approaches. This has stemmed from an acknowledgement that purely technocratic approaches to development programmes have often resulted in failure because they do not take into account the nature of political institutions. Nor do they consider the context in a particular developing country or the interests and incentives motivating powerful national actors. Policy processes are embedded in specific social, political and organisational contexts. Approaches that focus on implementing universal best practices in evidence-informed policymaking are unlikely to be successful. Success is far more likely through an approach that takes the local context as the starting point to understanding what issues are relevant to policymakers and developing contextually appropriate solutions. The authors of Chap. 8 reflect on policy reforms in the Indonesian knowledge sector and the use of politically smart, locally led approaches used to achieve those policy changes by a large-scale development programme.

In the final chapter, the editors synthesise the main conclusions from the various chapters and look at what lies ahead for Indonesia's knowledge sector. These are not easy times for putting forth an evidence-informed approach to policymaking. The emergence of a post-truth political discourse changes how citizens perceive and (mis)trust politicians and how the policymaking process appears to conspire against the use of evidence. However, the findings presented here confirm that intellectual capital and a policymaking process that values, demands and makes use of timely, high-quality knowledge and evidence to inform policy decisions are necessary to boost productivity and strengthen economic growth.

Overall, the findings show that Indonesia is amongst the middle-income countries that are beginning to invest in finding ways to demand, use and produce more and better-quality evidence to inform public policy. The authors remain optimistic that Indonesia has decided to use evidence and knowledge to strengthen economic development, improve social conditions and contribute to a stronger democracy – and hope that this volume will contribute to that development.

References

AusAID [Government of Australia. Australian Agency for International Development]. (2012). *Australia-Indonesia Partnership for Pro-Poor Policy: The knowledge sector initiative: Design document*. Jakarta. http://dfat.gov.au/about-us/publications/Documents/indo-ks-design.pdf. Accessed 11 Mar 2014.

Cairney, P. (2016). *The politics of evidence-based policy making*. Basingstoke: Palgrave Macmillan.

Carden, F. (2009). *Knowledge to policy: Making the most of development research*. London: Sage and IDRC.

Carden, F. (2017). *How do you evaluate a mental revolution?* (Working Paper 22). Jakarta: Knowledge Sector Initiative. http://www.ksi-indonesia.org/en/news/detail/how-do-you-evaluate-a-mental-revolution. Accessed 20 May 2017.

Datta, A., Jones, H., Febriany, V., Harris, D., Dewi, R. K., Wild, L., & Young, J. (2011). *The political economy of policy-making in Indonesia*. AusAID. Available at: http://dfat.gov.au/about-us/publications/Documents/indo-ks11-knowledge-policymaking.pdf. Accessed 20 May 2017.

Davies, H. T. O., Nutley, S., & Smith, P. (2000). Introducing evidence-based policy and practice in public services, In H. T. O. Davies, S. M. Nutley, & P. C. Smith (Ed.), *What works? Evidence-based policy and practice in public services*. Bristol: Policy Press.

Davies, P. (2012). The state of evidence-based policy evaluation and its role in policy formation. *National Institute Economic Review, 219*(1), 41–52.

Flynn, N. (1999). Modernizing British government. *Parliamentary Affairs, 52*(4), 582–597. https://doi.org/10.1093/pa/52.4.582.

Government of the United Kingdom, Cabinet Office. (1999). *Modernising government* (White Paper). London: Her Majesty's Stationery Office.

Indonesia Investments. (2016, February 6). *GDP in focus: Analysis of Indonesia's 5.04% economic growth in Q4-2015*. https://www.indonesia-investments.com/news/news-columns/gdp-in-focus-analysis-of-indonesia-s-5.04-economic-growth-in-2015/item6470? Accessed 18 March 2017.

Karetji, P. C. (2010). *Overview of the Indonesian knowledge sector*. Jakarta: AusAID. Available at: http://dfat.gov.au/about-us/publications/Documents/indo-ks8-overview.pdf. Accessed on 21 May 2017.

Leicester, G. (1999). The seven enemies of evidence-based policy. *Public Money and Management, 19*(1), 5–7.

Lindblom, C. E. (1968). *The policy-making process*. Englewood Cliffs: Prentice Hall.

Sackett, D. L., Rosenberg, W. M. C., Gray, J. A. M., Haynes, R. B., & Richardson, W. S. (1996). Evidence-based medicine: What it is and what it isn't. *BMJ, 312*(1996), 71. https://doi.org/10.1136/bmj.312.7023.7.

Schwab, K. (2016). *The fourth industrial revolution*. Geneva: World Economic Forum.

Shaxson, L. (2016). *Lessons for building and managing an evidence base for policy* (Working Paper 10). Jakarta: Knowledge Sector Initiative. http://www.ksi-indonesia.org/en/news/detail/lessons-for-building-and-managing-an-evidence-base-for-policy. Accessed 5 April 2017.

Sherlock, S. (2010). Knowledge for policy: Regulatory obstacles to the growth of a knowledge market in Indonesia. Jakarta: AusAID. http://dfat.gov.au/about-us/publications/Documents/indo-ks13-knowledge-to-govt.pdf. Accessed 9 June 2017.

Stuart, E., Samman, E., Avis, W., Berliner, T. (2015). *The data revolution. Finding the missing millions*. London: Overseas Development Institute. https://www.odi.org/publications/9476-data-revolution-finding-missing-millions. Accessed 10 Apr 2017.

Sumarto, S. (2011). *The SMERU research institute: History and lessons learned*. Jakarta: AusAID. Available at: http://dfat.gov.au/about-us/publications/Documents/indo-ks12-smeru.pdf. Accessed 22 May 2017.

Suryadarma, D., Pomeroy, J., Tanuwidjaja, S. (2010). *Economic factors underpinning constraints in Indonesia's knowledge sector*. Jakarta: AusAID. http://dfat.gov.au/about-us/publications/Documents/indo-ks2-economic-incentives.pdf. Accessed 23 May 2017.

Sutcliffe, S., & Court, J. (2005). *Evidence-based policymaking: What is it? How does it work? What relevance for developing countries?* London: Overseas Development Institute. https://www.odi.org/sites/odi.org.uk/files/odi-assets/publications-opinion-files/3683.pdf. Accessed 15 Mar 2017.

Weiss, C. (1979). The many meanings of research utilization. *Public Administration Review, 39*(5), 426–431.

Part I
Producing Knowledge for Policy

Chapter 2
Linking Academic Research and Policymaking

Budiati Prasetiamartati, Fred Carden, Siti Ruhanawati, Inaya Rakhmani, and Yanuar Nugroho

> *Whilst creativity, ideas and questioning are of value in their own right, economies and societies which invest in research generally show faster rates of growth in output and human development.*
>
> (Stern 2016)

1 Introduction

This volume explores the role of evidence in producing better public policy in Indonesia. This chapter builds on the importance of research to that process and more broadly to socio-economic development. It sees research as foundational to a strong, knowledge-intensive twenty-first-century economy. Here, we explore the challenges that Indonesian academics face in producing policy-relevant research.

B. Prasetiamartati (✉) · S. Ruhanawati
Australia-Indonesia Partnership for Pro-Poor Policy: The Knowledge Sector Initiative, Jakarta, Indonesia
e-mail: budiati@ksi-indonesia.org

F. Carden
Using Evidence Inc., Ottawa, ON, Canada
e-mail: fred@usingevidence.com

I. Rakhmani
Department of Communication, Faculty of Social and Political Sciences, University of Indonesia, Jakarta, Indonesia

Y. Nugroho
Analysis and Oversight of Strategic Issues on Social, Cultural, and Ecological Affairs, Jakarta, Indonesia

Executive Office of the President, Government of Indonesia, Jakarta, Indonesia

© Springer Nature Singapore Pte Ltd. 2018
A. Pellini et al. (eds.), *Knowledge, Politics and Policymaking in Indonesia*,
https://doi.org/10.1007/978-981-13-0167-4_2

When we think of development as more than mere survival, knowledge is important for understanding how to develop an economy and a society that not only grows economically but does so with equity and in an ecologically sustainable manner. Development that supports the growth and nurturing of human potential – growth that addresses major inequities – requires knowledge. It needs knowledge and evidence because in this increasingly complex world, it is no longer viable for a decision-maker to effectively determine development policy for his or her people without significant inputs from a range of people and perspectives. In this chapter, we consider primarily knowledge generated through formal scientific research. In a forthcoming volume, Nugroho, Antlöv and Carden recognise that knowledge takes many forms and comes from diverse sources, defined as formal knowledge, professional knowledge and local knowledge.

This discussion of the links between academic research and policymaking is based on some basic assumptions. First, universities play a crucial role in building knowledge through research on issues central to development and thus play a key role in generating and managing knowledge in an increasingly uncertain world. Maintaining and building the integrity of the research enterprise are crucial to its credibility and ultimately to its value in advancing development and supporting policymaking. Second, universities do not only produce researchers. They also serve as the training ground for policymakers and bureaucrats – decision-makers who are in a position to make use of evidence in their decisions (Ford 2012). Third, we assume that institutions and organisations tend to be weak at accumulating knowledge. As a result, people need to learn for themselves, and it is people who make up the institutions that accumulate knowledge, through their life experiences. People then influence the policies and practices of the organisations through which they engage. Fourth, organisations are at risk for confirmation bias, that is, listening only to the like-minded. Universities can ensure a space for the expression of diverse viewpoints. Finally, we work under the assumption that universities can play a role in nurturing, managing and documenting knowledge to help mitigate the challenges faced by many institutions in this regard.

Universities in Indonesia are weak and research within them even weaker. The Programme for International Student Assessment results, comparing the education outcomes of high school students (15 years of age) in a number of countries, ranked Indonesia 62nd out of 72 economies assessed (OECD 2016). This means that students start university at a significant disadvantage. Indonesian universities also receive poor rankings in international comparisons (Rakhmani et al. 2017). Little research is published – far less than in other economies in the region (see Pellini et al. 2016). Indonesia spends less than 0.2% of its GDP on research, at least ten times lower than other countries in the region.

These are indicators, or symptoms, of an overriding problem in Indonesian universities: the absence of a research culture. In the next sections of this chapter, we break this broad-based problem into three underlying causes that we believe to be important starting points, or levers of change, for addressing the lack of a research culture. The next section explores constraints in the institutional environment, section three examines limited financing for research and the fourth section addresses the issue of inadequate human resource management. In section five the authors provide some suggestions for addressing these issues.

There is no single problem that can be 'fixed' to improve the place of research in universities. And these three levers are not the only challenges to be addressed. There are many other, multifaceted challenges. It can never be known for certain that any one response will help to move a university closer to a strong research culture, hence the need for ongoing assessment and reflection on whether and how universities are reaching their potential and whether a focus on these levers continues to be relevant.

2 Universities as Knowledge Environments: The Teaching-Research Nexus

Ford (2012) noted that 'The most intractable barrier to research excellence in Indonesia is the incentive structure within higher education'. This section argues that Indonesian universities place low priority on the production of knowledge for more equitable development. Universities in low- and middle-income countries have a demonstrated lack of research productivity. In the Asian region, universities play a role in knowledge production that favours market mechanisms and/or individual consultancies (Mok 2008). This contributes to widening the gap between rich and poor and prolongs the exclusion of social groups. So why argue that knowledge production should be strengthened at universities to achieve an equitable society when they often fail to do so?

The authors argue that universities as knowledge producers matter because of their potential to foster interaction between their three core functions: teaching and learning, research and community engagement (or *tridarma perguruan tinggi*). The institutionalisation of knowledge transfer, generation and selection at universities can and must be directed towards equitable social development. The speed with which knowledge is generated and accumulated today is clearly unprecedented (Foray 2004; Tyfield 2012). This means that there is potential to enhance knowledge efficiency and quality, providing wider access to many. However, the desired effect of a more equitable society can only be achieved through the structural transformation of the institutions mandated to provide knowledge access to the public.

Some argue that in the case of Indonesia, universities are more apt to be market-oriented than having a clear public-service agenda (i.e. to be more focused on profit than the public good) (Hadiz and Dhakidae 2005; Karetji 2010; Guggenheim 2012; Rakhmani and Siregar 2016; Rosser 2016). Moreover, the precondition of quality knowledge generation that is central in this new economy is currently lacking due to bureaucratic constraints. These constraints involve limited funding for basic sciences, the stunting of critical thinking among academics and bureaucratisation of the academic career. Current conditions at Indonesian state universities show an imbalance between teaching, research and community engagement. This is because university income is used to pay faculty for teaching, but not for research (see

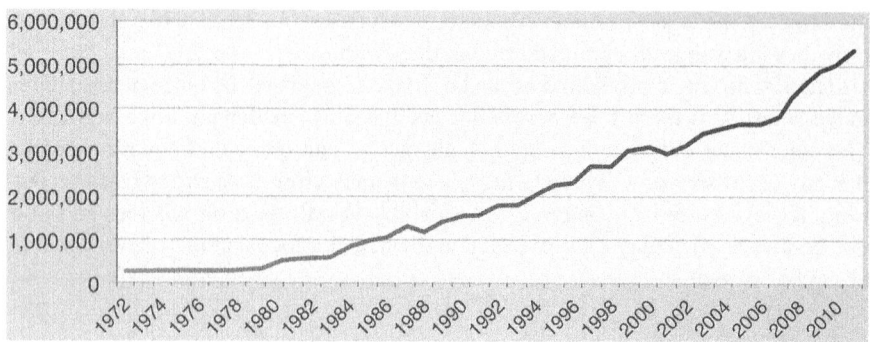

Fig. 2.1 Total tertiary enrolment (1972 to 2011). (Reproduced from World Bank World Development Indicators (cited in Rosser 2016, 10))

Rakhmani and Siregar 2016; Rosser 2016). This consistent imbalance has meant that Indonesian universities generally fail to carry out research.

Indonesian universities have yielded poor academic performance compared to countries with lower GDP (Guggenheim 2012; Rakhmani 2016). Rakhmani and Siregar, referring to Hadiz and Dhakidae (2005), note that 'poor performance in this respect has been linked to structural problems that are inherent to state universities and research institutions, whereby most research has, for the longest time, been confined to providing technocratic input for government development strategies' (2016, 1). This condition prevailed throughout much of the authoritarian New Order regime under President Soeharto (1967–1998), which systematically narrowed the role of state universities to the technocratic role of providing input for state programmes.

Since the early 2000s, state universities traditionally funded only through the state budget have been permitted to seek external income as autonomous state legal entities (Rakhmani and Siregar 2016). The assumption behind this policy change in 2000 was that authority to manage their own finances would allow state universities to improve the quality of academic performance. Instead, the outcome has been an increase of student intake – thereby increasing university income – with no significant change in teaching qualifications or support for research (Fig. 2.1). Consequently, academics take on increased teaching loads, either to secure higher income or respond to the demands of their department.

Moreover, a study by Rakhmani and Siregar shows that 51% of academic staff in major Indonesian state universities hold managerial positions – in addition to their role in teaching, research and community engagement (2016). This places research even further down on the priority list.

This is not to say that no research is carried out at Indonesian universities. Academic staff of major Indonesian state universities who do carry out research do so in such a way that their research network spans sectors, namely, state, private sector, international donors and universities (see Rakhmani and Siregar 2016). Significantly, 74% of the research carried out is thematically linked to governance. This may appear to suggest that the research produced is linked to policymaking (Ibid.). However, a closer look into the themes shows that research topics selected are driven by available funding. In other words, the market mechanism is the driving force within higher education institutions in the whole Asian region, not only Indonesia (Mok 2008). This is demonstrated in Indonesia by research reports at major state universities that are rarely turned into academic publications. Only 8% of academic staff at these universities have published in reputable, peer-reviewed, international academic journals (Rakhmani and Siregar 2016).

The structure and organisation of academic disciplines was inherited from the New Order regime and heavily favours teaching over research and academic publication. The single-discipline nature of academic pursuits has inhibited interaction and collaboration between researchers across disciplines and reduced the space for academics to carry out applied research (Nizam 2006; Wicaksono and Friawan 2011; Moeliodihardjo et al. 2012).

Current publication policies lack full appreciation of the complexity of peer review. The accreditation of journals by the former Directorate General of Higher Education (Direktorat Jenderal Pendidikan Tinggi – DJPT) also failed to place sufficient emphasis on the quality of peer review (Rakhmani et al. 2017), let alone address the lack of a peer-reviewed culture. This culture needs to be fostered by balancing, or properly appreciating, the connection between teaching and learning, research and community engagement.

The notion of *tridarma perguruan tinggi*[1] of Indonesian universities resonates with the idea of the teaching/research nexus identified in many studies (Neumann 1994; Colbeck 1998; Griffiths 2004; Robertson 2007; Simons and Elen 2007). A 2012 study by Horta et al. argues for complementarity between teaching and research, demonstrating through empirical data in the United States that by leveraging the link between teaching and research, academic activities can move beyond conventional teaching formats. The study's results show that students demonstrate higher output when research is at the centre of teaching activities, in what the authors call 'inquiry-based curricula'. Students become more actively involved in faculty research activities. This not only minimises the division of roles between faculty and students, it also reinforces the link between teaching and research as part of the same learning process. This, in turn, increases the productivity of scientific output at all levels (Griffiths 2004). With this in mind, in teaching social sciences and humanities, it becomes essential not only to stimulate critical inquiry and research among faculty and students but also with the wider community with which they engage and gather data. Thus, the next practical step would be to link the teaching/research nexus and evidence-based policymaking as one of the practical outputs.

3 Funding for Research

Carrying out research requires funding, but there is a lack of clarity on how much Indonesia actually invests in research and development (R&D). Recent estimates by the Ministry of Research, Technology and Higher Education show that gross

---

[1] Teaching and learning, research and community engagement

expenditure in R&D in 2015 amounted to 0.2% of GDP (Kompas 2016). This estimate is higher than the often-cited 2014 figure of 0.09% (Pappiptek LIPI 2014). The 2015 figure used a different methodology and included more variables than the 2014 figure, namely, salaries, allocation by local governments and research institutes. Neither figure covers contributions from the private sector, due to a lack of data. In any case, both figures demonstrate alarmingly low expenditure when compared to research funding expenditures in most expanding economies in the region (Fig. 2.2). In 2011, Malaysia was spending 1% of GDP, China 1.7%, Singapore 2.1% and Korea 3.7% (Tilley and Hidayat 2017).

Similarly alarming is that universities' share of gross expenditure on R&D stood at just 5.6% between 2000 and 2002 (OECD 2013, 172). This figure is miniscule, considering that most work done by Ph.D.-level researchers takes place at public universities. The implication is that most research is carried out outside the university and frequently by researchers without Ph.D. qualifications (Brodjonegoro and Greene 2012). Moreover, the majority of R&D funding in Indonesia (80%) comes from the government, compared to about 14% from the private sector. By contrast, research institutions in Malaysia, China, Japan, Korea and Singapore receive over 60% of their research investment from the private sector (Brodjonegoro and Greene 2012; Guggenheim 2012). Further, the Indonesian government contribution to R&D expenditure has declined precipitously over the past 35 years. The government's budget for 'science and technology' (which includes R&D, science services for information systems and statistical activities and education and training in universities, ministries and nonministerial institutions) as a share of the total state budget between 1969 and 2013 has been decreasing (Fig. 2.3).

In 2010 the Government of Indonesia issued Regulation No. 93, which included a measure allowing tax deductions for donations, including for funding research.

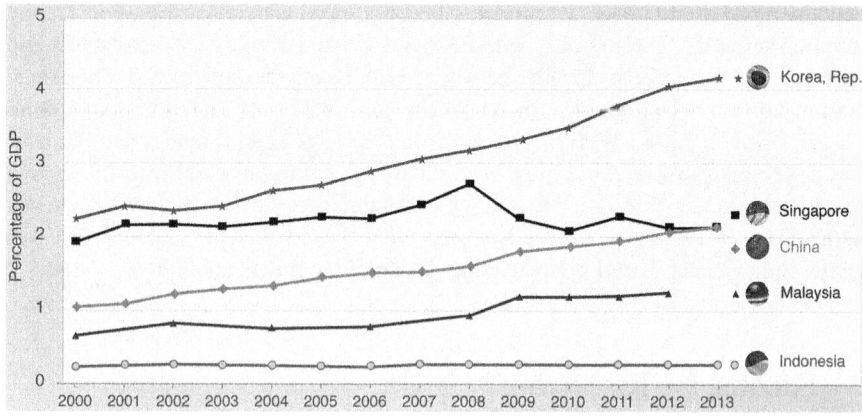

Fig. 2.2 Gross expenditure on R&D as a percentage of GDP (Indonesia's data contain only four original data points from different sources. Data for 2000 and 2001 are from UNESCO, 2009 from a national observation and 2013 from 'Science and Technology in Indonesia – in Brief' 2014, Pappiptek LIPI 2014. The data in between these observations are linear interpolations). (Reproduced from Tilley and Hidayat 2017)

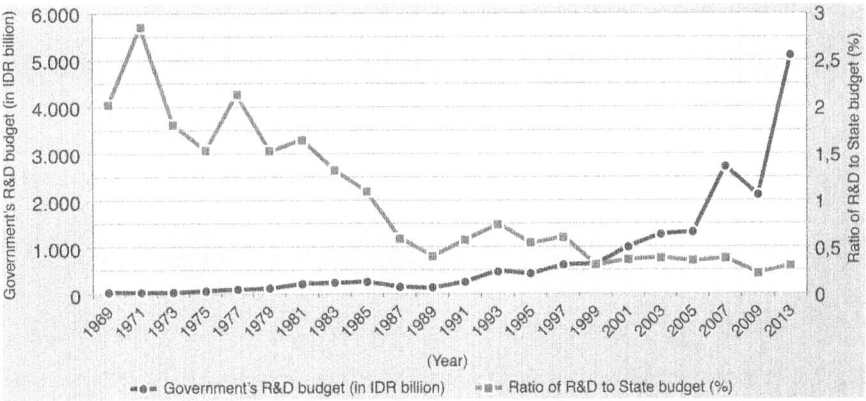

Fig. 2.3 Ratio of state science and technology and R&D budget to state budget, 1963–2013. (Reproduced from Pappitek LIPI 2014)

This was an attempt to incentivise private donations and funding for R&D. However, there have been very few applications of this regulation, and it is little known among potential donors from the private sector. Its use is further complicated by a general unwillingness among Indonesians, including the business sector, to interact with the tax office.

The main source of funding for public and private universities is grants provided by the state budget through the Ministry of Research, Technology and Higher Education (Kementerian Riset, Teknologi dan Pendidikan Tinggi – KemRistekDikti) and managed by the Directorate of Research and Community Service (Direktorat Riset dan Pengabdian Masyarakat – DRPM).[2] In 2017, DRPM was managing more than 17 different research grant schemes in three main areas: basic research, applied research and capacity-building research. In addition, DRPM allocates ten grants for community service that are directed to applied research in communities, ranging from community technology to collaborative research with local government or the private sector (DRPM 2016). This fragmentation of a small research funding allocation makes it difficult for academic staff to access the funds. Modes of disbursement add to the confusion. The 17 DRPM research grants are disbursed through two main channels: (1) directly to the university through the 'decentralised research grant' scheme (four grant schemes) and (2) through competitive national grants where academic staff have to apply for funds through their respective universities (13 grant schemes) (DRPM 2016; Rakhmani and Siregar 2016). Not all academic staff are

---

[2] The Ministry of Research, Technology and Higher Education (Kementerian Riset, Teknologi dan Pendidikan Tinggi – KemRistekDikti) is the regulatory body for Indonesia's higher education. In 2014, the Ministry was formed through a merger of Higher Education (formerly within the Ministry of Education and Culture) and the Ministry of Research and Technology. Before the merger, the body managing university research funding was the Directorate General of Higher Education (Direktorat Jenderal Pendidikan Tinggi – DJPT).

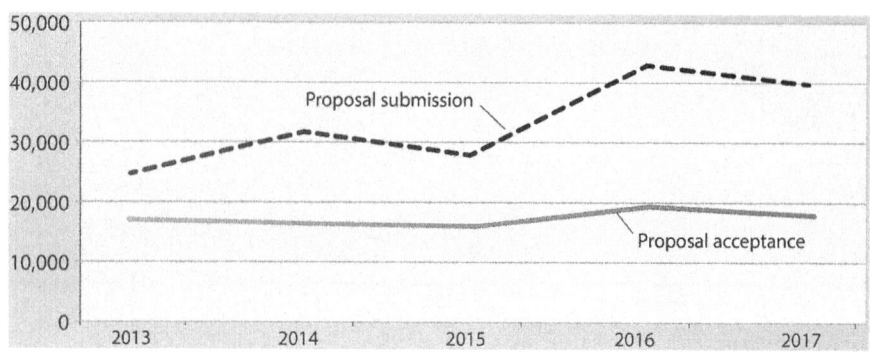

Fig. 2.4 Proposal submissions and acceptance to DRPM research grant scheme. (Adapted from DRPM 2017)

eligible to apply for the 17 research grants but rather depend on the DRPM's classification of university research capacity.

Grant amounts range from IDR 15 million to 200 million (US$1,100–15,000) per fiscal year, depending on the research scheme, according to DRPM data from January 2017. Due to the short time frame (1 fiscal year) allowed and the limited resources, a typical university research project produces no more than a report or very rarely a journal article, an academic briefing, an opinion piece or an article for public dissemination (Nugroho et al. 2016).

Funding for research is slowly increasing. Overall, DRPM research grants increased almost fourfold between 2006 and 2012 (from IDR 76 billion to nearly IDR 290 billion or US$21 million) (Moeliodihardjo et al. 2012). It continued to increase to IDR 1.2 trillion (US$90 million) in 2017, according to January data gathered by DRPM. In spite of this large-scale increase in funding, research grant funds allocated to DRPM remained low, merely 3% of the total Ministry of Research, Technology and Higher Education budget in 2016. However, this sum is spread across 269,351 academic staff in universities across Indonesia (PDDIKTI 2017). As shown in Fig. 2.4, due to limits on funding, between 2013 and 2017 on average, only 49% of proposals were funded (around 16,271 of 34,426 proposals).

Of all the types of research grants sought between 2013 and 2017, those for basic research received only 10–14% of the total managed by DRPM (Fig. 2.5), demonstrating the lack of funding for basic sciences mentioned above.

A major issue in research funding is that current Indonesian fiscal law and regulation discourages multi-year research programmes. Annual renewals are permitted, but the lack of initial multi-year commitments creates uncertainty, discouraging researchers from planning longer-term initiatives. DRPM allows some exceptions to these regulations, running some collaborative research grant schemes for up to three years, valued at up to IDR 1 billion (US$75,000) per year. However, even in these cases, the grants are evaluated annually, and there is no guarantee of continued funding. As a result, researchers tend to avoid applying for these schemes, even though they are sufficient to fund basic research.

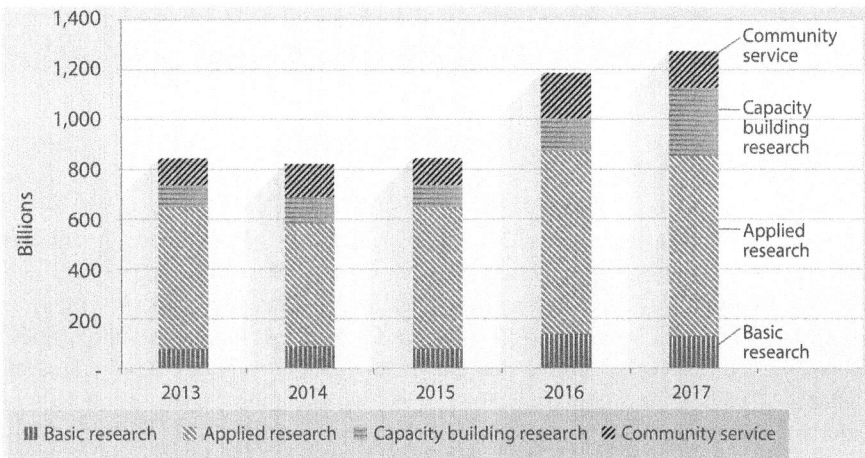

Fig. 2.5 DRPM research grant scheme. (Adapted from DRPM 2017)

State universities are considered government implementing units (*satuan kerja*) and must follow rigid reporting and budgeting guidelines and adhere to cumbersome bureaucratic procedures for all financial transactions. According to Brodjonegoro and Greene (2012), this has resulted in limiting the scope of research that is explorative, flexible and innovative.

Lack of clarity about research funding schemes, together with limited time frames for research, makes academic staff reluctant to risk their time by applying. Other challenges faced by academic staff are the requirement to spend the entire research budget in the same fiscal year, unpredictable timing of fund disbursements and onerous administrative and financial reporting demands (Rakhmani and Siregar 2016; Suradijono et al. 2017).

A significant shift in research funding has occurred as a result of efforts by the Indonesian Academy of Sciences (Akademi Ilmu Pengetahuan Indonesia – AIPI) to establish the Indonesian Science Fund (Dana Ilmu Pengetahuan Indonesia – DIPI) (Brodjonegoro and Greene 2012).[3] The Indonesian Science Fund was legally established in early 2016, confirming the Government of Indonesia's commitment to funding multi-year research projects. The Indonesian Science Fund is supported by Indonesia's Endowment Fund for Education under the Ministry of Finance. The Fund's regulatory framework also allows funding from external sources and has attracted financial support from the Australia-Indonesia Partnership for Pro-Poor Policy: the Knowledge Sector Initiative, the United States Agency for International Development and the UK Government (Sabarini 2016). Although it currently provides only a small fraction of the resources required for Indonesia's research needs, the Fund's significance lies in the modernising effect it can have on the country's approach to commissioning and fund-

---

[3] See also Chap. 7, Sect. 3.2.1.

ing multi-year research projects. Further discussion of the Indonesian Science Fund and other regulatory changes is presented in Chap. 7.

4 Careers in Research

Universities' human resource policies and regulations do not effectively support research and knowledge production. The Ministry of Research, Technology and Higher Education (Kementerian Riset, Teknologi dan Pendidikan Tinggi – KemRistekDikti) has set the goal of developing world-class Indonesian universities. This will require investment in teaching and the production of high-quality research capable of leading innovation in the nation and withstanding the tests applicable to international research.

To achieve this goal, it is important to recognise human resource management as a core area in higher education (AIPI 2017). Universities face several human resource challenges. The limited number of qualified Ph.Ds. teaching in universities in Indonesia has a significant negative effect on the quality of teaching and the capacity and potential for high-quality research. In Indonesia of 269,351 academic faculty, only 12% hold a Ph.D., while 15.2% hold only an undergraduate degree; the majority (63.8%) have master's level qualifications (see Fig. 2.6).

Academic staff at public universities are civil servants; hence the human resource policy is guided by national regulations designed to manage a bureaucracy, rather than a university.[4] The Indonesian bureaucracy relies on a centralised system of promotion, severely limiting the ability of a university to promote its values and manage faculty performance (AIPI 2017). International evidence shows that tertiary

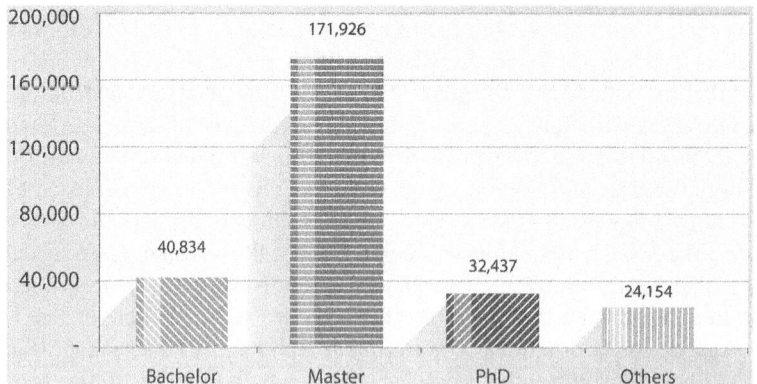

Fig. 2.6 Educational background of academic staff in Indonesia. (Adapted from PDDIKTI 2017)

---

[4]A relatively small number of autonomous universities have authority to manage their own resources.

education institutions need autonomy and academic freedom in order to thrive (Suryadarma and Jones 2013), something that is not possible under the current human resource structure and regulations.

The performance measurement system within the university sector is based on the *tridarma perguruan tinggi* mentioned earlier[5], which is regulated through Law No. 12/2012. All three core areas are considered individual obligations through the national academic credit system, known as Kum.[6] Under the Kum system, advancement is based on achieving a certain number of credit points. Most credits are awarded through teaching, leaving little incentive to accumulate credits through research or community service.

A further problem is the lack of a university-level performance assessment system to ensure implementation of the *tridarma perguruan tinggi*. Performance management systems in place do not capture staff performance, nor do they easily recognise broader issues, such as low levels of faculty training and the lack of university control over its human resources. In short, neither the skills nor the incentives are in place to boost the quality and quantity of research. So even if more resources for research were to become available, few faculty are in place to use them wisely.

There is an inherent contradiction in the law that governs universities. On the one hand, universities have the authority to manage academic staff; but on the other, the academic workload is managed centrally, making it impossible for universities to play a role in managing their staff (Suradijono et al. 2017).

Indonesian universities do not promote inter-institutional mobility. Nor do they engage in open international recruitment. Because of entry-level civil service requirements, there is a strong tendency among Indonesian academics to stay within their own home institutions. This tends to promote insularity and discourage innovation (Rakhmani and Siregar 2016). While new legislation permits open recruitment (Civil Service Law No.5/2014), very little use has been made of this provision (Ibid.). This could be mitigated through the engagement of international faculty, as it takes place in both Malaysia and Singapore. International faculty bring new ideas and diverse backgrounds that enrich debate and learning, as well as advancing academic publication (AIPI 2017). Ultimately, creating a more open and dynamic university sector would strengthen both research and teaching.

Salary and incentive systems at universities do not promote research and can even be seen to actively discourage it (Syafrudin et al. 2017). While some dedicated research staff are hired from time to time, there is a need to effectively link research

---

[5] Teaching and learning, research and community engagement

[6] The credit system is a tool for academic assessment. Kum system rules, faculty workload and promotion of academic staff are expected to increase the performance and productivity of academic staff in the implementation of tridarma (three main functions) of higher education. The legal basis for this system is the Joint Ministerial Decision between the Ministry of Education and Culture and the Head of the State Employment Body (Mendikbud and Kepala Badan Kepegawaian Negara) No. 61409/MPK/KP/99 and No. 181/1999 on the Operational Guidance on the Functional Title of Lecturer and Their Credit Values (Petunjuk Pelaksanaan Jabatan Fungsional Dosen dan Angka Kreditnya). This basis was recently renewed by Ministerial Regulation (Permendikbud) No. 92/2014, on the Technical Guidance on the Operationalisation of the Assessment of the Credit Values for Functional Position of Lecturer.

and teaching. This means that time for research needs to be incentivised, both on an ongoing basis as well as through mechanisms for release time to work on larger research initiatives. Sabbaticals could be one mechanism. At present, while these are permitted in principle, they are hindered by civil service regulations that restrict staff from taking leave (Rakhmani and Siregar 2016). Other mechanisms could also be introduced, such as buying out teaching time to focus on research for a given period of time. As noted earlier, this link between research and teaching not only produces new knowledge but also provides natural opportunities for mentoring junior researchers and enhancing publication (Suradijono et al. 2017). Moreover, it improves teaching and increases student engagement in the research enterprise, with the long-term benefits that implies. These mechanisms need to be managed within the university system to work effectively.

Without some restructuring of salary and incentive systems, faculty will continue to spend the bulk of their time in consulting and other activities outside the university (Nugroho et al. 2016). According to one study, as much as three-quarters of faculty time is spent on activities outside the university (Suryadarma and Jones 2013). As a result, the number of publications in international journals is very low (Pellini et al. 2016). While some universities do provide incentives for peer-reviewed publications and publication grants are available, these grants are usually too small to fund the necessary research and cover the time required to produce an article in an international journal (Nugroho et al. 2016; Suryadarma and Jones 2013).

In spite of these challenges, some bright spots are on the horizon. The government is taking steps to improve the state of Indonesian universities that could result in improving the environment for research. New regulations by the Ministry of Research, Technology and Higher Education (Kementerian Riset, Teknologi dan Pendidikan Tinggi – KemRistekDikti) on 'output-based research' open more space for increasing research incentives and reducing the administrative burden. Outputs for publication in an international journal will be valued differently than for a national journal.

Recently the government created a functioning mechanism for mid-level entry to the civil service. This could facilitate both inter-institutional mobility and the engagement of international faculty. As well, some universities (especially the autonomous universities) now have the opportunity to design the academic career path according to their particular needs and requirements. Progress along these lines could help make the case for giving more universities these opportunities.

5 The Way Forward: Reforming Research Culture and Connecting the Disconnected

The point of departure of this chapter is that strengthening the research culture in universities is of paramount importance to reviving the Indonesian knowledge sector and promoting informed policymaking processes. At present the link between the academic and policy worlds is broken. Not only does knowledge produced in the academy rarely inform policy, but overall, Indonesian universities do not have incentive systems in place either to fund research or to encourage academics to devote time to research.

Academic research has two important roles to play in informing policymaking: (1) produce policy-relevant knowledge and (2) provide academic training to future policymakers. However, these roles are impeded by multifaceted problems, at different levels and in various dimensions. Thus reframing the role of the university is an important part of strengthening its research culture.

Universities are not merely the arena in which knowledge production happens. They also serve as a medium through which knowledge production processes are shaped and reshaped. There is a symbiotic relationship between researchers and the university. The process of knowledge accumulation, which is very much the domain of researchers, cannot be successful unless the institution is supportive and nurtures a research culture. This can only become a reality with adequate funding for research. While resources cannot always dictate the quality of research outcomes, they are essential for research to take place.

In the introduction to this chapter, it was noted that the overriding challenge facing Indonesian universities is the absence of a research culture, which was then broken down into three subproblems/constraints. The next section suggested how to transform these challenges into levers of change that can contribute to reforming research in Indonesian universities and bringing that research closer to policymaking processes.

There is no silver bullet to address such complex problems, so rather than providing prescriptive recommendations, the authors reflect on some central issues and offer some key points for reform related to these levers of change as a way forward.

5.1 Universities as Research Environments

First, at a structural level, the reform agenda should be fundamentally directed towards enabling higher education institutions to give more prominence to research through its incentive structure and through interactive schemes with knowledge users. Ideas and initiatives that promote research may be challenged, as teaching is seen as the priority in Indonesian universities.

Several areas of change could be tested. The first concerns financial and nonfinancial rewards for peer-reviewing publications. Creating incentives for mentoring or peer review will contribute to improving research quality in academic institutions. A second area for piloting solutions is through incentives for undertaking multidisciplinary research. Faculties remain compartmentalised, but development problems tend to be multidisciplinary in nature and require multidisciplinary responses. A third area of experimentation and learning would be to find ways to enhance and diversify the interaction and collaboration between students and academic staff through joint research activities, peer review and mentoring support. Likewise, greater interaction between university-based researchers and, for example, policy researchers in think tanks or government units, as well as other actors in the knowledge sector, could be piloted. The creation of 'knowledge hubs' to facilitate interaction between universities and other actors in the knowledge sector, bringing together supply and demand, could be transformative.

The effort to link the administratively separated activities of teaching, research and community engagement into an integrated knowledge production process requires funding and organisational support (universities, schools, departments, study programmes, research centres) to transform existing practices and implement some of the measures suggested here. Without structural changes that foster these linkages, it is futile to argue that universities matter in the knowledge economy, and the achievement of a more equitable society will remain out of reach. Therefore, the authors of this chapter argue for a reform agenda, the first step of which is a focus on funding and career tracks that aim to nurture an academic culture in Indonesia. This reform agenda needs to appreciate both the prevailing bureaucratic model of Indonesian universities and the desired model of a knowledge ecosystem that deliberately interacts with knowledge users.

5.2   *Research Funding*

Section 3 presented evidence about the low level of government funding allocated for research. While this change will be among the most difficult, it has to be addressed; without it, the enabling conditions for quality research will not be in place. The formation of the Indonesian Science Fund, for example, is quite promising, but until it is fully operational and of adequate size and scope, much remains to be done. A clear allocation for research funding in support of development programmes and priorities is required to ensure better-informed development policies and practices. Research to facilitate evidence-informed policy demands specific funding allocations. Some funding also needs to be allocated for 'blue sky' research, to advance knowledge and expand the frontiers of human understanding of nature and society. The restructuring of funding for research must address both policy research and research policy.

To achieve fundamental reform, other key issues also need to be addressed. It is important to put in place a regulatory framework to allocate and reallocate state budgets for research. Institutional arrangements among existing research institutions are also required, to ensure coordinated and orchestrated efforts to ensure that the research budget is used wisely. An accountability mechanism is needed to ensure effective monitoring and oversight of research spending. Finally, although the government still holds the view that the education budget should be spent mostly for infrastructure and enrolment, the earmarked state budget should also be used to fund research. If accurately targeted, the funds could represent a significant increase in funding for research.

5.3 *Research as a Promising Career*

The third area of this reform agenda addresses the career track of researchers and academics. The Kum credit system (see Sect. 4 above) is outdated. The evidence reviewed here suggests that it is detrimental, rather than beneficial, to building research excellence within universities. Professorship and academic career promotion must be modernised. Universities should be encouraged to develop their own fairer, more competitive and merit-based research incentives and to reduce administrative loads. Mentoring and peer review systems need to be built institutionally within universities to strengthen interaction between senior and junior academics. A fair and supportive credit system is compatible with mentoring schemes, which are key to the production of qualified scientific outputs. Mentoring and peer review, when adequately promoted and supported by appropriate reward systems, will be instrumental to strengthening research culture in universities.

At the individual level, the reform agenda calls for strengthening relationships between teaching and research, including the use of research-based teaching materials. Teaching is more engaging when it relies on research findings that are not just new but relevant and contextual. Teaching can also inspire research, by involving students in testing new methods in the classroom or laboratory. This way, the prominence of research in the university is organically built and strengthened. One fundamental change with immediate impact would be policies on salary or remuneration for researchers and academics, which are currently not competitive with other occupations of similar standing. A reform in the recruitment and remuneration of researchers could make a significant difference, especially in ensuring that the best talents and minds remain in the knowledge sector.

Sabbatical leave, prominent outside Indonesia, could represent a quick win to boost spirits and send a message of change and reform to researchers. As a tactical and strategic reform, sabbatical leave requires neither legal changes nor specific arrangements by the central government (especially for autonomous universities). All it takes is a decision by the chancellor or rector – which is largely within the scope of university decision-makers. During their sabbatical, university academics could work in different sectors (e.g. government or business) or exchange their teaching time for research or publication. Thus appropriate schemes for sabbatical leave would provide university academics with 'fresh air' in their career: mobility, knowledge exchange, space for further academic reflection and publication, among others. This would benefit both the university and the researcher.

A note of caution: to successfully undertake these new tasks, universities will need to focus on the development and implementation of a *strategic human resource plan* that will eventually enhance their ability to contribute to a strong, knowledge-based economy.

6 Conclusions

The reform agenda proposed in this chapter aims to strengthen both the structure and practice of research (i.e. the research culture) in Indonesian universities. The proposed reforms can revitalise Indonesian universities as focal points of knowledge production that inform both the society and the policies through which it is governed. The principles of *tridarma perguruan tinggi*[7] offer opportunities for change and for bringing university research closer to policy processes.

A well-interpreted and implemented *tridarma perguruan tinggi* promotes not only teaching and research but also community engagement. Community engagement could represent the link between research on policy issues and development needs – in essence as a platform for exchange. This means using *tridarma perguruan tinggi* to overcome the bureaucratic nature of the university, reviving and revitalising it to achieve professionalisation. The hard fact is that such exchange never guarantees that evidence will inform all policies; but without it, there will never be an informed policy. This is how *tridarma perguruan tinggi* should be revived and given new meaning: from a norm to a platform for exchange between academicians and policymakers.

These challenges in reviving the research culture in Indonesian universities are not straightforward. The issues touched on are not the only issues, and as they are addressed, new issues will emerge. The authors see them, however, as key levers of change where continued efforts could lead to new respect for research within universities, and hope that we have convincingly argued how important it is to strengthen university research in today's knowledge economy. Some aspects outlined here are structural, some propose new modalities and some are intended to strengthen incentives and support for individual researchers. These changes represent an opportunity to foster the link between research and policy, so that universities can play a more important role in achieving an equitable society.

References

AIPI [Akademi Ilmu Pengetahuan Indonesia/Indonesian Academy of Sciences]. (2017). *Era Disrupsi: Peluang dan Tantangan Pendidikan Tinggi Indonesia* (Disruption era: Opportunities and challenges of Indonesian higher education). Jakarta: Indonesian Academy of Sciences.

Brodjonegoro, S. S., & Greene, M. P. (2012). *Creating an Indonesian science fund.* Jakarta: AIPI and World Bank. https://www.aipi.or.id/index.php?pg=detilpublikasi&pid=19&type=3. Accessed 14 June 2017.

Colbeck, C. (1998). Merging in a seamless blend: How faculty integrate teaching and research. *Journal of Higher Education, 69,* 647–671.

DRPM [Direktorat Riset dan Pengabdian Masyarakat/Directorate of Research and Community Services]. (2016). *Panduan Pelaksanaan Penelitian dan Pengabdian pada Masyarakat di Perguruan Tinggi* (Guidelines for implementation of research and Community Services in Universities). Jakarta: Ministry of Research, Technology and Higher Education.

---

[7] Teaching and learning, research and community engagement

DRPM [Direktorat Riset dan Pengabdian Masyarakat/Directorate of Research and Community Services]. (2017). *Rekap Penelitian Tahun 2013–2017* (Research recapitulation 2013–2017). Jakarta: Ministry of Research, Technology and Higher Education.

Foray, D. (2004). *Economics of knowledge.* Cambridge, MA/London: MIT Press.

Ford, M. (2012). *Mechanisms for building research capacity in Indonesia's knowledge sector through Australian universities.* Jakarta: AusAid. http://dfat.gov.au/about-us/publications/Documents/building-indonesian-research-capacity-aust-universities.pdf. Accessed 5 June 2017.

Griffiths, R. (2004). Knowledge production and the research–teaching nexus: The case of the built environment disciplines. *Studies in Higher Education, 29*(6), 709–726.

Guggenheim, S. (2012). Indonesia's quiet springtime: Knowledge, policy and reform. In A. Reid (Ed.), *Indonesia rising: The repositioning of Asia's third giant* (pp. 141–169). Singapore: ISEAS.

Hadiz, V. R., & Dhakidae, D. (2005). *Social science and power in Indonesia.* Singapore: Equinox Publishing.

Horta, H., Dautel, V., & Veloso, F. (2012). An output perspective on the teaching–research nexus: An analysis focusing on the United States higher education system. *Studies in Higher Education, 37*(2), 171–187.

Karetji, P. C. (2010). *Overview of the Indonesian knowledge sector.* Jakarta: AusAID. Available at: http://dfat.gov.au/about-us/publications/Documents/indo-ks8-overview.pdf. Accessed 5 June 2017.

Kompas. (2016, September 15). *Dana Riset Jadi 0,2 Persen PDB, tetapi Cuma Karena Perubahan Rumus Penghitungan* (Research funds became 0.2 percent of GDP, but only due to changes in the calculation formulas).

Moeliodihardjo, B. Y., Biemo, W., Brodjonegoro, S. S., & Hatakenaka, S. (2012). University, industry, and government partnership: Its present and future challenges in Indonesia. *Procedia – Social and Behavioral Sciences, 52*, 307–316. https://doi.org/10.1016/j.sbspro.2012.09.468.

Mok, K. (2008). Varieties of regulatory regimes in Asia: The liberalization of the higher education market and changing governance in Hong, Kong, Singapore, and Malaysia. *Pacific Review, 21*(2), 147–170.

Neumann, R. (1994). The teaching–research nexus: Applying a framework to university students' learning experiences. *European Journal of Education, 29*, 323–339.

Nizam, N. (2006). *Higher education in South East Asia-Indonesia.* https://repository.ugm.ac.id/32578/1/UNESCO_Rihed_Higher_Education_nizam.pdf. Accessed 5 June 2017.

Nugroho, Y., Prasetiamartati, B., & Ruhanawati, S. (2016). *Addressing barriers to university research* (Working Paper 8). Jakarta: Knowledge Sector Initiative. http://www.ksi-indonesia.org/en/news/detail/addressing-barriers-to-university-research. Accessed 5 June 2017.

OECD [Organisation for Economic Co-operation and Development]. (2013). *OECD reviews of innovation policy: Innovation in Southeast Asia.* https://doi.org/10.1787/9789264128712-en

OECD [Organisation for Economic Co-operation and Development]. (2016). *PISA 2015 results in focus.* Paris. https://www.oecd.org/pisa/pisa-2015-results-in-focus.pdf. Accessed 5 June 2017.

Pappiptek LIPI [Pusat Penelitian Perkembangan IPTEK Lembaga Ilmu Pengetahuan Indonesia]. (2014). *Buku Saku Indikator IPTEK Indonesia 2014* (Pocket book of science and technology indicators Indonesia). Jakarta: Pappiptek LIPI.

PDDIKTI [Pangkalan Data Pendidikan Tinggi]. (2017). *Jumlah Dosen Aktif Berdasarkan Jenjang Pendidikan Tertinggi* (Number of active academic staff based on highest education level). http://forlap.dikti.go.id/dosen/homegraphjenjang. Accessed 2 May 2017.

Pellini, A., Helen, T., & Carden, F. (2016, November 16). Indonesia's knowledge sector is catching up, but a large gap persists. *The Conversation.* https://theconversation.com/indonesias-knowledge-sector-is-catching-up-but-a-large-gap-persists-67937. Accessed 5 June 2017.

Rakhmani, I., & Siregar, F. (2016). *Reforming research in Indonesia: Policies and practices* (Working Paper No 72). Washington, DC: Global Development Network.

Rakhmani, I. (2016, February 3). *Insularity leaves Indonesia trailing behind in the world of social research.* Retrieved from The Conversation: https://theconversation.com/insularity-leaves-indonesia-trailing-behind-in-theworld-of-social-research-53973. Accessed 18 Apr 2018.

Rakhmani, I., Siregar, F., & Halim, M. (2017). *Policy journal diagnostic*. Jakarta: Knowledge Sector Initiative. http://www.ksi-indonesia.org/en/news/detail/policy-journal-diagnostic-study. Accessed 5 June 2017.

Robertson, J. (2007). Beyond the 'research/teaching nexus': Exploring the complexity of academic experience. *Studies in Higher Education, 32*(5), 541–556.

Rosser, A. (2016). Neo-liberalism and the politics of higher education policy in Indonesia. *Comparative Education, 52*(2), 109–135.

Sabarini, P. (2016, March 31). Indonesia launches its first multi-year funding scheme for scientific research. *The Conversation*. http://theconversation.com/indonesia-launches-its-first-multi-year-funding-scheme-for-scientific-research-56979. Accessed 5 June 2017.

Simons, M., & Elen, J. (2007). The 'research-teaching nexus' and 'education through research': An exploration of ambivalences. *Studies in Higher Education, 32*(5), 617–631.

Stern, L. N. (2016). *Building on success and learning from experience: An independent review of the research excellence framework*. London: Government of the United Kingdom. https://www.gov.uk/government/uploads/system/uploads/attachment_data/file/541338/ind-16-9-ref-stern-review.pdf. Accessed 5 June 2017.

Suradijono, S. H., Probandari, A., Syafrudin, D., Panggabean, H., & Kurniawan, T. (2017). *Addressing barriers to research in university: Cases from four Indonesian universities. KSI Diagnostic Study*. Jakarta: Knowledge Sector Initiative. http://www.ksi-indonesia.org/in/news/detail/diagnostic-study-of-four-universities. Accessed 14 June 2017.

Suryadarma, D., & Jones, G. W. (Eds.). (2013). *Education in Indonesia*. Singapore: Institute of Southeast Asian Studies.

Syafrudin, D., Nasuhi, H., Darmadi, D., Makruf, J., Umam, S., & Ropi, I. (2017). *Addressing barriers to research in university: A case study of State Islamic University Syarif Hidayatullah* (Kajian Diagnostik Mengatasi Hambatan Penelitian di Universitas: Studi Kasus UIN Syarif Hidayatullah). Jakarta: Knowledge Sector Initiative and Centre for Study of Islam and Society (PPIM) UIN. http://www.ksi-indonesia.org/in/news/detail/kajian-diagnostik-hambatan-penelitian-di-uin-syarief-hidayatullah. Accessed 14 June 2017.

Tilley, H., & Hidayat, D. (2017). *The knowledge sector in Indonesia: higher education and R&D expenditure. Infographic*. Jakarta: Knowledge Sector Initiative. http://www.ksi-indonesia.org/en/news/detail/higher-education-and-rd-expenditure. Accessed 5 June 2017.

Tyfield, D. (2012). A cultural political economy of research and innovation in an age of crisis. *Minerva, 50*(2), 149–167.

UNESCO [United Nations Educational, Scientific and Cultural Organization] Institute of Statistics. *Dataset: Science, technology and innovation*. http://data.uis.unesco.org. Accessed 20 Jan 2017.

Wicaksono, T. Y., & Friawan, D. (2011). Recent developments in higher education in Indonesia: Issues and challenges. In S. Armstrong & B. Chapman (Eds.), *Financing higher education and economic development in East Asia* (pp. 159–187). Canberra: Australian National University E-Press. http://www.oapen.org/download?type=document&docid=459234#page=167. Accessed 25 Jan 2017.

Chapter 3
The Role of Policy Research Institutes in Policymaking in Indonesia

Farini Pane, Irene Astuti Kuntjoro, Siti Ruhanawati, Tanty Nurhayati Djafar, and Kharisma Priyo Nugroho

1 Introduction

The role played by Indonesian policy research institutes (PRIs) in policymaking is evolving. Its features are largely shaped by the dynamic and complex relationships among state and non-state organisations and international development regimes. It emerges in different combinations in different periods; and the combinations shift over time. While many studies on the role of policy research institutes or think-tanks (McGann 2005; Bach et al. 2012; STATT 2012) conclude that PRIs play a vital role in the political and policy arenas of local- and national-level policymaking, the significance of the role and influence of Indonesian policy research institutes in the real world of policymaking is understudied.

Empirical evidence on this topic continues to be a challenge; important instances of success at both the national and subnational levels are usually based on analytical evaluations rather than precise measures of programme impact. Case studies, 'suc-

F. Pane (✉) · I. A. Kuntjoro · S. Ruhanawati
Indonesian Alliance for Policy Research (ARK Indonesia), Jakarta, Indonesia

T. N. Djafar
Australia-Indonesia Partnership for Pro-Poor Policy: The Knowledge Sector Initiative, Jakarta, Indonesia
e-mail: tdjafar@ksi-indonesia.org

K. P. Nugroho
Indonesian Alliance for Policy Research (ARK Indonesia), Jakarta, Indonesia

Winrock International, Bangkok, Thailand

© Springer Nature Singapore Pte Ltd. 2018
A. Pellini et al. (eds.), *Knowledge, Politics and Policymaking in Indonesia*,
https://doi.org/10.1007/978-981-13-0167-4_3

cess stories or smart practices' and other types of reports from development projects[1] provide evidence of influence by Indonesian PRIs in policymaking. However, these stories of influence in specific circumstances face inherent limitations when trying to explain the influence of PRIs in the real world of policymaking, because it is not linear. What these studies represent is limited to a series of logical propositions that serve as proxies of the relationships between PRIs and policymakers. Evidence on how that policy is actually made resides in the domain of bureaucratic knowledge that is both highly experiential and largely tacit. These studies face both technical and political limitations in uncovering the real drivers/incentives for policy change. Nevertheless, the cases help to identify some key features of the roles of Indonesian PRIs in policymaking, as described below.

2 General Framework

Indonesian PRIs and the policymaking realm co-exist within a general framework of research and policy relationships. Although the emergence, evolution and dynamics of Indonesian PRIs are context-specific and unique, their role in policymaking – in terms of how their knowledge products interact with policymaking regimes (i.e. process, structure and products of the policymaking process) – is similar to these processes in other countries. For example, the struggle of Indonesian PRIs to influence development policy echoes some international experiences described by Fred Carden in *Knowledge to Policy* (2009). Carden identified three critical moments (socio-economic crisis, transition and technology) when research can become exceptionally influential, which can be used to explain the situation in Indonesia:

- Indonesia's 1997–1999 economic and political crisis demonstrated a failure of government development policy during the previous decades. This situation forced policymakers to seek research advice from non-governmental organisations (NGOs) that they would previously have ignored or dismissed. But at the time, non-state actors were ill-prepared to present specific, practical solutions to policymakers' problems.
- Political systems undergoing transition (e.g. the decentralisation policy that resulted in direct elections for subnational leaders in the mid-2000s) have gener-

---

[1] See, for example, Yayasan Bakti's smart practices (http://bakti.or.id/en/smart-practices); the Australia-Indonesia Partnership for Pro-Poor Policy: the Knowledge Sector Initiative stories of change series (http://www.ksi-indonesia.org/en/news/index/stories-of-change); the Partnership for Governance Reform (Kemitraan) success story (http://www.kemitraan.or.id/success-story/); etc. These kinds of evidence, according to Hunt and Shackley (2009), fall within the category of 'fiducial science' that is produced as a service to users, rather than for its own ends, comprising that area of work which, in principle at least, provides the knowledge base for the production and implementation of policy decision-making and associated regulations. The audience is thus donors, government and other interest groups, rather than primarily academicians. Products are very often within the 'grey literature' and are frequently not peer reviewed (at least formally) but derive their authority from the status of their proponents and their use by significant policy actors.

ated new opportunities for researchers to influence policy both at national and sub-national levels. Regional Autonomy Watch (Komite Pemantauan Pelaksanaan Otonomi Daerah – KPPOD) is an example of an Indonesian PRI established in response to these opportunities.

- The advent and rapid spread of information technologies and social media have created a 'social media parliament', representing citizen voices and manifested in 'the wisdom of the crowd'. As a result, public opinion cannot be ignored by elected policymakers and civil servants, forcing them to explore new ways to respond and to search out knowledgeable advice.

The literature reflects the experience of Indonesian PRIs, in that the relationship between research and policymaking is not straightforward. Evidence-informed policymaking is a complex process in a complicated landscape of interaction and contestation, in which successful policy is a combination of politics, evidence and delivery (Hallsworth et al. 2011). The persistent failure of efforts to rationalise policymaking elsewhere through, for example, the professionalisation of policymaking applies also to Indonesia. Experience from Indonesian PRIs shows how repeated efforts to define and rationalise policymaking have frequently failed to have an impact, either because policymakers do not see research findings as central to their decision-making or because technical evidence is seen as less important than political evidence (public attitudes and the 'truth of the many' (Rose 2017)). In short, the relationship between research and policy is often tenuous and quite often fraught (Stone et al. 2001).

2.1 Individuals and Institutions

The role of Indonesian PRIs in policymaking varies, but in large measure, it is still a function of individuals within institutions. Scanlon and Alawiyah (2015) reported that the role of individuals in institutions, and within non-governmental organisations (NGOs) as a whole, is an important factor for understanding how the NGO sector functions, including its role in policymaking. An NGO is an institutionalised form of individual activists and personal politics (Antlöv et al. 2006; Antlöv et al. 2010; STATT 2012). As a part of the NGO sector, the role of Indonesian PRIs in policymaking has been driven by their activist staff and by individual relationships and patronage networks. Policymakers generally prefer to source evidence and advice from trusted individuals – often based on long-established relationships, shared social histories, friendships, ideology and/or political affiliations (Datta et al. 2011). In Indonesia, this situation is exacerbated by complicated public procurement regulations that prohibit the state from procuring research services from nonprofit organisations (see Chap. 7). As a result, policymakers prefer links with individuals to those with organisations, which nurture the informal nature of knowledge-to-policy processes in Indonesia. Informal networks become the main platform for information flows from experts and interest groups to decision-makers, helping them to identify what evidence they need.[2]

In a sense, the role of PRIs in Indonesian policymaking is not a function of how their knowledge products influence policy, nor the institutional relationships they build, but rather how individuals within an organisation work through their relationships and patronage networks to influence the policymaking process. Although this varies by region, according to a recent social network analysis among 400 Indonesian PRIs, most of the dominant actors are Jakarta-based NGOs and university-based think-tanks at the University of Indonesia and Gadjah Mada University (Lassa et al. 2017).

2.2 Relationship Between State and Civil Society

The role of PRIs in policymaking is situated within the dynamics of the political-economic relationship between Indonesia's state and non-state organisations. This constellation shapes the relationships between social science and power (Hadiz and Dhakidae 2005), the political economy of research and higher education (Rakhmani and Siregar 2016) and the history of science and politics of knowledge in modern Indonesia (Goss 2011). Thus, the social history (contextual emergence and evolution) of civil society movements in Indonesia is key to understanding the role of PRIs in policymaking and the politics of knowledge in modern Indonesia. This section provides a historical timeline of the role played by Indonesian PRIs in policymaking.

Colonial Period and Early Years of Indonesian State Goss (2011) provides historical data about the relationship between the state and civil society in terms of knowledge production during the colonial period. During the 1830s and 1840s, when the costs of the Java War, the Padri War in West Sumatra and the Belgian Revolution brought the Netherlands to the brink of bankruptcy, a new governor general of the Dutch East Indies, Johannes van den Bosch, was appointed to increase the exploitation of the colony's resources. This was achieved by requiring a portion of agricultural production to be devoted to export crops. Around one-fifth of village land had to be devoted to government crops for export, or, alternatively, peasants had to work in government-owned plantations for 60 days each year. This policy created demand for agriculture-related sciences, such as biology and other natural science disciplines.

In the early 1900s, Melchior Treub, an experimental biologist, equipped the Bogor Botanical Gardens in West Java with a laboratory that became famous among the European scientific community. It established a platform for knowledge production

---

[2] While notes from some Indonesian PRIs and government officials consider using individuals' network to be part of an advocacy or communication strategy, Carden (2009) sees that personal relationships can lead to misgovernment. Personal relationships can lead to a cronyism that will undermine good governance. For him, '…rule by insiderism and influence-peddling is a vice in any country, and it diminishes the prospects for research to influence policy. Researchers can compete in a policy contest of ideas, but not when the game is rigged by string pullers and special favours' (Ibid., 5).

on tropical environments, outside the realm of government. In the 1950s and 1960s, scientists of the newly established Republic of Indonesia considered how to craft a distinctly Indonesian biology. However, according to Goss, all of these efforts failed to create scientific enlightenment in Indonesia because knowledge production was effectively co-opted by the state. Scientific research was subordinated to the interests of the colonial government and then of the independent nation. By controlling the resources for research, the colonial state successfully isolated the scientific community from the public. As a result, a civil society-based scientific movement did not emerge, so there was no general support for the role of science in development.

Soeharto/New Order Era   Subordination of scientific research (including the social sciences) to the state continued into the New Order regime under President Soeharto (1967–1998). Hadiz and Dhakidae (2005) concluded that the role and development of the social sciences (civil society-based policy research institutes and universities) are matters of power. Not only the resources for research but also critical thinking and curiosity as the basis of social science research were controlled by the state. However, government and non-government intellectuals shared a need for think-tank organisations. Non-government intellectuals established the Institute for Social Economic Research Education and Information (Lembaga Penelitian, Pendidikan dan Penerangan Ekonmi dan Sosial – LP3ES) in 1971. In addition to influencing policymakers, their aim was to influence the discourse among Indonesian technocrats. The same year, government-affiliated intellectuals established the Center for Strategic and International Studies (CSIS).

The 1970s and 1980s saw the beginning of 'developmentalism' in Indonesia, as well as the consolidation of the New Order regime. Many government- and university-affiliated research centres (including the Indonesian Science Institute–or LIPI) were established, mainly in response to development challenges or problems. Civil society-based PRIs were limited in number during this period. Most civil society organisations (CSOs) were focused on either grass-roots public service delivery or operated as study clubs (Gordon 1998). Few were engaged in work to influence policy. Even the word 'advocacy' was considered politically taboo and categorised as a subversive activity.

End of the New Order Regime and Beginning of the Reformasi   The situation changed in the 1990s. For Lassa et al. (2017), between 1990 and 1999, at least 55 think-tanks were established, mostly by civil society members. Half of these started as part of the tremendous growth in the number of CSOs throughout Indonesia soon after the collapse of President Soeharto's New Order regime in 1998, when tens of thousands of new CSOs were established (Beittinger-Lee 2009). This boom in policy research organisations continued and gained momentum throughout the reform period (Reformasi) and the decentralisation of the state between 2005 and 2009. These changes show that the activities of civil society groups were interlinked with the power struggles, democratisation processes and international development trends of the time. The crisis sparked by Indonesia's economic and social crisis in 1998–1999 and the state's inability to provide sufficient security and services to citizens strengthened the long-standing demand for democracy. This contributed to the resignation of President Soeharto in 1998 and a shift in the international donor agenda for Indonesia, and also shaped the evolution of the country's CSOs and PRIs. Much has been written about Indonesia's civil society and its role in the process of democratisation and democratic consolidation. Development partners brought financial and technical support to Indonesian NGOs and established various programmes to strengthen democracy, civil society, good governance and the like with the hope that Indonesia's civil society would profit from the political opening.

3 From Non-governmental Organisations to Policy Research Institutes. From Service Delivery to Advocacy and Policy Research

Most Indonesian PRIs evolved from the NGO sector. During the authoritarian New Order regime, policymaking was tightly controlled. The government's development focus and that of its partners was on poverty reduction (Ganie-Rochman 2002; Antlöv et al. 2006), which meant that during the 1970s, Indonesian NGOs played an integral part in development activities, mainly through basic service delivery at the grass-roots level.

In the 1980s the notion of people's *participation* emerged at a time when progress on poverty reduction did not materialise as expected – or perhaps as a result of this failure. Some NGOs began to critique the social and political arrangements in place under President Soeharto's New Order regime. NGOs working on human rights issues started to promote the idea that people's participation is a fundamental right and that by ignoring popular participation in development processes, the state was violating basic political and economic rights of its citizen (Ibid.).

By the 1990s, advocacy around this issue provided NGOs with a viable opportunity to adopt a new, more critical role in promoting social transformation. NGOs voiced concerns about new and old social and political problems. Advocacy allowed NGOs to speak critically of the government – but precluded accusations of their involvement in political activity aimed at challenging the government due to the key idea of people's participation in development, which they promoted through their work at the local level and with communities. NGOs gained international support on several critical issues, such as human rights, women's participation and environmental sustainability (Ibid.).

Following President Soeharto's resignation in 1998, Indonesian governments became more open to the involvement of NGOs in development processes and to the use of knowledge from NGOs to inform policy decisions. The Reformasi era brought political reform in the form of new legislation and amendments to the constitution. During this period NGOs were a key driver of political, economic and social reforms, in particular on women's rights, anti-corruption, freedom of information and religious tolerance. In more technical sectors, such as health, education and finance, the role of NGOs was limited (Pisani et al. 2016).

The 2000s witnessed a shift in the international donor agenda in Indonesia. Assuming that the government was now more stable and capable of handling basic service delivery, development partners shifted their focus to issues such as good governance, regional autonomy and the justice sector.[3] Importantly, they shifted their engagement strategy to include the Indonesian government as their main counterpart. NGOs, which until then had often served as key implementing partners, had to adjust their agenda and strategies accordingly. Grass-roots service delivery NGOs (like Bina Swadaya, Dian Desa and the Appropriate Rural Technology Development Institute/Lembaga Pengembangan Teknologi Perdesaan – LPTP) shifted their strategies to become 'consulting contractors', with the government as one of their 'clients'. Some NGOs established a limited company (Perseroan Terbatas) as a way to access funding. Activists in advocacy NGOs shifted towards providing legal advocacy services (e.g. the Legal Aid Service Foundation – Lembaga Bantuan Hukum) or policy research (e.g. the Institute for Policy Research and Advocacy, Lembaga Studi dan Advokasi Masyarakat (ELSAM), and the Indonesian Centre for Law and Policy Studies, Pusat Studi Hukum dan Kebijakan Indonesia (PSHK).

In sum, the evolution of Indonesian NGOs towards a greater role in knowledge and evidence production could be summarised as:

1. Service delivery – NGO version 1.0 (1970s–1980s)
2. Advocacy work – NGO version 2.0 (1990s–2000s)
3. Knowledge production – NGO version 3.0 (2010–today)

From 2007 to 2014, most of the policy research institutes that evolved and developed are those that managed to develop core capabilities and skills in knowledge production such as project evaluations, assessments and research. It is interesting to note, however, that among those working in the knowledge sector, only a few function as knowledge *producers* – as identified from their peer-reviewed papers in academic journals (Sumarto 2011). Most of these organisations can be called 'knowledge crafters' who do not produce new knowledge, like universities, but rather synthesise and repackage knowledge gathered from external sources, thereby creating new forms of knowledge for different purposes and audiences.[4]

Knowledge crafters serve as a bridge between scientific knowledge and policymakers' needs for evidence. The synthesis and knowledge they generate and communicate to the public and policymakers can be considered as 'professional knowledge' based on synthesis and consolidation of secondary sources, connected to the context in which the policy operates (Nugroho et al. 2017).

---

[3] Human rights issues remained outside the bilateral and multilateral donors' agendas because they are like 'pebbles in the shoe' in building a development partnership with the government.

[4] See Chap. 4 for a review of the concepts of knowledge intermediation and knowledge brokering. Moreover some of the evidence about the development of the core capabilities of policy research organisations can be derived from datasets derived from the ca. 400 applications sent in 2012 to the Australia-Indonesia Partnership for Pro-Poor Policy: the Knowledge Sector Initiative in response to a call for proposals for the provision of core grants and the ca. 600 applications sent to the Australia-Indonesia Partnership for Pro-Poor Policy: the Knowledge Sector Initiative local knowledge grants in 2015 and the financial analysis of over 300 NGOs, a study funded by the Department of Foreign Affairs and Trade in 2015 (Scanlon and Alawiyah 2015).

4 Policy Research Institutes and the Policymaking System

As producer or crafter of knowledge, the role of PRIs in policymaking is also shaped
by the processes and political economy of the demand for evidence, i.e. the policymaking system. Different policymaking systems in different eras – colonial era,
early post-independence period (1945–1960s), early New Order (1970s and 1980s),
early post-Soeharto era (1999–2009) and 2010 and beyond – established different
roles for PRIs. Each period had unique characteristics that shaped the institutional
arrangements and strategies used by policy research institutes to influence
policymaking.

During the colonial era, knowledge was utilised to serve colonial and business
interests, which resulted, according to Goss (2011), in limited achievements among
Indonesian scientists in terms of knowledge production, as compared with their
international peers. In the two decades after independence, from 1945 to 1965, the
political focus was on national identity and crafting a distinctly Indonesian science
capability. In the early years of the New Order (1970s), the development agenda and
closed policymaking system forced Indonesian CSOs to play their role through
alternative 'policy implementation' by providing direct services to communities.
From the 1980s to the end of Soeharto's regime in 1998, 'advocacy' meant quick
mobilisation of supporters to a demonstration when direct action was deemed necessary. In the post-Soeharto era, relationships became more complex and rich, as
government began to acknowledge and attempt to use NGOs' expertise and legitimacy. NGOs, meanwhile, saw the government as neither too bad (to be the enemy)
nor too good (to be a friend).

The role of PRIs in policymaking is structured according to the type of policymaking process. In the centralistic policymaking system in place during the New
Order era, the role of PRIs like the LP3ES and CSIS was mainly to encourage
debate and discourse around policy options among the Jakarta elites who largely
controlled the policymaking process. In this situation, the public policymaking
model was the 'cyclical-linear' approach, a logical sequence of stages, as described
in Law No. 25/2004 on the National Development Planning System. As shown in
Fig. 3.1, the stages of Indonesian policy making are:

During the New Order, policy research institutes were mainly involved in the
'pre-decisional' stages (identifying the problem and building policymaker awareness). The decisional stage was primarily a political process in which PRIs were
seldom involved. New Order technocrats tried to structure the institutional arrangements for supporting better policymaking through the establishment of Research
and Development Units (Balitbangs) within ministries[5] and a dedicated ministry for
development policymaking (Bappenas). PRIs generally focused their advocacy
efforts on Bappenas, instead of the Balitbangs, because Balitbangs tended to be less
influential due to political, structural and technical barriers within ministries
(Cislowski and Purwadi 2011). Most Indonesian PRIs view Bappenas as the most

---

[5]On the role of Balitbangs, see also Chap. 4, Sect. 2.1.

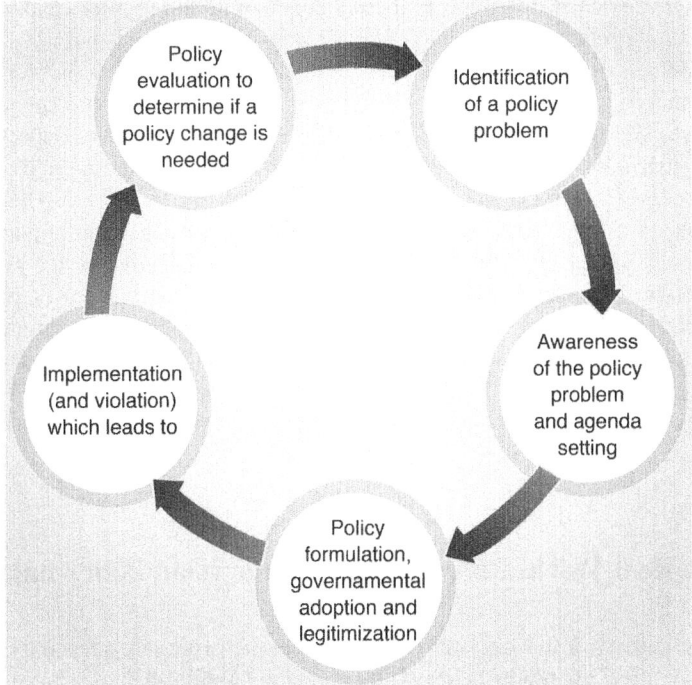

Fig. 3.1 Stages of Indonesian policymaking (Authors)

legitimate actor in the policy planning sector (Lassa et al. 2017). Targeting Bappenas means finding ways to channel policy research to inform the development planning agenda. Bappenas is also an important node because it deals with multiple policy issues across all development sectors (health, education, poverty, environment, etc.). A significant amount of high-level policy research is associated with Bappenas, which is the hub for strategic agreements with the development partners that often fund policy research in Indonesia.

Experiences documented since 2012 – through and by the PRIs[6] that collaborated with the Australia-Indonesia Partnership for Pro-Poor Policy: the Knowledge Sector Initiative – show that the policy process described in Law No. 25/2004 on the National Development Planning System is unrealistic. The PRIs note that in a decentralised public policymaking, policymakers engage different actors at different levels, making the distinct, linear stages unrealistic. The 'stages' of policymaking do not simply often overlap, they are often inseparable. This has led to a shift in focus by PRIs in the post-Soeharto era away from a unique focus on the pre-decisional stages. Today PRIs are spread across all stages of the policy cycle, including policy legitimation.

---

[6] See the list of the partners of the Knowledge Sector Initiative at http://www.ksi-indonesia.org/en/pages/ksi-partners.

A key lesson learned by PRIs in their attempts to influence policymaking is that their research products (i.e. technical knowledge) are necessary, but not sufficient, to exert influence. Researcher bias tends to neglect politics or treat it as something to be 'managed'. Most attempts by researchers to improve policymaking pay little attention to the role of politics, focusing instead on technocratic aspects alone. When politics is acknowledged, it is presented as something external to the targeted policy process, a 'context' that must be 'understood' or 'managed'. This attitude grows out of a long-standing researcher belief, or bias, that the application of 'higher' scientific criteria can resolve problems currently mired in the rather distasteful realm of politics. PRIs have learned that such a treatment of politics is unrealistic: policymaking can never be separated from politics. As outlined in the next section, some PRIs have begun to realise that instead of being a negative factor, politics can add value to policymaking. PRIs are now aware that policymakers draw on multiple sources of evidence and that their technical evidence and analysis are never 'pure' or above politics.

5   The Real-World Role of PRIs in Indonesian Policymaking

The social history of Indonesian PRIs shows that their roles are shaped by the context and political economy in which they operate. While their primary task is to conduct policy research – meaning that their main product is knowledge aimed at influencing policy – their role in the policymaking process goes beyond research.

This section provides specific examples of roles played by Indonesian PRIs. The examples are derived from the experiences of some of the 16 organisations that collaborated with the Australia-Indonesia Partnership for Pro-Poor Policy: the Knowledge Sector Initiative between 2013 and 2017.

Strategic Actors in the Development Community   Over the past 15 years, the most prominent PRIs in Indonesia have acted as strategic partners of bilateral and multilateral agencies working in international development. PRIs launched as a result of support by international NGOs[7] are not as strong in terms of volume of policy research as the PRIs that emerged from support from bilateral and multilateral development agencies. The latter have managed to bridge development partners' interests and bureaucrats' pragmatic needs for knowledge and policy reform. The demand for national PRIs to bridge this gap emerged because it is not politically possible for international development agencies to drive policy reform directly. At the same time, government officials tasked with executing policies and programmes need practical support from donors, as they are overwhelmed with a multitude of tasks and suffer from limited budgets and capabilities. Some Indonesian PRIs have made a conscious decision, for ideological reasons, to keep a certain

---

[7]The emergence and early growth of many Indonesian NGOs was associated with international organizations such as Oxfam, Ford Foundation, Cordaid, Misereor and ICCO.

distance from government agencies, but others have filled this gap and seized the opportunity to access funding and strengthen their capacity through support from international organisations. Some PRIs serve informally as trusted policy advisors to the government through personal network. When the government needs policy research, it asks a development partner to fund it and to support those institutions with which the government has close links.

Providing Data to Support CSO Coalition Advocacy Agendas Most policy advocacy initiatives in Indonesia are carried out through coalitions or networks, with a loose division of labour among members. In general, one or two people are responsible for conducting research or data analysis, as was the case for the Institute for Policy Research and Advocacy (Lembaga Studi dan Advokasi Masyarakat – ELSAM) in the example below.

ELSAM was part of a CSO coalition seeking to revise Law No. 13/2006 on the Protection of Witnesses and Victims, because in their view it created fundamental limitations on probes into past rights abuses and prevented the Witnesses and Victims Protection Agency from helping survivors. The new law (Law No. 31/2014), passed in October 2014, included a measure to step up the Agency's efforts to support victims of past human rights abuses. A key factor contributing to the successful outcome of this advocacy effort was the coalition's capacity to generate and communicate evidence supporting advocacy for policy change. The input to the legal draft provided by the coalition was widely acknowledged by policymakers. While most advocacy activities were conducted through a coalition, ELSAM played a critical role by providing regulatory reviews and drafting the bill. ELSAM also worked with its network of partner organisations at the subnational level to collect and analyse data on human rights violations. In addition, ELSAM provided a platform for data collection and managed a national database system.

Creating Public Pressure by Advocating Through the Media and Social Media At a time when politically appointed policymakers place public perceptions above the evidence provided by experts, the battle to influence policy has gone beyond the quality of evidence to include the issue of whose evidence matters. Policy research institutes in Indonesia are fully aware of these phenomena and know that their role in policymaking includes a mix of policy research and 'working politically'. Seknas Fitra is a PRI and state budget watchdog network that works intensively with the media (especially national opinion makers and newspapers) to inform and convince policymakers that the change agenda they advocate is supported by 'the many'. The strength of their argument lies not only with evidence generated from their research but also by legitimisation from the public.

Focused on a Core Research Agenda to Build Credibility One of the important features of effective policy research is the relevance of the research to the policy reform agenda. However, some Indonesian PRIs approach this proposition differently, allocating a certain proportion of their budget and resources to conducting policy research that may not be directly linked to the current policy reform agenda but is considered important and relevant in terms of the country's long-term social and economic development. They argue that policy research can accomplish more when it is unconstrained by policy goals and aligned with the mission of the research organisation. This is the case for the two examples provided below involving the SMERU Research Institute, the Sajogyo Institute, the SurveyMETER and the Centre for the Study of Islam and Society at the National Islamic University (Pusat Pengkajian Islam dan Masyarakat di Universitas Islam Negeri – PPIM UIN).

The SMERU Research Institute conducts economic research with a focus on poverty reduction. In early 2006 SMERU found that the income distribution gap in Indonesia was widening. SMERU researchers shared these result with policymakers at Bappenas and the National Team for the Acceleration of Poverty Reduction (Tim National Percepatan Penanggulangan Kemiskinan – TNP2K), which at the time had other policy reform priorities. SMERU's management decided to continue the study on income distribution because they considered this to be a key issue for poverty reduction. SMERU's research team thought that continuing their research would help to generate and accumulate evidence that could be used later on. Ten years later, in 2016, the income gap and disparities had continued to worsen, and the commodity boom in Indonesia had ended. This situation forced policymakers to seek research advice from SMERU on inequalities in Indonesia that they had previously ignored or dismissed. These abrupt attitudinal swings rewarded SMERU, which was prepared to present specific practical solutions to policymakers' problems. SMERU was capable of responding because of their accumulated knowledge; the group's credibility led the government to look to them for support.[8]

Research at the Sajogyo Institute focuses on agrarian policies, which they consider central to strengthening community development. The Institute's ability to maintain their focus on agrarian reforms has contributed to strengthening their legitimacy in this policy arena, which has resulted in the expansion of networks and linkages with policymakers. In 2013 the Corruption Eradication Commission research unit sought policy advice from Sajogyo Institute in relation to eradicating corruption in the natural resource management sector. The Corruption Eradication Commission research unit worked alongside Sajogyo Institute's researchers to collect empirical data on corruption cases in forestry and natural resources, conducting a joint analysis and co-producing a white paper on agrarian conflicts and corruption in the forestry sector. The two entities then collaborated on a second study to research and analyse cases of breakdowns in land certification processes reported by people in the district of Trenggalek District (East Java). The collaboration benefitted both partners; each gained exposure to new research methodologies for measuring corruption indicators. The Sajogyo Institute also gained access to a large amount of field data and information, while the research unit at the Corruption Eradication Commission gained a collaborative partnership yielding empirical research findings on forestry and natural resource issues (interview with staff of Sajogyo Institute).

---

[8] Authors' notes from a series of meeting with SMERU on inequalities in Indonesia, November to December 2016.

In 2013 SurveyMETER, a research institute established in 2002 in Yogyakarta and specialised in high-quality data collection and analysis, started an independent research project in 14 cities to assess the extent to which services and infrastructure in those municipalities were prepared to cope with the growing elderly population, as the average age of Indonesia's population is on the rise. The SurveyMETER research team conducted a roadshow to present their findings in all the cities. In the city of Balikpapan, SurveyMETER briefed the mayor, who invited the research team to be part of the Regional Government Task Force to provide policy recommendations to the local government on how to improve the services and infrastructures to meet the needs of elderly citizens. SurveyMETER's engagement with administrators of cities like Balikpapan has helped to inform policymakers' decision and turn policy recommendations into concrete plans and budgets (Suriastini et al. 2016a, b, c; Pellini et al. 2017).

Over the last few years, the Centre for the Study of Islam and Society at the National Islamic University (Pusat Pengkajian Islam dan Masyarakat di Universitas Islam Negeri – PPIM UIN) has gained considerable experience in communicating policy research results and recommendations to the public and policymakers. This has not always been the case. PPIM UIN researchers have traditionally concentrated their efforts on research, rather than communication or advocacy of their findings. However, since early 2015 evidence-based advocacy has gained a greater importance in the organisation. That year a new post was created: Director of Advocacy and Knowledge Management. An organisational policy was introduced requiring each research study to produce, in addition to the report requested by the client, a policy brief with clear policy recommendations. Social media is now widely used by the researchers of PPIM UIN. Two well-attended seminars in 2016 communicated research results on radicalism in Islamic text books and teachers that were covered by national news media such as Kompas, Tempo and *The Jakarta Post*. Policy briefs based on the results were also received positively by the ministers of Education and Religious Affairs, who both considered follow-up on PPIM UIN's recommendations. PPIM UIN also organised internal communications training that provided significant insights into the importance of research communication. Seven of the 15 full-time researchers at PPIM UIN have now received training in writing for journalistic publication and participated in research communication capacity development organised by the Tempo Institute in Jakarta. Senior researchers of PPIM UIN regularly contribute op-eds on Islam and society to national newspapers and are frequently interviewed by national television networks. PPIM UIN has introduced a policy to digitise all reports and knowledge products, including the *Studia Islamika* journal, which received awards from the Ministry of Research, Technology and Higher Education (Kementerian Riset, Teknologi dan Pendidikan Tinggi – KemRistekDikt) and is one of only two Indonesian journals registered by Scopus (Rakhmani et al. 2017).

These examples of the different roles that Indonesian PRIs can play in the policymaking process demonstrate that a mix of strategies and approaches are required to develop linkages and collaboration with policymakers and to establish a profile and reputation that enable involvement in policymaking discussions. Some PRIs decide to work quietly behind the scenes with great success and without much publicity. Others decide to communicate and use that approach to inform policymakers. The best tactic always depends on the principles of the organisation and the circumstances and the nature of the policy issue that the PRI seeks to address. The examples presented in this section also show that as knowledge crafters and knowledge providers, Indonesian PRIs' role in policymaking is often that of intermediary between the government and the public. Measuring their influence is not simple and depends on what counts as influence, particularly in the context of Indonesia's political economy, where many layers, actors and outside forces are at play in the decentralised policymaking process.

6   Conclusions

The role of Indonesian PRIs in policymaking processes is part of a dynamic relationship. It depends on internal factors – such as the state and civil society relationships and power struggles and the ongoing democratisation process – as well as external factors such as global development trends, the data revolution and international politics, in particular the emerging post-truth political discourse.[9] As research institutions, the core mandate of PRIs is to provide research-based evidence to inform policy decision and policy processes.

If the performance of Indonesia's PRIs were to be judged by the number of publications in peer-reviewed journals, they would be rated as weak or very weak. However, a better measure of their performance is the extent to which they make their research results available for use by policymakers (Ofir et al. 2016). Here many PRIs score high as they show a demonstrated capacity to reach policymakers and inform policy processes with a mix of strategic capacity, research skills and capacity to understand the political economy and work politically with the bureaucracy, development partners and funders.

A key message of this chapter is that Indonesia's policy process is driven by values and politics and that from the first post-independence government in the late 1940s to the present, governments have been applying *experimentalist* approaches to governance, largely informed by short-term political opportunities, a process of trial and error, but not so much by evidence and knowledge generated and communicated by PRIs. This approach reflects the lack of a 'pause and reflect' moment (Sabel and Zeitlin 2008).

Indonesia's PRIs adopt different roles in their attempts to inform policymaking. These roles depend on the policy context and circumstances. Key features of effective PRIs in Indonesia are their links with international bilateral and multilateral develop-

---

[9] Jonathan Rose (2017) defines this as a world in which truth is less important than public attitudes and everyone has their own (often incompatible) 'facts'.

ment agencies, credibility in a specific policy area, proactive stance in defining their policy research agendas, access to policymakers and ability to influence public opinion and acquire public legitimacy. As seen in the illustrations above, a combination of these skills and capabilities has given PRIs access to policymaking processes.

References

Antlöv, H., Ibrahim, R., & Van Tuijil, P. (2006). *NGO governance and accountability in Indonesia: Challenges in a newly democratizing country* (Resource Document). The International Center for Not-for-Profit Law. http://www.icnl.org/research/library/files/Indonesia/Peter_NGO%20 accountability%20in%20Indonesia%20July%2005%20version.pdf. Accessed 7 Mar 2017.

Antlöv, H., Brinkerhoff, D. W., & Rapp, E. (2010). Civil society capacity building for democratic reform: Experience and lessons from Indonesia. *VOLUNTAS: International Journal of Voluntary and Nonprofit Organizations, 21*(3), 417–439.

Bach, T., Niklasson, B., & Painter, M. (2012). The role of agencies in policy-making. *Journal of Policy and Society, 31*(3), 183–193.

Beittinger-Lee, V. (2009). *(Un)Civil society and political change in Indonesia: A contested arena.* Routledge: Studies on Civil Society in Asia.

Carden, F. (2009). *Knowledge to policy: Making the most of development research.* Thousand Oaks/Ottowa: Sage/International Development Research Centre.

Cislowski, H., & Purwadi, A. (2011). *Study of the role of Indonesian government research units ('balitbang') in bridging research and development policy* (Resource Document). Australian Department of Foreign Affairs and Trade. https://dfat.gov.au/about-us/publications/Documents/ indo-ks3-balitbang.pdf. Accessed 3 Mar 2017.

Datta, A., Jones, H., Febriany, V., Harris, D., Dewi, R. K., Wild, L., & Young, J. (2011). *The political economy of policy-making in Indonesia: Opportunities for improving the demand and use of knowledge* (Resource Document). Overseas Development Institute. http://www.odi.org.uk/ resources/details.asp?id=5985&title=policy-making-politicaleconomy-indonesia-knowledge. Accessed 3 Mar 2017.

ELSAM. (2016). *Mengembangkan prinsip-prinsip HAM di Kabupaten Sikka.* http://elsam. or.id/2016/09/mengembangkan-prinsip-prinsip-ham-di-kabupaten-sikka/. Accessed 12 Mar 2017.

Ganie-Rochman, M. (2002). *An uphill struggle: Advocacy NGOs under Soeharto's new order.* Pustaka Pelajar: LabSosio.

Gordon, J. (1998). NGOs, the environment and political pluralism in new order Indonesia. *Journal of the Southeast Asian Studies Student Association, 2*(2), 1–26.

Goss, A. (2011). *The floracrats: State-sponsored science and the failure of the enlightenment in Indonesia.* Madison: University of Wisconsin Press.

Hadiz, V. R., & Dhakidae, D. (2005). *Social science and power in Indonesia.* Equinox: Institute of Southeast Asian Studies.

Hallsworth, M., Parker, S., & Rutter, J. (2011). *Policymaking in the real world: Evidence and analysis* (Resource Document). Institute for Government. https://www.instituteforgovernment. org.uk/sites/default/files/publications/Policy%20making%20in%20the%20real%20world.pdf. Accessed 10 March 2017.

Hunt, J., & Shackley, S. (2009). Reconceiving science and policy: Academic, fiducial, and bureaucratic knowledge. *Minerva, 37*(2), 141–164.

Lassa, J. A., Davis, B., Nugroho, K., & Li, D. E. (2017). *Serendipity of think tanks networks and influence in Indonesia.* Manuscript Unpublished.

McGann, J. G. (2005). *Think tanks and policy advice in the United States: Academics, advisors, and advocates.* London: Routledge.

Nugroho, K., Carden, F., & Antlöv, H. (2017, forthcoming). *Local knowledge matters: Power, context and policymaking in Indonesia.*

Ofir, Z., Schwandt, T., Duggan, C., & McLean, R. (2016). *Research quality plus. A holistic approach to evaluating research* (Resource Document). International Developer Research Center. https://www.idrc.ca/sites/default/files/sp/Documents%20EN/Research-Quality-Plus-A-Holistic-Approach-to-Evaluating-Research.pdf. Accesses 5 Mar 2017.

Pellini, A., Djafar, T. N., & Suriastini, N. W. (2017). *Is measuring policy influence like measuring thin air? The experience of SurveyMETER in producing three episode studies of research-based policy influence* (Working Paper 18). Jakarta: Knowledge Sector Initiative. https://goo.gl/7K94WB. Accessed 25 Mar 2017.

Pisani, E., Kok, M. O., & Nugroho, K. (2016). Indonesia's road to universal health coverage: A political journey. *Health Policy and Planning, 32*(2), 267–276. https://doi.org/10.1093/heapol/czw120.

Rakhmani, I., & Siregar, F. (2016). *Reforming research in Indonesia: Policies and practice* (Resource Document). Global Development Network. http://cipg.or.id/reforming-research/. Accessed 2 Mar 2017.

Rakhmani, I., Ruhanawati, S., Darmadi, D., & Pellini, A. (2017, forthcoming). *Religious studies as evidence for policy: Insights from the Centre for the Study of Islam and Society in Indonesia* (Working Paper). Jakarta: Knowledge Sector Initiative.

Rose, J. (2017). Brexit, trump, and post-truth politics. *Public Integrity, 19*, 1–4. https://doi.org/10.1080/10999922.2017.1285540.

Sabel, C. F., & Zeitlin, J. (2008). Learning from difference: The new architecture of experimentalist governance in the EU. *European Law Journal, 14*, 271–327.

Scanlon, M. M., & Alawiyah, T. (2015). *The NGO sector in Indonesia: Context, concepts and an updated profile* (Resource Document). Australian Department of Foreign Affairs and Trade. http://www.ksi-indonesia.org/files/1450222914$1$11C1$.pdf. Accessed 20 March 2017.

STATT. (2012). *NGO sector review finding report* (Resource Document). Australian Department of Foreign Affairs and Trade. https://dfat.gov.au/about-us/publications/Documents/indo-ks15-ngo-sector-review-phase1.pdf. Accessed 20 Mar 2017.

Stone, D., Maxwell, S., & Keating, M. (2001). *Bridging research and policy* (Resource Document). Warwick University. http://www2.warwick.ac.uk/fac/soc/pais/research/researchcentres/csgr/research/keytopic/other/bridging.pdf. Accessed 18 Mar 2017.

Sumarto, S. (2011). *The SMERU research institute: History and lessons learned.* Report to Australia-Indonesia Partnership on Revitalising Indonesia's Knowledge Sector for Development. Jakarta: Knowledge Sector Initiative.

Suriastini, N. W., Pellini, A., Sikoki, B., Fauzan, J., & Rahayu, T. (2016a). *Building partnerships for designing policy: Episode study of Jakarta declaration on dementia- and Age-Friendly City* (Working Paper). Yogyakarta: SurveyMETER.

Suriastini, N. W., Pellini, A., Sikoki, B., Fauzan, J., Pujiastuti, S., & Sukamtiningsih (2016b). *Data that inspires policy: Episode study of City of Balikpapan's experience towards age-Friendly City 2030* (Working Paper). Yogyakarta: SurveyMETER.

Suriastini, N. W., Pellini, A., Sikoki, B., Fauzan, J., Dwiyanti, D. H., & Lestari, S. (2016c). *Information strengthens policy: Episode study of the commitment of Denpasar City in integrating policies of Child-Friendly City, Age-Friendly City, and Green Open Spaces of Healthy City* (Working Paper). Yogyakarta: SurveyMETER.

Chapter 4
Brokering Knowledge and Policy Analysis Within the Indonesian Public Sector

Arnaldo Pellini, Agus Pramusinto, and Iskhak Fatonie

1 Introduction

Three main groups of actors give life to a knowledge sector: *policymakers*, who demand and make use of knowledge and evidence to inform their decisions (see Chap. 6); *knowledge producers*, such as universities, think-tanks, and government analysis units; and *data analytics providers*, who generate and communicate various types of evidence to inform the policy process (see Chaps. 1, 2 and 6). While these groups of actors, with different strengths and capabilities, exist in any knowledge sector, the linkages between knowledge producers and policymakers cannot be taken for granted because, as noted by Lindquist (2009), they are inherently loosely coupled and serendipitous.

Another set of actors that play a vital role in a knowledge sector are *intermediaries* – individuals or organisations who facilitate communication, synthesis and collaboration between knowledge producers and policymakers (Guston 2001).

This chapter is about intermediaries and the role they play in the process of transforming knowledge into policy in Indonesia, with a specific focus on knowledge intermediaries within the government bureaucracy. Other chapters touch on the role

A. Pellini (✉) . I. Fatonie
Overseas Development Institute, London, UK
e-mail: a.pellini@odi.org.uk; ifatonie@ksi-indonesia.org

A. Pramusinto
Public Policy and Administration, Universitas Gadjah Mada, Yogyakarta, Indonesia
e-mail: aguspramusinto@ugm.ac.id

© Springer Nature Singapore Pte Ltd. 2018
A. Pellini et al. (eds.), *Knowledge, Politics and Policymaking in Indonesia*,
https://doi.org/10.1007/978-981-13-0167-4_4

of intermediaries outside government institutions. Chapter 2, for example, focuses on the role of policy research organisations and non-governmental think-tanks. Here the focus is on individuals and units within the bureaucracy and the considerable efforts and investments made by the Government of Indonesia during the last 5 years to strengthen policy research and analysis. The passage of Law No. 5/2014 on the Indonesian Civil Service is particularly significant in this respect. The Law marked the end of 4 years of intense and difficult political negotiations and represented a key step toward modernising the bureaucracy and transforming 'the Indonesian civil service into a world-class government administration more prepared to face challenges as the Asian Century looms' (Effendi 2011). Section 3 of this chapter places special focus on one of the key measures introduced by the new law: the role of policy analysts (*Jabatan Fungsional Analis Kebijakan*).

1.1 Evidence-Informed Policymaking and Knowledge Intermediation

Davies (2012) describes the objective of evidence-informed policymaking as being quite straightforward: 'to help policymakers make better decisions, and achieve better outcomes, by using existing evidence more effectively, and undertaking new research, evaluation and analysis where knowledge about effective policy initiatives and policy implementation is lacking' (41). Translating this objective into practice, however, is not as straightforward. For Davies some of the key challenges are as follows: (i) evidence alone does not tell users what to do, although it provides a basis upon which policymakers can form a judgement; (ii) researchers and policymakers often have different notions of the time required to generate sound evidence and what constitutes sound evidence; and (iii) evidence is only one of the many factors that contribute to policy decisions, which are also influenced by politics and the beliefs, ideology, individual experience and expertise of policymakers. Milani (2005) underlines the political nature of policy decisions and argues that policy decisions are rarely the direct outcome of social science research; rather they are the result of conflicting pressures by social actors, entrepreneurs, social interest groups, political parties and the media.

Given these challenges, the objective of evidence-informed policymaking is not to provide the *absolute best evidence* to policymakers but, more realistically, to provide policymakers with *access to the best available evidence* at key moments (Davies 2012). Knowledge intermediaries have a vital role to play here – through analysis of policy options, synthesis of existing evidence, summarising research results, outreach to knowledge producers, bringing stakeholders together to discuss and debate existing evidence, etc. Roth (2003) describes them as acting as brokers who try to meet the needs of both knowledge producers and decision-makers by enabling access to different types of types of evidence (e.g. research-generated evidence, administrative data, statistics, data analytics and citizen knowledge).

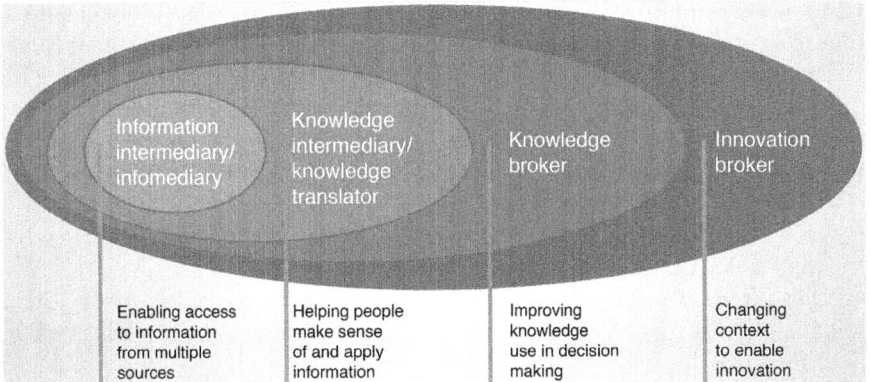

Fig. 4.1 From information intermediary to innovation broker. (Reproduced from Fisher 2010)

The roots of the analysis of the role of knowledge intermediaries in decision-making processes lie in early studies of boundary organisations, that is, organisations able to cross the gap between different expertise areas of expertise and to act beyond the boundaries of a specific sector or domain by encouraging a flow of information and the ability of these organisations to link science and policy in applied research settings (e.g. Guston 1999; Guston et al. 2000). In the evidence-informed policymaking space, analysis and research about the role of intermediary actors have improved understanding of the subtle, but important, differences in the meaning of knowledge intermediation, depending on the degree of engagement by intermediary actors in policymaking processes (Fig. 4.1).

Fisher describes a range of intermediary roles starting from the relatively simple and narrow function of making information available to decision-makers to a more substantial role of helping to transform information into *knowledge* and assist policymakers to make informed decisions (the centre of Fig. 4.1), to an even more complex role in which knowledge brokers contribute explicitly to the use of knowledge in policy decisions, enabling changes in the policymaking context.

Shaxson and Bielak (2012) draw on Fisher's analysis to (i) categorise the different knowledge functions and roles in knowledge-to-policy processes and (ii) describe different modalities of collaboration between knowledge intermediaries/ brokers and policymakers that help to assess the degree of complexity of a knowledge sector and evidence-informed policymaking system. They argue that the linear knowledge transfer (or communication) approach to incorporating evidence into policy is insufficient to capture the complex processes involved in making the best evidence available to policymakers. They list several knowledge processes that occur when informing policy decisions:

- *Knowledge management*: the process of ensuring that knowledge is available by collecting and storing different types of knowledge, to be accessed when needed

- *Knowledge transfer*: a one-way process of sharing knowledge, similar to a teacher-student relationship, which can involve the mutual exploration of a policy issue or problem
- *Knowledge translation*: the process of translating knowledge from one format to another so that the receiver can understand it
- *Knowledge exchange*: a two-way process of sharing knowledge between different groups of people or networks
- *Knowledge brokering*: a two-way exchange of knowledge about a policy issue or problem that can foster collective learning
- *Knowledge mobilisation*: a two-way process that makes use of the existing stock of knowledge to create new knowledge that contributes to fostering policy change

Shaxson and Bielak (Ibid.) then take these knowledge processes and merge them into Fisher's 2010 illustration of the differences between intermediation and brokering. They describe different degrees of complexity of intermediation in policy processes, which the authors cluster under the name 'K* Framework' (or K-Star Framework, depicted in Fig. 4.2).

Starting from the left of the figure, *information intermediaries* support and enable access to information from multiple sources, directing policy actors to the sources of evidence by communicating the information to them. *Knowledge translators* take different sources of evidence and analyse them to understand the implications of the information and try to answer the 'so what?' question. They act as 'translators' because they communicate the findings of their analysis to policymak-

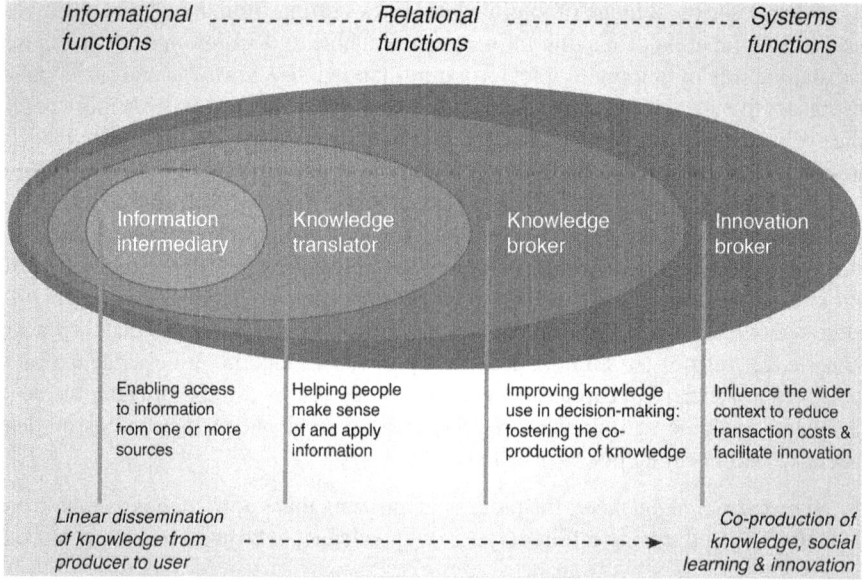

Fig. 4.2 The K* Framework. (Reproduced from Shaxson and Bielak 2012)

ers, going beyond the original evidence. *Knowledge brokers* are individuals, teams or organisations that link the source of information with analysis and with users, trying to foster collaboration and co-production of analysis and knowledge between evidence producers and policymakers. The most advanced role is that of the *innovation broker*, defined as individuals, teams or organisations that actively seek to influence the policy context by establishing collaborations to co-create knowledge and by facilitating innovative solutions to policy problems.

The more interconnected the role of intermediaries, the more interconnected will be the process and systems for making use of evidence in policy processes. Moreover, knowledge intermediaries play a crucial role in creating demand for information, analysis and evidence, thereby contributing to generating or strengthening a culture of information and use of evidence for policy decision-making (Fisher 2010).

The effectiveness of the role played by knowledge intermediaries and brokers depends on two crucial factors. The first is the enabling environment – the set of rules and regulations that legitimise their role within the bureaucracy and provide them with the resources and support required to perform their responsibilities. The second factor, as noted by Mark Considine, is that knowledge intermediaries are equipped with a mix of hard skills in policy analysis, data gathering and interpretation of trends, as well as soft skills, such as interaction with a variety of stakeholders and good understanding of stakeholders' needs and concerns, how their current agenda relates to the social or economic situation they face and how they have tried to solve problems in the past (Pellini 2017). Policy analysis skills are particularly critical in a modern bureaucracy. For MacRae (1991), without policy analysis produced by intermediaries, research-based evidence would be used less for policy choice than for pre-decision enlightenment.

This section stresses the importance of knowledge intermediation (and brokering) in policy processes. It establishes that different degrees of engagement characterise the role of intermediaries in the policy process and that intermediaries can be individuals or organisations and inside or outside government. They are neither policymakers nor researchers but share a commitment to producing policy-relevant data, research or analysis (Lindquist 2001).

The degree to which a bureaucracy has developed its capabilities from the simple intermediation of information to knowledge intermediation and brokering is an indicator of its maturity and a recognition that is has developed the systems and capabilities required to provide policymakers with the *best available evidence* when policy decisions are required.

The next section turns to Indonesia and the experience of some of the partners of the Australia-Indonesia Partnership for Pro-Poor Policy: The Knowledge Sector Initiative, describing the evolution of the intermediation of evidence and policy analysis in policymaking. It reviews the experience of Balitbangs, the research and development units in ministries and local governments, some of which have been in existence for more than 40 years but have struggled to perform as strong knowledge intermediaries. Section 3 discusses the recent reforms undertaken by the Government of Indonesia, through the passage on 14 June 2014 of Law No. 5/2014 on the

Indonesian Civil Service, and establishment of the role of policy analysts through enactment of Ministerial Regulation of Administrative and Bureaucracy Reform No. 45/2013, on the functional position of policy analyst. The final section presents the authors' conclusions.

2 Knowledge Intermediation and Policy Analysis in Indonesia

General Soeharto's highly centralised government ruled Indonesia for 31 years, from the ousting of President Sukarno in 1967 until Soeharto's resignation in 1998. Under a centralised and authoritarian form of government, the policy cycle was controlled at the centre. Public policies were designed and decided by government actors; there was very little, if any, public participation in discussions around public policy formulation from citizens, civil society, non-government actors or the private sector (Jackson and Pye 1978; Crouch 1979; King 1982; Emmerson 2001; Shiraishi 2006).

The institutional set-up of Soeharto's New Order government restricted the flow of information within the bureaucracy to top-down lines of control and encouraged senior officials to grow their sphere of influence through personal skills, wealth and connections. This arrangement enabled President Soeharto to accumulate and distribute authority and maintain political order. Decisions were made by policymakers in Jakarta and implemented by local governments with little or no formal autonomy (Datta et al. 2017). New Order authoritarianism suppressed critical thinking and shut down spaces for policy contestation, although it encouraged technocratic input to policies. Political intervention in the bureaucracy was commonplace; for instance, promotion criteria were usually based on the approval of bureaucratic higher-ups rather than on merit. In addition, an unattractive compensation and benefit system contributed to the poor performance of government officials (Tjiptoherijanto 2007). As a result, the quality of Indonesia's bureaucracy was among the worst in the world, and the country had very poor development indicators (Gie 2003).

President Soeharto resigned in May 1998 due to pressure from civil unrest and following 12 months of severe economic crisis caused by the Asian financial crisis (Lloyd and Smith 2001). His resignation led to a rapid transition to democratic governance (known as *Reformasi*), which was rolled out by several presidents, namely, Habibie, Wahid and Megawati (Shiraishi2006). This period brought very significant changes to Indonesia's political landscape. In June 1999, President Habibie presided over the first multiparty general election in three decades. The same year he also launched the drafting of a new law on regional autonomy, aimed at devolving considerable power to local governments, including power over policy decision-making, budget allocation and control over local resources and activities (Lay 2003; Pratikno 2003; Green 2005). Law 22/1999 on Local Government and Law 25/1999 on Fiscal Balance between Central and Local Government were passed in 1999, implemented in January 2001 and revised in 2004 through the passage of Laws 32 and 33, and more recently through Law 23/2014 on Local Government. Laws 22/1999 and 23/1999 transferred powers and financing to the regions in all sectors except those deemed to be the exclusive jurisdiction of the central government (foreign affairs, judicial affairs, monetary matters and religious affairs). Around one-third of the national budget and three million civil servants were transferred to local governments. The budget figures remain about the same today, even though the number of subnational civil servants has increased (Datta et al. 2017). Overall the implementation of the decentralization reforms started without a well-developed transition or implementation plan and with very little capacity among local governments to take on the new responsibilities (Green 2005; Dixon and Hakim 2009).

In recent years President Joko Widodo, who was elected president in 2014, has attempted to follow through on his election promise to continue, and accelerate, the reform and modernisation of the bureaucracy. For example, in 2016 President Joko Widodo instructed the Minister of Home Affairs to annul thousands of local regulations (*peraturan daerah*) that were not effective or that duplicated each other (Kuwado 2016).

These were significant political and institutional changes because they all open up opportunities for greater demand for evidence. This call for more evidence is not new but has been renewed under the administration of President Joko Widodo and his insistence on developing processes and systems within the bureaucracy to demonstrate the results of public policies and programmes and the use of the state budget. Balitbangs (i.e. research and development units within ministries) have been in place since 1969 but have not been very effective in informing policy decisions. According to Cislowski and Purwadi (2011), Balitbangs are not the only units within ministries that conduct research. Other units may procure research from universities or carry out their own research. This can create overlap in terms of production and synthesis of research and other types of evidence within ministries. More recently, Law No. 5/2014 on the Indonesian Civil Service aims to modernise the Indonesian bureaucracy, applying principles of meritocracy and establishing the role of policy analyst. Another example is Law No. 23/2014 on Local Governments, which established Balitbangda within local governments and mandates them to assist in local policy decisions. Several ministries (Ministry for National Development Planning/National Development Planning Agency (Kementerian Perencanaan Pembangunan Nasional/Badan Perencanaan Pembangunan Nasional – Bappenas), Ministry of Finance, Ministry of Education and Culture have established, over the last few years, rapid response units to provide ministers with fast, succinct policy analysis and advice.

It has been 19 years since the resignation of President Soeharto and 16 years since the start of decentralization reforms. From the point of view of demand for evidence by elected and non-elected leaders at all levels of government – who determine Indonesia's policy priorities and are instrumental in approving budget allocations and regulations affecting knowledge suppliers – Karetji (2010) argues that Indonesia is transitioning from a past of low accountability and top-down decision-making to today's decentralised governance. The shift has involved a limited but growing demand for evidence as the country is moving towards a future scenario characterised by solid democratic rule, democratic decentralisation, leadership guided by accountability to citizens, and government organisations that actively demand different types of evidence from internal and external sources. This means that central government organisations require (and will require more and more) data and analysis oriented toward supporting macro-level policymaking. Local governments, meanwhile, will require an increasing amount of data and locally relevant analysis as inputs to social development interventions.

The next sections review some Indonesian experiences with knowledge intermediation within the government bureaucracy, before describing more in depth the role of policy analysts.

2.1 Knowledge Production and Intermediation Within the Government: Role and Challenges of Balitbangs

Every ministry in Indonesia has a Balitbang responsible for the development of research plans and programmes in its particular sector (see, e.g. Minister of Education and Culture Decree no. 36/2010 and Minister of Health Decree no. 1144 /2010). The research results can then be used to inform internal policy decisions or help to advance knowledge in a specific sector.

These research units have been in place for many years; for example, the Balitbang at the Ministry of Education and Culture and the Ministry of Health was established in 1969 and 1975, respectively. Balitbangs are fairly large organisations. The Balitbang at the Ministry of Education and Culture (Kementerian Pendidikan dan Kebudayaan – Kemdikbud) consists of 1,166 staff in Jakarta and regional offices. The unit at the Ministry of Health (*Kementerian Kesehatan*) has about 420 staff in Jakarta (Cislowski and Purwadi 2011). They are organised as research centres that may have a thematic focus. For example, the Balitbang at the Ministry of Education has a Policy Research Centre, a Curriculum and Book Centre and an Educational Assessment Centre.

At the local level, Balitbangs are one of the several local government units (*Satuan Kerja Pemerintah Daerah* – SKPDs) located in both provinces and districts. Similar to the ministerial Balitbangs, local-level Balitbangs assist district heads and line agencies with research and analysis to inform local policy decisions.

In their analysis of the ministerial Balitbangs at the ministries of education and health, Cislowski and Purwadi (2011) found that while budget allocations to Balitbangs were increasing, they represented a very small percentage of ministry budgets. For example, the Education Balitbang saw its budget increase from 1.59%

of the total ministry budget in 2009 to 2.22% in 2011. That corresponded to Indonesian rupiahs (IDR) 1,232,000,000 for 2011 (approximately to US$135,800,[1] or US$323 per staff member annually). Not much, considering that the Ministry of Education and Culture is one of the largest recipients of state budget allocations.[2] In 2009 Balitbangs at the Ministry of Health received 1.95% of the ministry budget; in 2011 the percentage dropped to 1.07%, although the amount grew to IDR 540,041,000, representing approximately US$59,540[3] for that year, or US$51 annually per staff member (Ibid.).

The limited availability of budget funding for Balitbangs is also evident at the local level, as shown in this example from a Balitbang in a district in East Java province with 27 staff members.[4] In 2016 the Balitbang received around IDR 1,000,000,000 (c. US$74,850),[5] which was allocated to the work of the secretariat and the Balitbangs' four divisions, each of which is divided into three subdivisions. The Balitbang thus had 12 sub-divisions in total. Of the total budget, the secretariat received IDR 500 million (c. US$37,000) for salaries and other operational costs. Each division received IDR 125 million (c. US$9,350), leaving each sub-division with the challenge of operating for a year with the equivalent of US$3,100.

2.1.1 Challenges Facing Balitbangs

The figures above highlight a critical problem for Balitbangs: funding. The data show that budget allocations are too small to produce and communicate high-quality research that can be used by a ministry or the government at large to inform policy decisions. Limited funding also makes it difficult to attract qualified staff, as salaries are not competitive and are pegged to the civil servants' remuneration framework. Between 26% and 31% of the staff at the two Balitbangs in health and education lack an undergraduate degree; 43% to 44% possess an undergraduate degree. The remaining 23% to 29% have postgraduate qualifications, mainly Masters' degrees (Cislowski and Purwadi 2011).

Other issues also contribute to the limited influence of Balitbangs in evidence-based policy processes.

A mix of regulatory barriers and established practices hinders the capability of ministries and local governments to strengthen the role of Balitbangs. These include

---

[1] Exchange rate on 31/12/2011 1 US$ = 9,070 IDR. See http://www.exchange-rates.org/Rate/USD/IDR/12-31-2011

[2] At number seven, after Public Works and Housing, Defense, Police, Health, Religious Affairs (Negara 2016)

[3] Exchange rate on 31/12/2011 1 US$ = 9,070 IDR. See http://www.exchange-rates.org/Rate/USD/IDR/12-31-2011.

[4] Name of the district withheld

[5] Average exchange rate in 2016 1 US$ = 13,360 IDR. Available at http://www.exchangerates.org.uk/USD-IDR-exchange-rate-history.html

the rigid 1-year budget cycle, which impedes the conducted multi-year research and studies (see also Chap. 7), the vested interests of various agencies and individuals in commissioning their own research and the tendency of development partners to work directly with directorates within ministries, bypassing the Balitbangs. Other obstacles include the absence of a grand strategy within ministries that clearly describes their need for evidence and the resources to produce and procure it, with the help of Balitbangs, the separation between *functional* staff (specialists) and *structural* staff (administrative staff). Lastly, ministries and local governments must cope with the complexity and ambiguity of the decree on procurement, which leaves Balitbangs unsure whether or not they can procure research from universities and think-tanks (see Chap. 7) (Cislowski and Purwadi 2011; Sherlock 2010).

To conclude, using the K* Framework (Fig. 3.2), Balitbangs appear to function mainly as information intermediaries. They are better positioned than external think-tanks, for example, to link to policy formulation and implementation processes, as well as to decision-makers and senior policymakers in ministries and local government. However, they struggle. The capacity and resources to conduct high-quality research and inform policy are simply not available, which poses the question of whether Balitbangs are necessary at all or whether another type of organisation or actor is required to provide the research, evidence and policy analysis needed by policymakers.

2.2 Experimenting with the Government Think-Tank Model

Government think-tanks are an alternative model for providing governments with evidence and analysis. Being embedded in the government structure brings several benefits, such as a strong understanding of government programmes and priorities, which helps to tailor advice to actual policy needs and coordinate across government departments (Mackenzie et al. 2015). Given the structural problems faced by Balitbangs, Indonesian governments have been looking into this option for some years.

When President Joko Widodo announced his first cabinet on 26 October 2014, he used the opportunity to describe it as a 'working cabinet' and to make certain structural changes, including removing Bappenas from the Coordinating Ministry of Economic Affairs and requiring that it report directly to the president and assume the role of national 'think-tank'.

This followed other attempts to incorporate a think-tank function into the government, a gap that different presidents have also tried to fill. For example, in December 2009, at the beginning of his second term, President Susilo Bambang Yudhoyono established the 'President's Delivery Unit of Development Monitoring and Oversight', known as UKP4 (Unit Kerja Presiden Bidang Pengawasan dan Pengendalian). At that time, this was understood as a sign that President Yudhoyono believed that Bappenas was not doing its job of oversight and general evaluation. UKP4, sitting directly under the president, was seen as more powerful and well-positioned to provide both timely feedback on outcomes and forward-looking strategic advice.

The decision to bring Bappenas directly under President Joko Widodo's office is a sign that he wants to strengthen its role. Whether Bappenas is able to perform the new think-tank role in addition to its responsibility for planning, and to some extent budget allocation, is yet to be seen. What is clear, however, is that, internally, there have been attempts to develop a think-tank-type unit to better coordinate the research, analysis and monitoring of development plans that Bappenas is mandated to carry out.

The Policy Analysis Unit was established in late 2010 as a pilot to support Bappenas in producing quick turnaround policy products to support Indonesia's role in national, regional and international development forums. The Unit's establishment was supported with funding and technical assistance through a programme funded by the Australian Government Development Agency (AusAID), from 2011 to mid-2013.[6] In 2012, the Policy Analysis Unit was renamed 'Policy Analysis Team', with an executive secretary to manage the production, coordination and communication of policy products. The goal was to allow for greater ownership of policy analysis across the different working units in Bappenas. The support continued when the Australia-Indonesia Partnership for Pro-Poor Policy: The Knowledge Sector Initiative, a joint programme of the Indonesian and Australian governments, was launched in May 2013. The Knowledge Sector Initiative seeks to improve the lives of the Indonesian people through better quality public policies that make better use of research, analysis and evidence. In late 2014 an internal reorganisation at Bappenas resulted in the renaming of the Policy Analysis Team into its Bahasa Indonesian wording Tim Analisis Kebijakan (TAK) and the appointment of a new executive secretary. The fourth iteration of the unit occurred in early 2016, when the new Minister of Bappenas, Sofyan Djalil, established the Centre for Policy Analysis (Pusat Analisis Kebijakan, PAK) as a structural unit within Bappenas. The Centre for Policy Analysis reports directly to the Minister, receives a budget allocation and is headed by an echelon two official.[7]

The Centre for Policy Analysis represents a step in the direction of transforming Bappenas into a national think-tank. It is an opportunity, but there are capability challenges. The new Centre for Policy Analysis has a clear intermediary function within Bappenas, which appears to be more than a simple information intermediary function. The team provides briefs to senior officials, which shows that team members can act as knowledge translators, using the terminology of the K* Framework. They also engage with external research institutes and universities,

---

[6] The Knowledge Sector Initiative began to develop a working relationship with the Policy Analysis Team on 1 July 2013 with the transition of the contractual support to the Knowledge Sector Initiative.

[7] Indonesian public servants work in a highly structured hierarchy. The ministers head this organisation and are appointed by the president. Beneath them is the public service hierarchy which is organised in both echelons and grades. A person's management position within the hierarchy is indicated by their echelon, with echelon 1 indicating the highest and echelon 5 the lowest management positions. Secretaries-General and Directors-General are assigned as echelon 1 officials. Directors and heads of central support units are usually assigned as echelon two, as are the head of bureau in the Secretariats-General.

with which they collaborate to produce cross-cutting analysis that is packaged into accessible knowledge products (memos, policy briefs, position papers, etc.) and submitted to the Minister of Bappenas and the Executive Office of the President (Kantor Staf Presiden). In this case, the Centre for Policy Analysis acts as a knowledge translator. The challenge lies in the fact that except for a small core team of full-time staff (*structural* positions), the Centre's team is formed by functional staff serving on a voluntary basis from across Bappenas, limiting continuity. A second problem is the absence of a strong internal management process for overseeing and monitoring research activities, which has resulted in delays and insufficient quality assurance for final research outputs. A third problem is the lack of clear selection criteria for collaboration with research partners based on organisational or research capacity (Utama 2017).

3 Policy Analysts as Professional Knowledge Intermediaries Within Government

The passage of Law No. 5/2014 on the Indonesian Civil Service marked a significant step in the direction of modernising the Indonesian civil service and bureaucracy to meet the policymaking and other needs of a modern economy. The Law includes provisions for a stronger policy analysis function within the bureaucracy, which is assigned by Article 44 to the National Institute of Public Administration (Lembaga Administrasi Negara – LAN). The main role and responsibilities of policy analysts are described in the Ministerial Regulation of Administrative and Bureaucracy Reform No. 45/2013 on 'Functional Position of Policy Analysts' and comprise identifying policy problems, forecasting, developing policy recommendations and monitoring and evaluating policy implementation (Fatonie 2017). Two government organisations are assigned responsibility for policy analysts. The Ministry of State Administrative and Bureaucratic Reform (Kementerian Pendayagunaan Aparatur Negara dan Reformasi Birokrasi) issued a decree that establishes policy analysis as a *functional* position in the civil service and defines modalities for the recruitment of policy analysts from within the bureaucracy. The LAN is mandated to design and provide training for and accreditation of policy analysts. The target set by the government is to have at least 6,000 trained and accredited policy analysts by 2019, working at both the national and subnational levels (informant interview 2016). The total number of policy analysts across the bureaucracy when all the positions will be assigned is expected to be close to 200,000 (informant interview 2016).

As noted by Fatonie (2017), policy analysts can play a key knowledge intermediation role between knowledge producers in universities, Balitbangs or think-tanks and policymakers and civil servants, which until now was missing in Indonesia. The

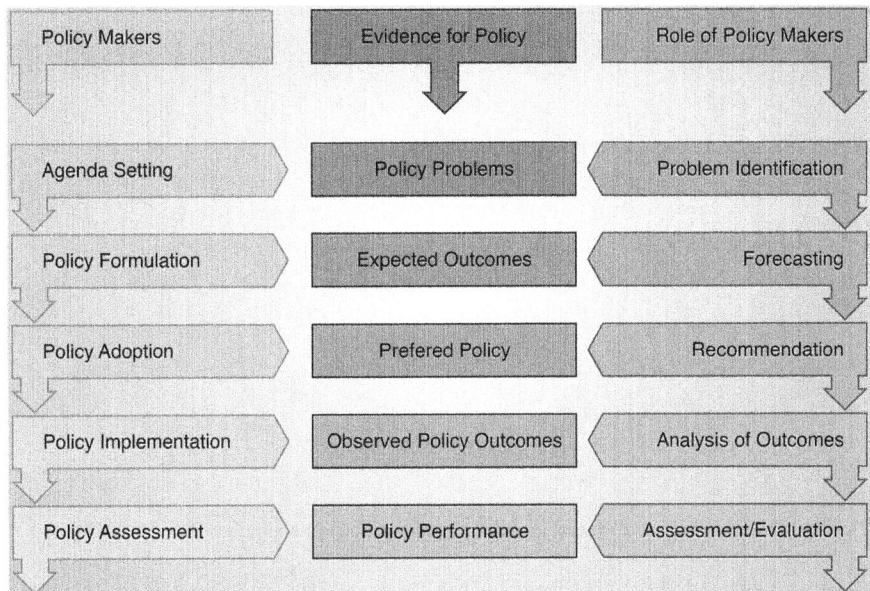

Fig. 4.3 Role of policy analysts and the types of evidence they can generate to inform the policy process. (Reproduced from Kumorotomo et al. 2013)

role of policy analyst is important during each phase of the policy cycle,[8] and one of the expected outcomes from the insertion of policy analysis in government organisations is that more evidence will be used to inform policy decisions. This is expected to occur as a result of their closer involvement in policymaking through problem identification, forecasting, providing policy recommendations, analysis of policy outcomes and assessment or evaluation of policy performance, as depicted in the green column of Fig. 4.3 (Dunn 2004, Fatonie 2017).

As shown in the figure, the evidence produced by policy analysts can help to clarify the nature and political economy of policy problems and the expected outcomes of different policy options, as well as to provide criteria for comparing different policy options and alternatives. While policies are being tested and implemented, policy analysts can assess their outcomes and impact. To provide these inputs, policy analysts must know where to find the data and be able to analyse the data and transform it into evidence, which is then synthesised and communicated to policymakers (see Fig. 4.4). At a minimum, they may play the role of information intermediaries, but hopefully, with time, they can become more involved in policymaking processes and take up the role of knowledge brokers described in Fig. 4.2.

Good policy analysis requires skills. Since 2015, the LAN has trained and certified about 100 civil servants from ministries and local governments (e.g. from the

---

[8]Academic Paper on Functional Position of Policy Analyst in Indonesia, University of Gadjah Mada (UGM) and National Institute of Public Administration (LAN), December 2013

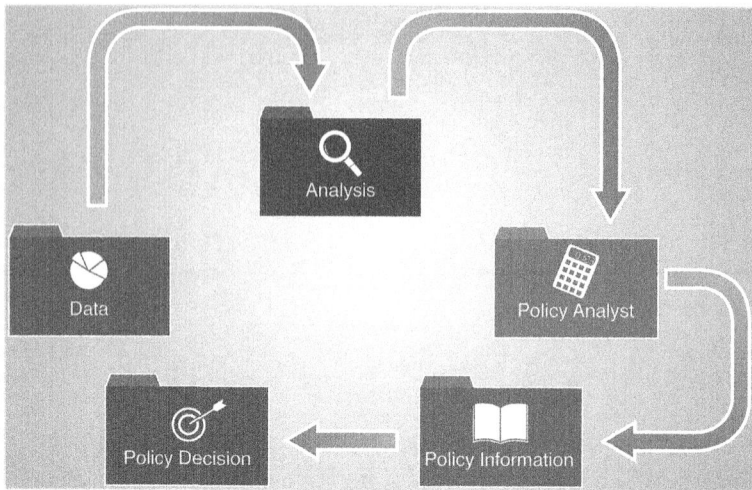

Fig. 4.4 The knowledge translation process. (Reproduced from Kumorotomo et al. 2013)

Ministry of Communication and Information, Secretariat General of the Indonesian House of Representatives, National Resilience Agency and Ministry of Home Affairs) as policy analysts. There are two types of application and certification processes for policy analysts. The first is through a competency test for junior civil servants. The second is through job transfer or promotion (also known as 'inpassing') for mid-level to senior civil servants.

The target of 6,000 policy analysts by 2019 is very ambitious and will test the capacity of the LAN to prepare this new cadre of civil servants. To realise this plan, the LAN has established collaboration with some top-level universities (University of Gadjah Mada, University of Diponegoro and University of Indonesia) to conduct training for policy analysts. The training programme lasts for three weeks and involves classroom-style teaching provided by institute staff and academics.

3.1 Opportunities and Challenges for Policy Analysts

Section 3.1 explains that the role of knowledge intermediaries can involve different degrees of complexity and sophistication, depending on the enabling environment in which they perform their role. Thus, there is scope for experimentation with different degrees of complexity in undertaking policy analysis – if one important challenge can be overcome.

In June 2016, the Ministry of State Administrative and Bureaucratic Reform (Kementerian Pendayagunaan Aparatur Negara dan Reformasi Birokrasi) issued a decree that regulates the job grading (*kelas jabatan*) of policy analysts, organising them into four categories: beginner, junior, mid-level and senior. The position of policy analyst is a *functional* position, and the four categories determine the applicable remuneration level and additional incentives. The post's status as a functional position carries a risk of overlapping with the tasks and role of other functional positions, which are basically advisory roles (e.g. expert staff or *staf ahli*). As a result, some questions remain to be clarified, such as the difference between the role of a policy analyst, a development planner in Bappenas and a researcher working, for example, in a ministerial Balitbang. All three perform (to various degrees) research and analysis and could be asked to produce a research synthesis or policy brief. These overlaps need to be resolved because they raise the risk of limiting the added value to policy processes that policy analysis can bring. Without a clear distinction of roles, skills and responsibilities, policy analysis can be relegated to a secondary role – which will not attract potential candidates.

The second option assumes that policy analysts are posted in a specific unit and dedicated to any local government department (dinas). They can work collectively and be assigned to serve any local agency that needs their expertise in making policy recommendations. Based on this model, a unit containing policy analysts could be established so that a local government may need only 10–15 policy analysts who work collectively. However, the consequence would be that policy recommendations cannot be delivered as quickly as with the first model. In addition, the limited number of policy analysts and their separate offices, distant from those of decision-makers, is liable to inhibit communication between policymakers and policy analysts.

The recruitment of policy analysts, particularly at senior level, may pose a challenge. Junior policy analysts are nominated by the ministry or agency where they work. They then receive training to equip them with the technical and policy competencies required. But recruiting senior civil servants as policy analysts may be more challenging, as senior officials who hold a *structural* position may be reluctant to exchange their role, where they can exert some authority, for a *functional* role as policy analyst, which is mainly advisory.

The continuing development of a culture of demand and use of evidence in policymaking will be a key success factor for the role of policy analyst. Without demand from policymakers and civil servants, the analysis produced by analysts does not have a client. Although demand for evidence-based research is slowly growing within Indonesia's bureaucracy, policy decisions are still made based on perceptions or intuition and without a strong appetite for critical evidence (Nur Rochmi 2015).

4 Conclusions

Various attempts have been made to strengthen the knowledge intermediation function within Indonesia's government organisations over the last few decades. The results have been modest. Balitbangs have not been able to move beyond the role of information intermediaries. In response to this situation, the Ministry of State Administrative and Bureaucratic Reform (Kementerian Pendayagunaan Aparatur

Negara dan Reformasi Birokrasi) is conducting an assessment aimed at deciding whether and how to revitalise the role of Balitbangs or whether they should be dismantled.

The strengthening of Bappenas' role as the national think-tank – and within Bappenas of the role of think-tank units such as the PAK – is a work in progress and may require considerable structural reform, as well as increased organisation and research and analysis capacity. Politics will also play an important role in this regard.

The establishment of the policy analyst position is a promising step toward modernising Indonesia's bureaucracy and developing a system for introducing more evidence and analysis into policy decisions. The training curriculum developed by the LAN focuses on the analytical skills required for policy analysis and knowledge of the policy cycle. With time, it should also include greater emphasis on the soft skills mentioned by Considine (see Sect. 1.1) that are required to interact with different stakeholders and understand the political economy of current policy agendas.

The newly established Indonesian Policy Analysts Association (*Asosiasi Analis Kebijakan Indonesia* – AAKI), founded in September 2016, includes 110 policy analysts in ministries and local governments and is a very promising initiative to strengthen the role, functions and visibility of policy analysts. The objective of the Association is to become a hub not only for policy analysts but also for other knowledge producers and intermediaries (e.g. in Balitbangs, policy analysis units in ministries, NGOs and CSOs, and research and development units in the private sector, universities and the media) who play a role in policy research and evidence-informed policymaking.

Policy analysis creates an opportunity to develop the knowledge-brokering function within government entities described by Fisher (2010) and Shaxson and Bielak (2012). This can help to strengthen the demand for and use of evidence in the policy cycle in Indonesia and ensure the development of spaces where government organisations actively demand analysis and evidence (Karetji 2010) and, as noted by Shaxson (2014), internal and external stakeholders discuss what evidence is needed to help address policy priorities.

References

Cislowski, H., & Purwadi, A. (2011). *Study of the role of Indonesian government research units ('Balitbangs') in bridging research and development policy*. Jakarta: AusAID.

Crouch, H. (1979). Patrimonialism and military rule in Indonesia. *World Politics, 31*(4), 571–587.

Datta, A., Nurbani, R., Satria, G., Antlöv, H., Fatonie, I., & Sabri, R. (2017, forthcoming). *Policy, change and paradox in Indonesia: Implications for the use of knowledge* (Working Paper). Jakarta: Knowledge Sector Initiative.

Davies, P. (2012). The state of evidence-based policy evaluation and its role in policy formation. *National Institute Economic Review, 219*(1), 41–52.

Dixon, G., & Hakim, D. (2009). Making Indonesia's budget decentralisation work: The challenge of linking planning and budgeting at the local level. *International Public Management Review, 10*(1), 119–169.

Dunn, W. N. (2004). *Public policy analysis: An introduction.* Upper Saddle River: Pearson-Prentice Hall.

Effendi, S. (2011). Finally, a new civil service law. *The Jakarta Post.* http://www.thejakartapost.com/news/2014/02/03/finally-a-new-civil-service-law.html. Accessed on 25 Apr 2017.

Emmerson, D. K. (2001). *Indonesia beyond Soeharto: Negara, Ekonomi, Masyarakat.* Jakarta: Gramedia.

Fatonie, I. (2017). *End of intervention report: Support to the National Institute of Public Administration (LAN) on strengthening the capacity of policy analysts. Internal report.* Jakarta: Knowledge Sector Initiative.

Fisher, C. (2010). *Knowledge brokering and intermediary concepts.* Analysis of an e-discussion on the Knowledge Brokers' Forum. http://www.preventionweb.net/files/workspace/33381_knowledgebrokeringandintermediaryco.pdf. Accessed 21 Apr 2017.

Gie, K. K. (2003). *Reformasi Birokrasi dalam Mengefektifkan Kinerja Pegawai Pemerintahan* (Bureaucratic reform toward a more effective government official's performance). Jakarta: Workshop Gerakan Pemberantasan Korupsi, PBNU.

Green, K. (2005). *Decentralization and good governance: The case of Indonesia.* Munich Personal RePEc Archive. https://mpra.ub.uni-muenchen.de/18097/1/Decentralization_and_Good_Governance-The_Case_of_Indonesia.pdf. Accessed 2 Apr 2017.

Guston, D. (1999). Stabilizing the boundary between politics and science: The role of the office of technology transfer as a boundary organization. *Social Studies of Science, 29,* 87–111.

Guston, D. (2001). Boundary organizations in environmental policy and science: An introduction. *Science Technology and Human Values, 26*(4), 299–408.

Guston, D., Clark, W., Keating, K., Cash, D. Moser, S., & Powers, C. (2000). *Report of the workshop on boundary organizations in environmental policy and science,* 9–10 December 1999, John F. Kennedy School of Government at Harvard University. https://www.hks.harvard.edu/gea/pubs/huru1.pdf. Accessed 15 Apr 2017.

Jackson, K. D., & Pye, W. (1978). *Political power and communications in Indonesia.* Berkeley: University of California Press.

Karetji, P. C. (2010). *Overview of the Indonesian knowledge sector.* Jakarta: AusAID.

King, D. Y. (1982). Indonesia's new order as a bureaucratic polity, a neopatrimonial regime or a bureaucratic authoritarian regime: What difference does it make? In B. Anderson & A. Kahin (Eds.), *Interpreting Indonesian politics: Thirteen contributions to the debate.* Ithaca: Cornell University Press.

Kumorotomo, W., Purwanto, E. A., Pramusinto, A., Widaningrum, A., Dwiputrianti, S., & Rahmalia, M. (2013). *Naskah akademik jabatan fungsional analis kebijakan* (Academic Paper on Policy Analysts as a Functional Position). Jakarta/Yogkjakarta: National Institute of Public Administration/University of Gadjah Mada.

Kuwado, F. J. (2016, June 13). *Jokowi: 3.143 Perda Bermasalah Telah Dibatalkan* (Jokowi: 3.143 local regulations have been cancelled). *Kompas.com.* http://nasional.kompas.com/read/2016/06/13/17215521/jokowi.3.143.perda.bermasalah.telah.dibatalkan. Accessed 15 Apr 2017.

Lay, C. (2003). Otonomi daerah dan keindonesiaan. In A. G. Karim (Ed.), *Kompleksitas Persoalan Otonomi Daerah di Indonesia* (pp. 3–32). Yogyakarta: Pustaka Pelajar.

Lindquist, E. A. (2001). *Discerning policy influence: Framework for a strategic evaluation of IDRC-supported research.* International Development Research Center. http://www.bettere-valuation.org/sites/default/files/discerning_policy.pdf. Accessed 19 Apr 2017.

Lindquist, E. A. (2009). *There's more to policy than alignment.* Research Report. Canadian Policy Research Networks Inc. http://observgo.uquebec.ca/observgo/fichiers/80533_RCRPP_A.pdf. Accessed 22 Apr 2017.

Lloyd, G. J., & Smith, S. L. (2001). Thoughts on Indonesian history. In J. L. Gayson & S. L. Smith (Eds.), *Indonesia today: Challenges of history* (pp. 1–13). Lanham: Rowman & Littlefield.

Mackenzie, J., Pellini, A., & Sutiyo, W. (2015). *Establishing government think tanks: An overview of comparative models* (Working Paper 4). Jakarta: Knowledge Sector Initiative.

MacRae, D. (1991). Policy analysis and knowledge use. *Knowledge and Policy, 4*(3), 27–40. https://doi.org/10.1007/BF02693086.

Milani, C. R. S. (2005). *Evidence-based policy research: Critical review of some international programmes on relationships between social science research and policy-making* (Policy Papers No. 18). UNESCO. http://unesdoc.unesco.org/images/0018/001834/183415e.pdf. Accessed 30 Apr 2017.

Negara, S. D. (2016). Indonesia's 2016 budget: Optimism amidst global uncertainties. *Perspective, 2016*(3), 1–13. https://www.iseas.edu.sg/images/pdf/ISEAS_Perspective_2016_3.pdf. Accessed 2 May 2017.

Nur Rochmi, M. (2015). *Studi pembelajaran pelatihan Calon Analis Kebijakan (CAK)* (transl. Lessons learned from the training for policy analysts). Report. Jakarta: National Institute of Public Administration (LAN) and Knowledge Sector Initiative.

Pellini, A. (2017). Knowledge sector interview with Professor Mark Considine. *Knowledge Sector Interviews.* http://www.ksi-indonesia.org/en/news/detail/knowledge-sector-interview-with-professor-mark-considine-by-arnaldo-pellini. Accessed 2 Apr 2017.

Pratikno. (2003). Desentralisasi, pilihan yang tidak final. In A. G. Karim (Ed.), *Kompleksitas Persoalan Otonomi Daerah di Indonesia* (pp. 33–56). Yogyakarta: Pustaka Pelajar.

Roth, J. (2003). Enabling knowledge creation: Learning from an R&D organization. *Journal of Knowledge Management, 7*(1), 32.

Shaxson, L. (2014). *Investing in evidence: Lessons from the UK Department for Environment, Food and Rural Affairs* (Working Paper 2). Jakarta: Knowledge Sector Initiative. http://www.ksi-indonesia.org/files/1421384737$1$QBTM0U$.pdf. Accessed on 15 May 2016.

Shaxson, L., & Bielak, A. (2012). *Expanding our understanding of K*.* A concept paper emerging from the K* conference held in Hamilton, Ontario, Canada, April 2012. United Nations University. http://www.alnap.org/resource/10031.aspx. Accessed 10 Apr 2017.

Sherlock, S. (2010). *Knowledge for policy: Regulatory obstacles to the growth of a knowledge market in Indonesia.* Jakarta: AusAID.

Shiraishi, T. (2006). *Technocracy in Indonesia: A preliminary analysis* (RIETI Discussion Paper Series). Research Institute for Economy, Trade & Industry. http://www.rieti.go.jp/jp/publications/dp/06e008.pdf. Accessed 21 Apr 2017.

Tjiptoherijanto, P. (2007). Civil service reform in Indonesia. *International Public Management Review, 8*(2), 31–44.

Utama, S. (2017). *End of intervention report: Bappenas Policy Analysis Team (PAT) and Tim Analisis Kebijakan (TAK). Internal report.* Jakarta: Knowledge Sector Initiative.

Part II
Knowledge and the Politics
of Policymaking

Chapter 5
How and When Do Policymakers Use Evidence? Taking Politics into Account

Elisabeth Jackson, Endah Bayu Purnawati, and Louise Shaxson

1 Introduction

The preceding chapter discussed how to ensure that policymakers have access to the best available evidence at key moments and the role of knowledge intermediaries in facilitating that access, using both 'hard' (disciplinary) and 'soft' (relationship-building) skills. But this is not a passive process in which policymakers simply rely on the right evidence to appear at the right time. A hard and careful look permits identification of the signals policymakers send out about what issues they are considering and what evidence they need to help them address their policy goals and to manage any opportunities and risks that might arise. These signals, collectively, can be understood as the 'demand' for evidence. This chapter discusses how to improve the demand for evidence within the Indonesian context, focusing on key policy planning processes at the national and subnational levels. As this demand becomes more clearly articulated, it becomes easier for others to see and understand what is needed and how it can be provided most effectively.

Demand for evidence is shaped by a mixture of individual skills, organisational relationships and organisational processes. The latter two are very much shaped by politics, that is, by the power relationships created within the bureaucracy. At the individual level, policymakers need technical skills in sourcing, evaluating and inter-

E. Jackson (✉)
Australia-Indonesia Partnership for Pro-Poor Policy: The Knowledge Sector Initiative,
Jakarta, Indonesia
e-mail: eljackson@ksi-indonesia.org

E. B. Purnawati
Global Green Growth Institute, Jakarta, Indonesia
e-mail: endah.purnawati@gggi.org

L. Shaxson
Overseas Development Institute, London, UK
e-mail: l.shaxson@odi.org.uk

© Springer Nature Singapore Pte Ltd. 2018
A. Pellini et al. (eds.), *Knowledge, Politics and Policymaking in Indonesia*,
https://doi.org/10.1007/978-981-13-0167-4_5

preting evidence – such as the ability to appraise the quality of a research report or to synthesise the results of several related studies. But policymakers generally work in teams, and collectively their interests, values and beliefs influence what evidence is considered to be credible and useful and is therefore put forward for consideration in decision-making processes. Powerful groups (such as business lobby groups) or highly regarded experts (such as scientists) can play a significant role in determining what evidence is listened to and what is excluded (Jones et al. 2012).

Organisational politics also shape the demand for evidence. Government ministries and departments are complex organisations: power is embedded in the organisational structures and processes that dictate what evidence is needed at what points in the decision-making process (Farid 2017). For instance, a technical guideline is an operational form of power because it specifies what is to be done, in what order, using what evidence (Ibid.).

Several recent studies have examined key aspects of the demand for evidence, including the political economy of policymaking in Indonesia (Datta et al. 2011), national policymakers' acquisition of research evidence (Datta et al. 2016) and subnational governments' use of evidence in policymaking (Sutmuller and Setiono 2011; Zhang 2015). However, significant gaps remain for gaining a full understanding of the factors shaping demand for evidence in Indonesia.

This chapter examines the factors that shape how evidence is used in Indonesia's planning processes, with a focus on the national 5-year development plan (Rencana Pembangunan Jangka Menengah Nasional – RPJMN) and regional 5-year plans (Rencana Pembangunan Jangka Menengah Daerah – RPJMD). Although some policies will emerge outside these processes in response to emerging events, these planning documents provide a structure through which to analyse the factors that influence how and when Indonesian policymakers seek out and utilise evidence. The authors use a broad definition of 'evidence', encompassing statistical and administrative data, research evidence, evidence from policy implementation and evaluation and the views and experiences of citizens and other stakeholders (Wills et al. 2016). The chapter draws from three frameworks that describe (i) policymakers' capacities and motivations (Newman et al. 2012); (ii) how their interests, values and beliefs affect what evidence is perceived to be credible (Jones et al. 2012); and (iii) organisational issues that influence how evidence is sourced, interpreted and used (Shaxson et al. 2016).

The chapter begins with a brief outline of national and regional development planning processes, highlighting the main points at which evidence is required.[1] It then discusses the individual, organisational and contextual factors that influence that demand, before reviewing approaches to building individual and organisational capacity that have been used successfully in other middle-income countries. The chapter concludes with suggestions on how these approaches could be adapted to the Indonesian context.

---

[1]The chapter focuses on the executive body of government. For those interested to see how the legislature demands and uses evidence, see Sherlock (2010) and Sherlock and Djani (2015).

2 Policymaking Processes in Indonesia

Indonesia has a range of formal processes for regular planning and budgeting and for developing national and subnational laws and regulations. Two main formal policy processes take place at the national level: long- and medium-term development planning and the development of laws and regulations. All development planning is the responsibility of the Ministry for National Development Planning/National Development Planning Agency (Kementerian Perencanaan Pembangunan Nasional/Badan Perencanaan Pembangunan Nasional – Bappenas) and its subnational counterparts, the Bappedas. The current long-term national development plan (Rencana Pembangunan Jangka Panjang Nasional – RPJPN) was prepared in 2005. It sets out Indonesia's priorities for achieving a nation that is self-reliant, progressive, just and prosperous, through efforts to improve innovation and competitiveness, ensure equitable and sustainable development, maintain peace and stability, uphold democracy and justice and improve Indonesia's global influence. It is closely linked to the long-term regional development plans (Rencana Pembangunan Jangka Panjang Daerah – RPJPD), which set out similar goals for decentralised regional governments.

Bappenas uses the RPJPN to prepare 5-year plans that outline different focus areas for development. These plans are based on an evaluation of achievements under the previous 5-year plan and an assessment of the current context and key issues. They draw on background studies either commissioned or conducted by Bappenas.[2] Preparation of the national plan is also aligned with the electoral cycle, ensuring that its priorities and targets are informed by the president's priorities. Bappenas then uses the RPJMN to prepare annual plans (Rencana Kerja Pemerintah – RKP) that outline national development objectives, sector priorities and performance indicators and targets. The annual plans also set out indicative funding levels for ministerial and cross-ministerial programmes in each sector. Once the RKP has been finalised, responsibility shifts to the Ministry of Finance, which uses it to guide the development of the annual state budget (Anggaran Pendapatan dan Belanja Negara – APBN). At the subnational level, elected leaders formulate regional 5-year plans (Rencana Pembangunan Jangka Menengah Daerah – RPJMD), which draw from the RPJPD, and regional Bappedas use the 5-year plans to formulate their annual plans, which guide the development of regional budgets.

At the national level, sectoral ministries then use the RPJMN to formulate their 5-year strategic plans, which guide the development of annual sectoral work plans and which, in turn, refer back to the RKP. A similar process takes place at the subnational level: the RPJMD is used by local governments to formulate regional annual work plans, which shape the 5-year strategic plans of regional working units. The local government units (Satuan Kerja Pemerintah Daerah – SKPD) develop the sectoral work plans from that. This complex system is set out in Fig. 5.1.

---

[2] Bappenas funds are often limited, leading to requests for development partners' assistance for these studies.

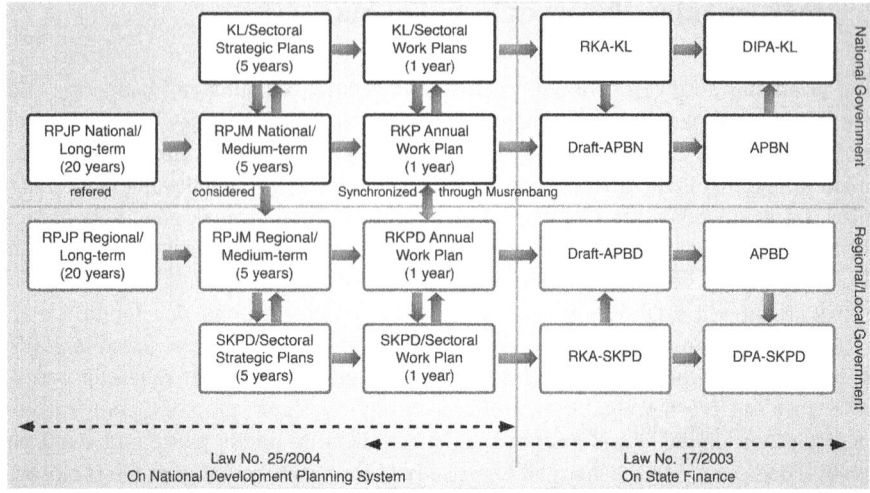

Fig. 5.1 Indonesia's integrated system of planning and budgeting at national and regional/local levels (Reproduced from Bappenas 2013) (see slide 4 at http://perpustakaan.bappenas.go.id/lontar/file?file=digital/138227-%5B_Konten_%5D-Konten%20C9673.ppt)

Responsibility for monitoring the plans lies mainly with Bappenas, which oversees implementation of the RPJMN by sectoral ministries and liaises closely with staff at the Office of the President's Staff (Kantor Staf Presiden – KSP) to monitor priority development programmes. Sectoral and annual work programmes at both the national and subnational levels are linked to specific budgeting processes led by the Ministry of Finance.

These processes incorporate evidence to varying degrees and at different points in the process (Datta et al. 2011; Sheppard 2012). Law 25/2004 on the National Development Planning System mandates the use of evidence in formulating RPJMN and RPJMD, including evidence gathered for strategic planning by ministries/agencies and subnational governments. The RPJMN process is fixed: consultative development planning forums (musrenbang) are required from the lowest level of government within a province up to the national level. This bottom-up process is designed to ensure that citizens' aspirations and proposals are filtered through to national policies.

However, the musrenbang process is widely considered to be ineffective (Kompas Online 2008), in particular because it places greater emphasis on procedure than on ensuring participation by all stakeholders. This results in a degree of 'elite capture', meaning that diverse priorities at the village, municipal and district levels are not transparently or effectively reflected, and evidence that comes directly from citizens tends to be under-represented in both provincial and national-level plans.

Once the RPJMN and RPJMD have been finalised, Law No. 12/2011 on the formulation of laws and regulations requires the use of academic papers (naskah akademik) in all policy formulation processes. These papers, based on research or legal studies, are published and intended to improve accountability for addressing policy concerns. They follow a tightly specified format that outlines the legal need to address the problem, the theoretical and empirical background and an analysis of existing laws and regulations.[3] But while the planning process is well specified, and the RPJMN provides a checklist for how to produce 'outputs' of the policy process, little emphasis is placed on using evidence to assess what works and what does not (Wasono and Maulana 2018).

The RPJMN is a tightly prescribed process, which tends to restrict the sources of evidence used to develop the laws and regulations that flow from it; as Datta et al. (2011) suggest, such 'formal bureaucratic rules… provide weak incentives for policy-makers to invest in, demand and use knowledge in order to produce good outputs and outcomes'. There may be more leeway to strengthen the use of evidence in the development of laws and regulations through building coalitions with like-minded people to provide the best available evidence during the formulation of academic papers. For example, between 2007 and 2013 a group of civil society organisations worked collaboratively with lawmakers to provide an 'alternative' academic paper to the draft submitted by the government as evidence, leading to the passage of Law 6/2014 on Villages. They succeeded in influencing the expert staff and lawmakers in the national parliament by providing necessary evidence during the legislation process (Pellini et al. 2014).

3 Factors Influencing Policymakers' Ability to Search for and Use Evidence

In their study of the acquisition of research evidence by the Indonesian executive branch, Datta et al. (2016) identify a range of barriers to acquiring and using research evidence within government departments. Some of these are concerned with the supply of research evidence, such as the length of time required to produce research, poor quality and lack of policy relevance of research and limited expertise on some policy issues. This section focuses on three additional factors: (i) individual factors, such as individual policymakers' skills, knowledge and attitudes; (ii) organisational factors such as inadequate funding for policy research, lack of reliable data, challenges in procuring research and limited discretion to act on research findings; and (iii) factors related to the policy environment.

---

[3] The full text of Law No. 12/2011 is available at http://kelembagaan.ristekdikti.go.id/wp-content/uploads/2016/08/UU-12-Tahun-2011.pdf. The implementing regulations for the law are outlined in Presidential Regulation (PP) No. 87/2014, available at https://www.setneg.go.id/index.php?option=com_perundangan&id=404372&task=detail&catid=6&Itemid=42&tahun=2014.

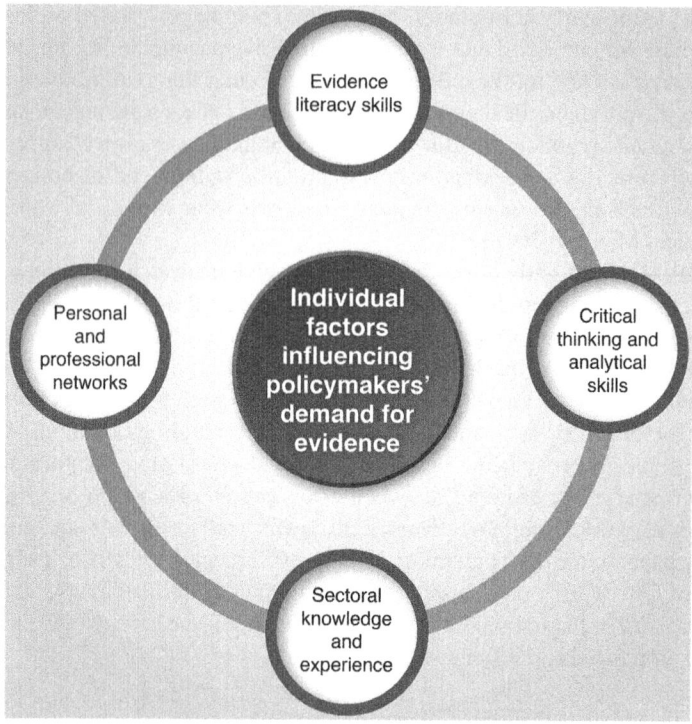

Fig. 5.2 Individual factors shaping policymakers' demand for evidence (Reproduced from Newman et al. 2012)

3.1 Individual Factors

A range of skills, knowledge, resources and attitudes shape policymakers' capacity and motivation to seek and use evidence. These include critical thinking and ana-lytical skills, evidence literacy skills, sectoral knowledge and experience and per-sonal and professional networks (Newman et al. 2012) (see Fig. 5.2).

The level and mixture of capacities that policymakers need differ according to seniority and the types of decisions they are required to make. Within the executive, senior decision-makers such as ministers, deputy ministers and directors general need to be able to consider evidence and apply it to policy problems. Directors, heads of sub-directorates and special and expert staff need to be able to synthesise and evaluate evidence both to inform their own decision-making and to feed into decision-making by more senior officials. Moreover, since officials at the director-ate and sub-directorate level are usually responsible for commissioning research evidence (Datta et al. 2011), they need to be able to identify and articulate evidence needs, develop terms of reference, evaluate the quality of research products and determine their implications for policy. Finally, a range of staff, including those within individual directorates and sub-directorates and in research and development units (Balitbang), need the skills and knowledge to be able to identify relevant information, assess its quality and present it in the form of a summary or policy brief (Ibid.). Individual people's attitudes towards evidence and their capacity to handle it effectively can have a major impact on overall organisational capacity, as discussed below.

3.2 Skills in Evidence Literacy

Finding, evaluating and using evidence in policymaking requires a range of high-level cognitive skills, including the ability to identify and synthesise often highly technical information from a range of sources, evaluate the quality of evidence and arguments and apply the results to concrete policy problems. Yet Indonesia's education system does not adequately equip graduates with critical thinking and analytical skills or information literacy skills. Recent data collected as part of the OECD Survey of Adult Skills, for example, reveals low levels of literacy proficiency – defined as the ability to understand, evaluate, use and engage with written texts – among Indonesian adults. In the survey, adults in Jakarta who had completed tertiary qualifications of between 2 and 4 years scored only slightly above the OECD average for those who did not complete upper secondary school and 20% below the OECD average for those with a tertiary education (OECD 2016; Pritchett 2016).

Although learning continues throughout a person's career, these results suggest that Indonesian graduates – including those who enter the civil service – begin their working life with a deficit in some of the key skills required to critically search for, assess and apply evidence. This situation is likely to be exacerbated at the subnational level, given that Indonesia's best universities are located in major cities and towns on Java and that positions in the subnational civil service tend to be filled with graduates of local universities. In addition, poorly designed entrance examination and recruitment processes based on nepotism and patronage mean that the most suitable candidates are not always selected (Turner et al. 2009; Blunt et al. 2012), although recently introduced changes – including the use of an online candidate registration system and computer-assisted testing – aim to make recruitment more transparent.[4]

3.3 Critical Thinking and Analytical Skills

Figure 5.3 shows that while the majority of civil servants at the national level hold an undergraduate degree, this is not the case at the provincial or district levels. Data from the National Civil Service Commission show that in 2016 just over 6% of Indonesia's 4.5 million civil servants – including over 1.7 million teachers, as well as health workers and other technical roles – have a master's degree, while 0.3%

---

[4] See http://www.bkn.go.id/produk/cat-bkn.

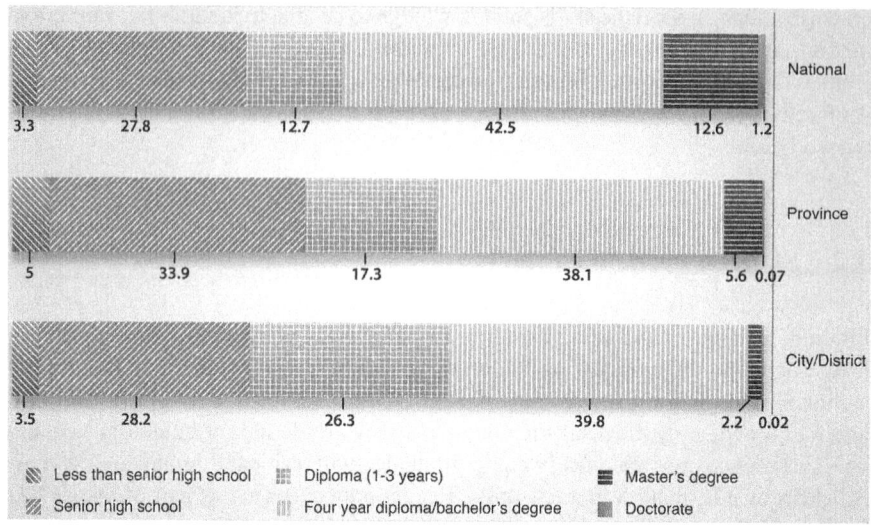

Fig. 5.3 Educational qualifications of civil servants at national, provincial and district levels, 2013 (Reproduced from SIPAN 2017)

Table 5.1 Samples of structural positions with educational background in select ministries

	Highest level of education	Minister/ deputy minister	Echelon 1/ DG level	Echelon 2/ director level
Bappenas	Bachelors	–	–	–
	Masters	–	6	29
	Doctorates	1	10	19
Kementan (Ministry of Agriculture)	Bachelors	–	–	–
	Masters	–	8	49
	Doctorates	1	8	41
Kemenko PMK (Coordinating Ministry for Human Development and Culture)	Bachelors	1	3	?
	Masters	–	6	24
	Doctorates	–	5	6

have a doctorate.[5] A further 46% have an undergraduate degree, the minimum qualification required for employment at the two highest ranks of the public service (BPS 2016; www.bkn.go.id). Within national-level ministries and agencies, senior policy officials often have higher degrees. Table 5.1 below shows three examples of degrees obtained by officials at the top three levels of the hierarchy, based on information from ministry websites in January 2017. The highest concentrations of people with

---

[5] This is in part a result of generous scholarship schemes from the Indonesian government as well as several foreign governments, which have enabled many civil servants to pursue postgraduate education overseas, including in Japan, the United States, the Netherlands, Australia and the United Kingdom.

advanced degrees are in the Ministry of Education and Culture, the National Development Planning Agency, the Coordinating Ministry for Economic Affairs, the Coordinating Ministry for Human Development and Culture and the National Institute of Public Administration.[6]

At the most senior levels of the civil service educational qualifications (which link to capacity for critical thinking and analysis) are higher. For example, at Bappenas, the Coordinating Ministry for Human Development and Culture and the Ministry of Agriculture most deputy ministers, directors general and directors have master's degrees and many have doctorates, including from overseas institutions.

At the national level, job-specific training is implemented by the education and training centres (Pusat Pendidikan dan Pelatihan – Pusdiklat) of the relevant ministry or agency, while the National Institute of Public Administration (Lembaga Administrasi Negara – LAN) manages compulsory leadership training for staff seeking promotion. LAN courses, which are linked to promotion to more senior roles (with associated increases in base salaries and allowances), have in the past tended to focus on general management and administrative skills (Turner et al. 2009). To some extent this is a legacy of the suppression of critical thinking and scholarship within universities, research organisations and civil society during the 32-year rule of President Soeharto (1967–1998). During this time, scholarship was directed towards reinforcing state-sanctioned interpretations of social and economic development (Hadiz and Dhakidae 2005; Nugroho 2005).

However, this is changing: LAN has revised the curriculum for its leadership and pre-service training programmes to emphasise professional competency, and the Ministry of State Administrative and Bureaucratic Reform (Kementerian Pendayagunaan Aparatur Negara dan Reformasi Birokrasi) has requested that all government agencies develop competency standards for all positions and a 5-year plan for developing employee competencies (LAN 2015a, b). The policy analyst role, which is described in Chap. 4, is an important step towards improving formal analytical skills, such as data gathering and interpreting trends, as well as soft skills for analysis and interaction with different stakeholders. However, at the subnational level, budgets for technical training are often limited, leading to lack of staff with the requisite skills (Turner et al. 2009; World Bank 2009; Tjiptoherijanto 2014).

3.4 Sectoral Knowledge and Experience

In the 2011 study by Datta and others, some informants noted that while inadequate training of technical and managerial staff was a challenge, an even greater challenge was the way that civil service staff were categorised, supervised, remunerated and promoted. As in many other countries, encouraging policymakers to build up their sectoral knowledge relationships is not easy. Indonesia requires civil servants

---

[6] See http://sipan.menpan.go.id/. Based on 2013 data.

holding positions in echelons two to four[7] to move to different posts every 3 years, to build breadth of experience and prevent capture by special interests. The policy is not always enforced uniformly across government institutions, although in general one-third of these officials are moved each year in ministries and other state institutions. These staff members are not only rotated within their ministry or agency but often between different geographical locations. Rotation between different directorates general within the same ministry is rare (World Bank 2009). Senior officials, such as deputy ministers and directors general, can provide some continuity, but where lower-level officials do not have an educational background in a particular policy area (e.g. health), they may lack the technical ability to generate and interpret evidence (Datta et al. 2011).

3.5 Personal and Professional Networks

Personal networks are an important resource in most professions, providing access to information, influence, goods and services. In Indonesia, personal networks and patron-client relationships were central to the organisation of power within the political and bureaucratic elite at both the national and subnational levels during the Soeharto period. This pattern persisted into the *Reformasi* era, beginning in 1998.[8]

The importance of personal networks is reflected in the evidence-seeking behaviour among policymakers in national ministries and agencies. A survey of mid-level and senior policymakers found that expert advice, accessed through personal networks, was the second most preferred type of knowledge after statistical and administrative data (Datta et al. 2016; see also Sherlock 2010; Datta et al. 2011). These sorts of informal networks help build social capital because they are based on relationships of trust; evidence acquired in this way is seen by policymakers as highly credible (Datta et al. 2011). In addition to professional connections with current and former colleagues, networks may be based on shared educational experiences (school or university), family and kin relationships, membership in a religious organisation or congregation, ethnicity and cultural background, political affiliation, membership in professional associations, involvement in non-profit organisations and business connections.

Professional networks tend to rely on connections to individuals rather than to organisations. Production of background documents for RPJMN and RPJMD, for

---

[7]The Indonesian public service is a tightly structured hierarchy. Ministers are appointed by the president. Beneath them, public servants are organised in both echelons and grades, with echelon 1 indicating the highest and echelon 5 the lowest management positions. Secretaries general and directors general are echelon 1. Directors and heads of central support units are usually echelon 2, as are the head of bureaux in the secretariats general.

[8]The cases described in Aspinall and Sukmajati (2016), for example, underscore the importance of legislative candidates' personal networks in electoral competition at the local level (see also Buehler 2009). Significantly, a high proportion of candidates in local legislative elections come from the ranks of the bureaucracy (Buehler 2010, 2013; Mietzner 2010).

example, is often contracted out to individual consultants rather than institutions. This may be related to the fact that under Presidential Regulation No. 54/2010, it is easier to contract an individual via direct appointment than to appoint civil society organisations or universities via open tender (see also Chap. 7).

3.6   Organisational Factors

Shaxson et al. (2016) outline a series of organisational factors influencing the demand for evidence. These include the organisational systems and processes and the different cultures of evidence that collide with or reinforce each other to shape the demand for evidence, as depicted in Fig. 5.4.

Organisational Systems and Processes   As noted above, the RPJMN and RPJMD provide the overarching framework for planning, sourcing and interpreting evidence in the Indonesian policy process. Their planning and budgeting processes are quite rigid, and the tendency is to simply add new policies on top of existing ones. Although regulatory review is a mandatory part of the academic papers that support

Fig. 5.4 Organisational influences on policymakers' demand for evidence. (Adapted from Shaxson et al. 2016)

RPJMN, it is often not done well, resulting in a large number of overlapping or inconsistent regulations (Wasono and Maulana 2018).

In a study of five districts in three provinces, Zhang (2015) notes the limited funding for policy research in local governments, indicating that research is not a priority. Even though there is a requirement to have background studies or evaluation to inform the RPJMD processes, this is being overlooked, as the cycle of planning and budgeting has become simply a repetitive process driven by administrative and compliance concerns. The strength of the planning and budgeting system – and the weakness of processes of monitoring and evaluating outcomes – means that policymakers are more worried about whether the relevant plans and budgets meet legislative requirements than whether the quality of those policies will improve the welfare of their citizens.

Cultures of Evidence The formal planning and budgeting processes for RPJMN and RPJMD guide policymakers towards a highly structured and somewhat restrictive approach to defining what evidence is sought and how it is used. Combined with the challenges of engaging with external organisations around evidence (as outlined in Chap. 7), this has in the past generated an introverted culture of evidence with a strongly hierarchical flavour. In addition, a weak commitment to policy evaluation within Indonesian ministries denotes a culture of using evidence to demonstrate compliance with a plan, rather than delivery of outcomes for the economy, environment and society. Furthermore, an inflexible budgeting process means that officials cannot easily mobilise resources if requests arise during the financial year, for example, for commissioning studies and research, monitoring implementation or holding public consultations. The default is to turn to development partners to commission specific pieces of evidence, reinforcing a culture of dependency on others.

The bureaucratic culture remains strong at the subnational level, where policymakers receive orders from the top and have little discretion in interpreting goals or designing specific policies (Karetji 2010). However, this too is changing: as decentralisation gives more authority to local governments, many local leaders are beginning to demonstrate innovative approaches to governance. The election of figures such as Ridwan Kamil in Bandung or Nurdin in Bantaeng shows that despite rigid directives from the central government, it is still possible to find innovative ways to serve the public.[9]

Data Quality At an organisational level, the quality of statistical and administrative data is problematic. Most obviously, computer and Internet skills vary widely across the country, and Internet access is often highly problematic in archipelagic Indonesia. This means that access to and use of administrative evidence varies widely by geography. At a more macro level, there are other concerns. District, provincial and national data are often mismatched: while data from the National Statistics Office (Badan Pusat Statistik – BPS) is widely used as the official reference data for min-

---

[9] *Tempo* magazine has named the ten most influential regional heads in Indonesia based on a number of criteria, including efforts to tackle corruption and innovation in good governance. See https://nasional. tempo.co/read/news/2017/03/03/173852419/tempo-beri-penghargaan-10-kepala-daerah-teladan-2017.

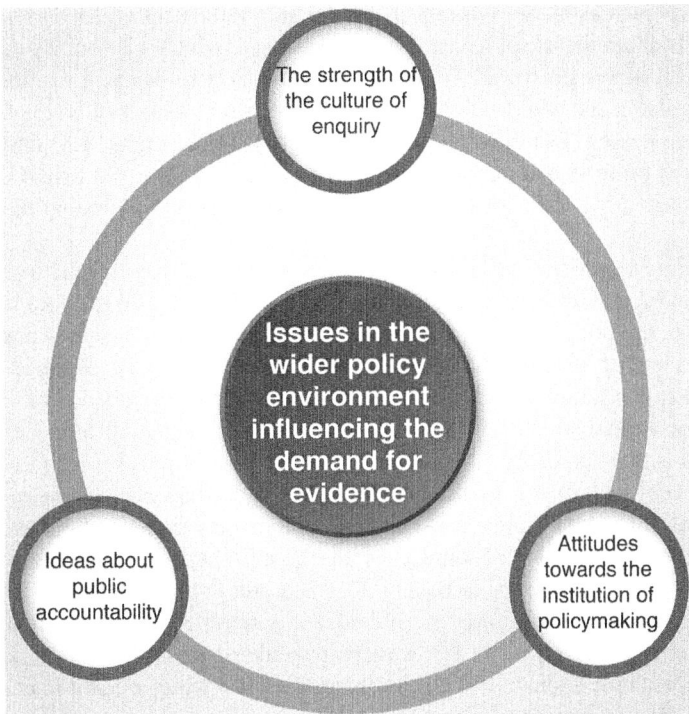

Fig. 5.5 Issues in the wider policy environment influencing policymakers' demand for evidence. (Adapted from Broadbent 2012)

istries and subnational governments, each ministry also produces its own data in accordance with its specific needs. In the same way that policy coordination between ministries and agencies is poor, so is data coordination, which makes data sharing problematic. The Office of the President's Staff (Kantor Staf Presiden – KSP) is currently developing a comprehensive regulation on data governance – Satu Data (One Data) – with the aim of developing a single reference point for administrative and statistical data in Indonesia (see also Chap. 6).[10]

3.7   The Wider Policy Environment

The broader policy environment affects demand for evidence and consists of various factors in both formal and informal institutions within a country or region (Broadbent 2012). Here it is conceptualised as three issues, as depicted in Fig. 5.5. First is the strength of the culture of enquiry and how this is developed through

---

[10] The draft regulation is currently being developed. See http://opengovindonesia.org/front/detail/news/forum-konsultasi-publik-rancangan-peraturan-presiden-satu-data-indonesia-upaya-konkret-pemerintah-merangkul-publik-dalam-proses-pembuatan-kebijakan.

institutions such as higher education. This culture influences wider societal values and beliefs about the use of research and the extent to which it is socially acceptable to challenge power structures. The second is attitudes towards the institution of policymaking itself, and what and who should drive it, which shapes the role of research in these processes. The third related issue is public ideas about accountability: to what extent policymakers are held accountable for the 'quality' of their decisions and scrutinised by other state or civil society organisations, including the popular media.

Very little empirical research on the effects of the wider policy environment on the demand for evidence has been undertaken. Jones et al. (2012) note that using evidence in the policy process has as much to do with issues of power and politics as it does with problem-solving and rational debate. This echoes Farid's (2017) observation in relation to technical guidelines: that power is embedded in positions and organisational structures. Different groups of people hold different values and base their actions on different belief systems, not always in their own rational self-interest. They may use evidence as ammunition to win an argument or to build broad coalitions to promote a particular cause; they may even withhold evidence to simplify decision-making. Their values and beliefs shape how problems are conceived and presented (see also Bacchi 2012) and serve to bind coalitions together, giving weight to particular aspects of evidence and to people with particular types of knowledge or expertise. In this way, policymakers' interests, values and beliefs influence what they perceive to be credible evidence – which may or may not coincide with the perceptions of others in the policy process.

Since 1998 the political context in Indonesia has been changing. The introduction of direct elections for president and vice president has affected notions of accountability, political competition and the changing role of civil society. Although there is no formal requirement to report on progress towards key policy goals, evidence is increasingly demanded as part of public accountability. For example, the Indonesian Forum for Budget Transparency (Sekretariat Nasional Forum Indonesia Untuk Transparansi Anggaran – SEKNAS FITRA), a 13-member network of civil society organisations from five regions, advocates for the Indonesian government to open up national and subnational budgeting processes to the public. Since 1998 it has produced evidence on issues of gender, inclusiveness and budget transparency to encourage wide scrutiny of the national budget (Rakhmani et al. 2017).

At the subnational level, decentralisation and direct elections for provincial governors, mayors and district heads have brought government and policymaking closer to the people. While there is not a strong culture of enquiry in Indonesia and while it is generally not acceptable to challenge authority, there is an emerging culture of critique and protest in some segments of the population (Karetji 2010). This raises the potential for greater accountability, as politicians strive to provide evidence to demonstrate that they are responsive to public aspirations. In some places civil society plays an important watchdog role, but this depends heavily on the presence or absence of local civil society organisations.

4 Other Countries' Approaches to Improving Policymakers' Demand for Evidence

Strengthening the 'demand' for evidence is a relatively new area of work within wider efforts to strengthen state capability in Indonesia. The previous analysis portrays the complexity of the Indonesian policy environment in relation to how evidence is sought and used. Shaxson et al. (2016) set out a range of different issues that could be addressed at the individual, team and organisational levels to ensure that evidence is gathered, interpreted and used effectively. These might include training policy officials in searching for and appraising the quality of evidence; creating spaces for debate with people and organisations using different types of evidence; building independent advisory committees to advise departments on the effective use of evidence; and training officials in how to communicate complex, uncertain or rapidly changing evidence.

This section reviews approaches to building individual and organisational capacity to demand and use evidence that have been used in other countries. Drawing from other countries' experience provides a useful source of ideas for how to address specific issues and build organisational cultures and systems for increasing policymakers' demand for evidence.

4.1 Strengthening Personal Awareness and Skills for Using Evidence

Improving the capacity of individuals to source, appraise, interpret and use evidence has been done in two ways: through the provision of dedicated training and through on-the-job mentoring. Training is delivered in two main ways – as part of the wider curriculum within civil service colleges that conduct mandatory training for public servants (government officials and parliamentarians) and training in specific methodologies, such as evaluation, by specialist providers.

Many countries have civil service colleges, and designing curricula specifically related to evidence could be an effective way to reach many officials simultaneously, particularly if attendance at specific courses is mandatory as part of the promotion process. Training several people from the same organisation can be beneficial, because they can form a core group with a common understanding, able to take forward the evidence agenda when they return to their home ministries. In Ghana, for example, the Civil Service Training Centre developed a training programme to build capacity of mid-level civil servants in areas such as searching for evidence, assessing and appraising its quality and communicating it effectively (Government of Ghana 2017; Ademokun et al. 2016). The University of Cape Town's Graduate School of Development Policy and Practice runs a similar course for senior civil servants covering the different uses of evidence in decision-making processes, examples of specific tools that can be used and the institutional cultures required to support more effective use of evidence (UCT n.d.). Training can also be given on specific methodological issues, such as on managing, designing and conducting impact evaluations (Wotela 2017) – although the level of technical skills required prior to taking these courses is often very high, so they may only be accessible to one or two people in a ministry.

Another form of transferring skills is on-the-job mentoring, that is, linking individual policymakers to individual evidence specialists. While mentoring has long been used in organisational development and capacity-building efforts, formal programmes to establish mentoring arrangements specifically for evidence-related issues are scarce. In South Africa, the University of Johannesburg set up such a programme and found that aside from ensuring that what is learnt during training can be put to immediate, practical use, this approach also helped to create networks of like-minded people that can expand into institutional relationships over time (Langer et al. 2015).

The Forum Kajian Pembangunan (Development Study Forum)[11] was jointly organised between the Government of Indonesia, think-tanks, civil society organisations and development partners in a relatively formal setting. However, less formal and more participatory processes to increase awareness can be a useful precursor to more formal training programmes, such as curriculum development and mentoring. In Canada, the Partnership Group for Science and Engineering hosts a series of breakfast meetings at which parliamentarians are given brief presentations about new research findings and interaction with scientists is encouraged (PAGSE n.d.). This informal style of breakfast meeting is intended to help break down barriers and encourage discussion.

4.2   Strengthening Organisational Approaches to Using Evidence

Personal skills and behaviours to improve the use of evidence need to be supported and reinforced by wider forces that influence how people work and how they interact with each other to source, appraise, synthesise, interpret and communicate evidence. But because of how different cultures of evidence interact, stimulating demand also means strengthening organisations, cultivating appropriate relationships and influencing the wider context (Newman et al. 2012; Punton et al. 2016). Strengthening the demand for evidence is not a simple matter of implementing training courses. The way individual people incorporate better use of evidence is influenced by processes specific to their organisation, as was seen with the RPJMN process.

---

[11] Forum Kajian Pembangunan was initiated by the Australian National University's Indonesia Project. Seminars or discussions are hosted by participating organisations in Indonesia, such as government agencies, research institutes or development partners. The seminars are also an opportunity to disseminate new research findings. Further information on Forum Kajian Pembangunan is available at www.fkpindonesia.org.

In South Africa, the Biodiversity and Conservation policy team of the Department of Environmental Affairs was finding it challenging to access the evidence they needed when they needed it. They were keen to develop relationships across the environment sector to generate greater awareness of what the key policy questions were and what evidence would be needed to answer them. In 2016 the team developed the first National Biodiversity Research and Evidence Strategy and Implementation Plan, which worked with a wide group of stakeholders to set out the key policy questions for biodiversity and conservation policy in the short, medium and long term, so that the research community would be better able to target their evidence to meet policy needs (Department of Environmental Affairs 2016). Clarifying the key policy questions was seen as an important way of signalling what evidence was needed and building relationships with external evidence providers and intermediaries.

Also in South Africa, since 2012 the Department of Planning, Monitoring and Evaluation (DPME) has developed and implemented a national evaluation system to support policy evaluations and to ensure that the findings from such evaluations are actively used to improve policymaking (DPME 2011, 2016). Drawing on the experience of the Sistema Nacional De Evaluación De Gestión Y Resultados (SINERGIA) in Colombia (Cassidy and Tsui 2017a), over the past 5 years the DPME has worked to build the capacity of line ministries to commission, monitor, interpret and use the evidence that emerges from evaluations of policies, plans, projects and programmes (Goldman et al. 2015). Different types of evaluation are conducted, depending on what is relevant to a particular policy or programme; an important part of the system is DPME's support to line ministries to inform programme managers and help them use the information effectively to support change. From the start, DPME worked to create buy-in from ministries, to ensure that the national evaluation system reflected real demand for evaluation evidence and was not seen as a top-down approach by central government (Ibid.). The national evaluation system intends to cover all provincial governments and all central government departments and may ultimately also work with metropolitan areas and state-owned companies (DPME 2016).

In the United Kingdom, the Department of Environment, Food and Rural Affairs (Defra) has produced a series of 'evidence investment strategies', which set out how Defra ensures that policy development and implementation is well supported by evidence. Over time the department has experimented with different organisational structures, systems and processes to improve the quality of the evidence it uses and to improve the flow of evidence to policy teams and senior decision-makers (Defra 2014; Shaxson 2014; Shaxson et al. 2016).

Finland's Government Policy Analysis Unit sits in the Office of the Prime Minister and is responsible for commissioning research and presenting evidence to inform government decisions on future strategic and economic policies. A linked organisation, the Strategic Research Council, funds long-term multidisciplinary research across multiple ministries, to prevent such research from being undertaken in ministerial 'silos' (Cassidy and Tsui 2017b).

5   Conclusions

The demand for evidence in Indonesian policymaking is shaped by the complex interplay of several factors, but the politics of evidence are slowly changing. Levels of technical evidence-related skills in both national and subnational governments are low and inconsistent, and although training in technical (as opposed to administrative) aspects of policymaking is improving, the heavy bureaucratic requirements of the RPJMN and RPJMD processes, as well as procurement restrictions, discourage an open and innovative approach to acquiring, appraising and using evidence. However, the increasing demand from civil society for demonstrable progress is instilling a greater sense of need to use evidence effectively to show how government is delivering outcomes for citizens. The international examples above show that although it is important to learn lessons from others, ultimately Indonesia will need to develop its own tailored approach to strengthening evidence-informed policymaking within government.

Training and skills development will continue to be key to ensuring that the new policy analyst function performs well. For maximum benefit, it should be extended to the wider network of analysts throughout national and subnational governments who perform similar roles. While the numbers remain low in the initial phase, formal training could be complemented by a programme of peer-to-peer support. This would help strengthen the informal relationships that play an important part in building social capital to find the evidence needed at the time it is needed. But as the numbers grow, the challenge will be to develop capacity-development processes that balance the need for consistent levels and types of skills with local-level innovations that respond to local needs for evidence.

Strengthening demand is ultimately as much about strengthening the quality of the processes through which evidence is sourced, appraised, interpreted and used as it is about the quality of the evidence itself. This means that developing organisational processes for improving the use of evidence will help ensure that once trained, people return to work in organisations that are receptive to the principles of evidence-informed policymaking. The international examples given above emphasise the need to think strategically about what evidence is likely to be needed and build relationships that will deliver that evidence effectively.

To achieve that end, greater collaboration with non-governmental knowledge producers will be increasingly important in Indonesia, to ensure that evidence reflects the voices of civil society. Amending procurement regulations to allow government to commission research from a range of organisations would broaden the range of evidence provided, and encouraging officials involved in policymaking to attend seminars and conferences where they could engage with these organisations in person would strengthen relationships and thereby enrich the search for evidence.

Monitoring and evaluating policy is a notable weakness in Indonesia. While efforts to improve the consistency and quality of administrative data are under way, this will not – in itself – strengthen the demand for evidence. Indonesian civil society still has a relatively weak voice in policy debates, but it is growing. Strengthening its calls for holding the government accountable for its promises could be one of the most effective ways to ensure that policymakers actively seek out evidence and use it to diagnose problems, reflect on what has been achieved in the past and make evidence-informed plans for the future.

References

Ademokun, A., Dennis, A., Hayter, E., Richards, C., Runceanu, L.-E., Cassidy, C., Liebnitzky, J., Suliman, S., & Kovacs, M. (2016). *Evidence-informed policymaking toolkit*. Oxford: INASP.

Aspinall, E., & Sukmajati, M. (Eds.). (2016). *Electoral dynamics in Indonesia: Money politics, patronage and clientelism at the grassroots*. Singapore: NUS Press.

Bacchi, C. (2012). Introducing the 'What's the Problem Represented to be?' approach. In A. Bletsas & C. Beasley (Eds.), *Engaging with Carol Bacchi: Strategic interventions and exchanges* (pp. 21–24). Adelaide: The University of Adelaide Press.

Badan Kepegawaian Negara. (2017). *Computer assisted test*. http://cat.bkn.go.id/

Bappenas. (2013). *Presentation delivered by the Minister of Bappenas at Musrenbang RPJMD for West Java province in Bandung, 10 September* (Resource Document). http://perpustakaan. bappenas.go.id/lontar/file?file=digital/138227-%5B_Konten_%5D-Konten%20C9673.ppt. Accessed 3 Apr 2017.

Blunt, P., Turner, M., & Lindroth, H. (2012). Patronage, service delivery, and social justice in Indonesia. *International Journal of Public Administration, 35*(3), 214–220.

BPS [Badan Pusat Statistik]. (2016). *Statistik Politik Tahun 2016 (2016 political statistics)*. Jakarta: Badan Pusat Statistik.

Broadbent, E. (2012). *Politics of research-based evidence in African policy debates: Synthesis of case study findings*. Report. Evidence-based Policy in Development Network. https://www.odi.org/sites/odi.org.uk/files/odi-assets/publications-opinion-files/9118.pdf. Accessed 2 June 2017.

Buehler, M. (2009). The rising importance of personal networks in Indonesian local politics: An analysis of the district government head elections in South Sulawesi in 2005. In M. Erb & P. Sulistyanto (Eds.), *Deepening democracy in Indonesia* (pp. 101–124). Singapore: Institute of Southeast Asian Studies.

Buehler, M. (2010). Decentralisation and local democracy in Indonesia: The marginalization of the public sphere. In E. Aspinall & M. Mietzner (Eds.), *Problems of democratization in Indonesia: Elections, institutions and society* (pp. 267–285). Singapore: Institute of Southeast Asian Studies.

Buehler, M. (2013). Married with children. *Inside Indonesia* 112 (April–June). http://www.insideindonesia.org/feature-editions/married-with-children. Accessed 2 June 2017.

Cassidy, C., & Tsui, J. (2017a). *Global evidence policy units Colombia: Sinergia*. Jakarta: Knowledge Sector Initiative. http://www.ksiindonesia.org/en/news/detail/evidence-policy-unit-in-colombia-sinergia. Accessed 25 May 2017.

Cassidy, C., & Tsui, J. (2017b). *Global evidence policy units. Finland: Government Policy Analysis Unit Politiikka-analyysiyksikkö*. Jakarta: Knowledge Sector Initiative. http://www.ksi-indonesia.org/en/news/detail/evidence-policy-unit-in-finland-the-government-policy-analysis-unitpolitiikka-analyysiyksikk-. Accessed 25 May 2017.

Datta, A., Jones, H., Febriany, V., Harris, D., Dewi, R. K., Wild, L., & Young, J. (2011). *The political economy of policy-making in Indonesia: Opportunities for improving the demand and use of knowledge* (Resource Document). Overseas Development Institute. http://www.odi.org.uk/resources/details.asp?id=5985&title=policy-making-politicaleconomy-indonesia-knowledge. Accessed 15 May 2017.

Datta, A. Hendytio, M. K., Perkasa, V., & Basuki, T. (2016). *The acquisition of research knowledge by national-level decision makers in Indonesia* (Working Paper 16). Jakarta: Knowledge Sector Initiative.

Defra [Department of Environment, Food and Rural Affairs]. (2014). *Making the most of our evidence: A strategy for Defra and its network*. London: Department of Environment, Food and Rural Affairs.

Department of Environmental Affairs. (2016). *National biodiversity research and evidence strategy (2015–2016): Strategy document*. Pretoria: Department of Environmental Affairs.

DPME. (2011). *National evaluation policy framework*. Pretoria: Department of Planning, Monitoring and Evaluation. http://www.dpme.gov.za/keyfocusareas/evaluationsSite/Evaluations/National%20Evaluation%20Policy%20Framework%2011%2011%2025.pdf. Accessed 18 July 2017.

DPME. (2016). *National evaluation plan 2016–2017 to 2018–2019*. Pretoria: Department of Planning, Monitoring and Evaluation. http://www.dpme.gov.za/keyfocusareas/evaluationsSite/Evaluations/National%20Evaluation%20Plan%202016-17%2016.03.31.pdf. Accessed 18 July 2017.

Farid, H. (2017). *Distribution of power through inclusive bureaucracy. KSI interview 31/03/2017*. http://www.ksi-indonesia.org/en/news/detail/hilmar-farid--distribution-of-power-through--inclusive-bureaucracy. Accessed 3 June 2017.

Goldman, I., Mathe, J., Jacob, C., Hercules, A., Amisi, M., Buthelezi, T., Narsee, H., Ntakumba, S., & Sadan, M. (2015). Developing South Africa's national evaluation policy and system: First lessons learned. *African Evaluation Journal, 3*(1), 9.

Government of Ghana. (2017). *GIMPA ends INASP's VakaYiko evidence informed policy making toolkit trial*. http://www.ghana.gov.gh/index.php/media-center/news/3371-gimpa-ends-vakayiko-s-evidence-informed-policy-making-toolkit-trial. Accessed 18 July 2017.

Hadiz, V. R., & Dhakidae, D. (2005). Introduction. In V. R. Hadiz & D. Dhakidae (Eds.), *Social science and power in Indonesia* (pp. 1–30). Jakarta/Singapore: Equinox Publishing/Institute of Southeast Asian Studies.

Jones, H., Jones, N., Shaxson, L., & Walker, D. (2012). *Knowledge, policy and power in international development: A practical guide*. Bristol: The Policy Press.

Karetji, P. C. (2010). *Overview of the Indonesian knowledge sector*. Jakarta: AusAID. Available at: http://dfat.gov.au/about-us/publications/Documents/indo-ks8-overview.pdf. Accessed 10 May 2017.

Kompas Online. (2008). Musrenbang dinilai tidak efektif serap aspirasi (National development planning consultations ineffective in capturing aspirations). http://nasional.kompas.com/read/2008/11/25/01372556/musrenbang.dinilai.tidak.efektif.serap.aspirasi. Accessed 4 Apr 2017.

LAN [Lembaga Administrasi Negara]. (2015a). *Modul pelatihan analis kebijakan (Policy analyst training module)*. Jakarta: Lembaga Administrasi Negara.

LAN [Lembaga Administrasi Negara]. (2015b). *Laporan tahunan 2015* (Annual report 2015). Jakarta: Lembaga Administrasi Negara.

Langer, L., Stewart, R., Erasmus, Y., & de Wet, T. (2015). Walking the last mile on the long road to evidence-informed development: building capacity to use research evidence. *Journal of Development Effectiveness, 7*(4), 1–9.

Mietzner, M. (2010). Indonesia's direct elections: Empowering the electorate or entrenching the New Order oligarchy? In E. Aspinall & G. Fealy (Eds.), *Indonesia: Soeharto's new order and its legacy* (pp. 173–190). Canberra: ANU E-Press.

Newman, K., Fisher, C., & Shaxson, L. (2012). Stimulating demand for research evidence: What role for capacity building? *IDS Bulletin, 43*(5), 17–24.

Nugroho, H. (2005). The political economy of higher education: The university as an arena for the struggle for power. In V. R. Hadiz & D. Dhakidae (Eds.), *Social science and power in Indonesia* (pp. 143–166). Jakarta/Singapore: Equinox Publishing/Institute of Southeast Asian Studies.

OECD [Organisation for Economic Co-operation and Development]. (2016). *Skills matter: Further results from the survey of adult skills*. Paris: OECD Publishing.

PAGSE. (n.d.). *Bacon and Eggheads*. http://pagse.org/en/breakfasts.htm. Accessed 18 July 2017.

Pellini, A., Angelina, M., & Purnawati, E. (2014). *Working politically: A story of change about the contribution of research evidence to the new village law in Indonesia*. Jakarta: Knowledge Sector Initiative.

Pritchett, L. (2016). *The need for a pivot to learning: New data on adult skills from Indonesia*. Research in Improving Systems of Education [RISE] blog, 9 August. http://www.riseprogramme.org/content/need-pivot-learning-new-data-adult-skills-indonesia. Accessed 8 June 2017.

Punton, M., Lloyd, R., & Vogel, I. (2016). *Insights from the evidence: what works to build capacity for evidence-informed policy making, for whom, and why?* Brighton: ITAD.

Rakhmani, I., Pellini, A., & Nurhidayat, Y. (2017). *Linking values and research evidence for policy advocacy: The journey of the Indonesian Forum for Budget Transparency (Working Paper 19)*. Jakarta: Knowledge Sector Initiative.

Shaxson, L. (2014). *Investing in Evidence : Lessons from the UK's Department of Environment, Food and Rural Affairs (Working Paper 2)*. Jakarta: Knowledge Sector Initiative.

Shaxson, L., Datta, A., Tshangela, M., & Matomela, B. (2016). *Understanding the organisational context for evidence-informed policy-making*. Report. Pretoria/London: Department of Environmental Affairs/Overseas Development Institute.

Sheppard, J. (2012). *Indonesia: Government capacity to assure high quality regulation*. Background report for OECD review of regulatory reform in Indonesia. Paris: OECD Publishing.

Sherlock, S. (2010). *Knowledge for policy: Regulatory obstacles to the growth of a knowledge market in Indonesia*. Jakarta: AusAID. Available at http://dfat.gov.au/about-us/publications/Documents/indo-ks13-knowledge-to-govt.pdf. Accessed 10 July 2017.

Sherlock, S., & Djani, L. (2015). *Update on constraints in the enabling environment to the provision of knowledge in executive and legislative government*. Jakarta: Knowledge Sector Initiative.

SIMPAN [Sistem Informasi Pendayagunaan Aparatur Negara]. (2017). http://sipan.menpan.go.id/. Accessed 8 June 2017.

Sutmuller, P. M., & Setiono, I. (2011). *Diagnostic on evidence-based public policy formulation under decentralisation*. Jakarta: AusAID. Available at http://dfat.gov.au/about-us/publications/Documents/indo-ks6-decentralisation.pdf. Accessed 9 May 2017.

Tempo Online. (2017, March 3). *Tempo beri penghargaan 10 kepala daerah teladan* (Tempo gives awards to 10 influential regional heads). https://nasional.tempo.co/read/news/2017/03/03/173852419/tempo-beri-penghargaan-10-kepala-daerah-teladan-2017. Accessed 10 June 2017.

Tjiptoherijanto, P. (2014). *Reform of the Indonesian civil service: Racing with decentralization* (Working Paper in Economics and Business IV:2). Depok: Faculty of Economics, University of Indonesia.

Turner, M., Imbaruddin, A., & Sutiyono, W. (2009). Human resource management: The forgotten dimension of decentralisation in Indonesia. *Bulletin of Indonesian Economic Studies, 45*(2), 231–249.

UCT [University of Cape Town]. (n.d.). *Evidence-based policy-making and implementation*. http://www.gsdpp.uct.ac.za/gsdpp/courses/evidence_based_policy_making_implementation. Accessed 24 June 2017.

Wasono, A., & Maulana, M. (2018). *Critical study on development planning and budgeting in Indonesia (Working Paper 27)*. Jakarta: Knowledge Sector Initiative.

Wills, A., Tshangela, M., Shaxson, L., Datta, A., & Matomela, B. (2016). *Guidelines and good practices for evidence-informed policymaking in a government department*. Report. Pretoria/London: Department of Environmental Affairs/Overseas Development Institute.

World Bank. (2009). *Support to civil service reform in Indonesia: Report from a programming mission to Jakarta*. Washington, DC/Jakarta: The World Bank.

Wotela, K. (2017). A proposed monitoring and evaluation curriculum based on a model that institutionalizes monitoring and evaluation. *African Evaluation Journal, 5*(1), 8 pages. 10/4102/aej.v5i1.186.

Zhang, D. (2015). *Do local governments in Indonesia produce evidence-based policies?* Jakarta: The Australia Indonesia Partnership for Decentralisation/Department of Foreign Affairs and Trade.

Chapter 6
Data Innovation for Policymaking in Indonesia

Arnaldo Pellini, Diastika Rahwidiati, and George Hodge

1 Introduction

In February 2015, Kenneth Benoit and Kenneth Cukier presented at a public lecture at the London School of Economics on the impact of big data on social science research, in which they stated that 'the ubiquity of big data has the potential to transform the way we approach social science'.

According to the United Nations Global Pulse, the United Nations Secretary-General's flagship innovation initiative on big data, 'the volume of data produced globally means that 90 per cent of all the data in existence today – back to the invention of the Phoenician alphabet – has been generated during the past 2 years alone' (United Nations Global Pulse 2016).

Indeed, growth has been exponential. In 1995 less than 1% of the world's population used the Internet. Today that figure has risen to around 46% (Internet Live Stats 2017).[1] The milestone of 1 billion Internet users was reached in 2005; the second billion was reached in 2010 and the third in 2014 (Fig. 6.1).

Today more households own a mobile phone than have access to electricity or clean water (United Nations Global Pulse 2016). This means that more and more individuals and organisations are at the same time producers, owners and consumers of data (Ibid.). We are living through a data revolution that offers unprecedented

---

[1] 'Internet users' is defined as an individual who can access the Internet at home via any device type and connection (Internet Live Stats 2017).

A. Pellini (✉)
Overseas Development Institute, London, UK
e-mail: a.pellini@odi.org.uk

D. Rahwidiati · G. Hodge
Pulse Lab Jakarta, Jakarta, Indonesia
e-mail: diastika.rahwidiati@un.or.id; george.hodge@un.or.id

© Springer Nature Singapore Pte Ltd. 2018
A. Pellini et al. (eds.), *Knowledge, Politics and Policymaking in Indonesia*,
https://doi.org/10.1007/978-981-13-0167-4_6

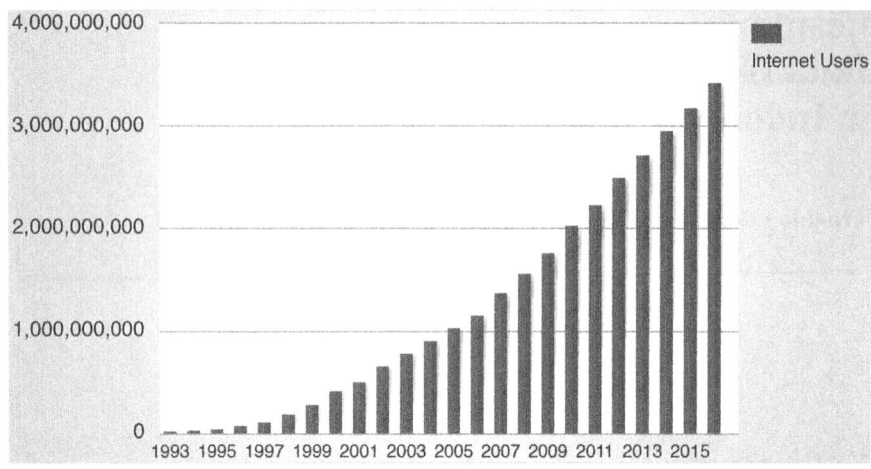

Fig. 6.1 Global Internet users (Reproduced from Internet Live Stats 2017)

opportunities to learn about human behaviour, as noted in the United Nations white paper on 'Big Data for Development: Challenges & Opportunities' (United Nations Global Pulse 2012).

The data revolution has been defined as:

> An explosion in the volume of data, speed with which data are produced, the number of producers of data, the dissemination of data, and the range of things on which there are data, coming from new technologies such as mobile phones and the Internet of things and from other sources, such as qualitative data, citizen-generated data, and perceptions data. (IEAGDRSD 2014)

The data revolution not only has the potential to transform society and social science research, as argued by Benoit and Cukier (2015), but also to transform what is at the core of this book: evidence-informed policymaking processes and systems.

Broadly speaking, policy makers rely on five main types of evidence: (1) statistical data (e.g. from national statistical offices); (2) administrative data (e.g. from government sources, such as hospitals and schools); (3) research-based evidence (e.g. from universities or think-tanks); (4) evidence from citizens (e.g. from feedback or complaint systems) and other stakeholders, such as private sector analysis; and (5) evidence from evaluations conducted by government or non-governmental institutions (Shaxson 2016).

The remarkable progress in new information technology for collecting and analysing data is changing the way policy makers can source and use evidence, adding real-time big data analytics to their evidence toolkits. Data analytics, defined here as the systematic computational analysis of data, provides relevant, accessible and timely data to policy makers and civil servants to better inform their choices and decisions on, for example, extending public services into remote communities or implementing programmes and policies more efficiently (Stuart et al. 2015).

The scale and size of the datasets that can be processed by big data tools is unprecedented and cannot be matched by any research sampling technique or census. A vast amount of metadata can be collected, for example, about the ways citizen move, what they buy, what information they search for online or what they think about public services. The raw data can then be analysed more quickly and more cheaply than was the case for traditional research approaches. This is extremely appealing to governments because it creates new, quicker and cheaper ways to gather information, identify problems and monitor the progress of public programmes and policies. The scientific research methods traditionally used to generate evidence for policy can seem dated.

With the data revolution, the size of the dataset has grown so much that only astronomical scale measures can be used to capture the volume of data. Scales like petabytes, exabytes and zettabytes (Benoit and Cukier 2015) are finding their way into policy parlance. Khoso (2016) estimates that 2.5 exabytes of data are produced *every day*. That is the equivalent to 530,000,000 million songs, or the memory storage of 150,000,000 iPhones, or the hard-disk capacity of five million laptops or 90 years' worth of high-definition videos.

This led Chris Anderson, the former editor-in-chief of *Wired* magazine, to argue that with big data we no longer need to understand the causes leading to effects; instead, correlation is sufficient to derive conclusions and new knowledge. 'Who knows why people do what they do? The point is that we can track it, measure it with great fidelity. The numbers speak for themselves' (Anderson 2008).

Anderson's point spurred a vigorous debate. Timmer (2008), for example, argued that correlations merit a scientist's attention, but it is the mechanism that explains these correlations that helps us to generate hypotheses, make predictions and develop practical applications. Similarly, Tim Harford (2014) wrote in an article published in the *Financial Times* that Anderson's faith in big data is at best an optimistic oversimplification. Harford quoted David Spiegelhalter, Winton Professor of the Public Understanding of Risk at Cambridge University, who stated that relying solely on correlations is 'absolute nonsense'.

The debate rages. What is not under discussion is that the data revolution is ongoing. It presents great opportunities, as well as numerous technical and legislative challenges. This means that if governments and policy makers are to use evidence from big data to improve the well-being of citizens and societies, they need to learn and understand what data analytics (such as descriptive analysis or machine learning) can and cannot offer, as well as the risks involved with using big data for public policy and evidence-based policymaking.

1.1 Benefits and Opportunities

Philip Davies (2012) has argued that the objective of evidence-based policymaking is not to provide the *absolute best evidence* to policy makers but, more realistically, to provide policy makers with access to the *best available* evidence at a given point in time (see Chap. 1, Sect. 1).

While imperfect information is part of the reality of policymaking, the problem is that the best available evidence that governments have at their disposal to inform public policy decisions is often poor, and there is much that governments do not know, as highlighted in the examples below.

Carr-Hill (2013) estimates that as many as 350 million people worldwide are not covered by traditional household surveys. This means that there could be as many as 25% more people living on less than US$ 1.25 a day than the 1.1 billion people estimated by the Organisation for Economic Co-operation and Development (OECD) in 2013. According to the United Nations Educational, Scientific and Cultural Organization (UNESCO), official universal primary education enrolment statistics may overstate children's school attendance at the appropriate age by about 10% (UNESCO 2010). Infant mortality is another example of the unavailability of reliable data. More than 100 countries do not have functioning systems to register births or deaths, meaning that fewer than one in five births occur in countries with complete civil registration systems. The remainder occur either in countries with incomplete registries or with no data at all (World Bank and World Health Organization 2014). Data and knowledge are also lacking about such basic information as how many people live in cities; how many girls are married before the age of 18; what percentage of the world's poor are women; what are the outcomes of primary-level basic education in sub-Saharan Africa, South-East Asia or Latin America; how many street children are there worldwide; and how many people in the world are hungry (Stuart et al. 2015).

The list is long. Without these data it is difficult for governments to be confident about policy decisions and allocations to state budgets for public programmes and public services. Policy decisions will always be based on imperfect information, but data innovation – defined as the use of new or nontraditional data sources and methods to gain a more nuanced understanding of our complex world – can help to reduce some of the unknowns in unprecedented ways.

The data revolution is enabling a dramatic expansion in the amount of data that governments can collect. It is making it cheaper to store and process raw data, so that their analysis can be translated into evidence for use by policy decision-makers and government units (United Nations Global Pulse 2016). Data analytics methods can help to overcome the limitations of survey-based data collection and statistical analysis (Stuart et al. 2015). Data innovation and the spread of mobile phone technology are making the political debate more participatory. Such tools provide space for marginalised groups to become part of the policy discussion by developing a shared sense of identity or a common platform through which they can articulate their problems and views on existing policies and programmes (United Nations Global Pulse 2016). Information and communication technologies have opened new channels of communication that provide new and cheaper ways for citizens and civil society groups to generate evidence and establish social networks, play a role in policy processes and demand greater accountability from policy makers and civil servants in national and local government (IEAGDRSD 2014).

Visualisation techniques and technology for data can create new ways to synthesise and communicate data analytics, serving as powerful catalysts for group discussion and further scrutiny of data (Bollier 2010). Margetts (2013) maintains that data innovation offers policy makers a chance to design and implement policies and programmes that are more citizen-focused and based on better understanding of citizens' problems and needs. New information systems can also help to monitor and quickly respond to feedback or alerts during emergencies, such as floods and other natural disasters, as well as to easily record citizens' experience of public services through social networking platforms.

To sum up, as elaborated at the New Zealand Data Futures Forum (2014a), the new data environment provides many benefits to governments: competitive advantage through innovation and a world-leading data environment; business opportunities through new markets and an expanded knowledge sector; better public services arising from data-driven efficiencies and better targeting; better places to live, work and play – smart cities and optimal use of natural resources; everyday life transformed through automation, personalised services and informed choices; and increased transparency, generating greater trust and empowered citizens.

The opportunities are there, but so are perils and challenges.

1.2 Perils and Challenges

Rapid advances in data innovation and information technology are challenging governments to find ways to maximise their potential for informing public policy and minimising risks. For Lips and Mansell (2015), strong, long-term vision and political leadership are critical success factors for the mobilisation of human and financial resources, along with the adoption and use of data-driven innovation and evidence for policymaking. Leadership is necessary because data innovation requires governments to invest in both large-scale information systems and institutional capacity within the bureaucracy to manage and utilise these systems.

Data innovation can be disruptive and shift power balances within governments, which can result in resistance against evidence and reduced uptake of data analytics in policy development processes. Lipps and Mansell (Ibid.) offer an instructional example from New Zealand. Since 2006 the government has been committed to developing new, evidence-based approaches to investing in social policy and service provision. The Ministry of Social Development championed sharing, integration and use of social sector data to inform funding decisions and increase the efficiency of social programmes. In 2011 the Ministry built up its data integration and analytics capability to better understand which social services have the greatest positive impact on the most vulnerable communities, in order to redirect service provision to particular groups. This initiative encountered considerable resistance from social sector agencies. One reason expressed by government agencies concerned privacy risks linked to sharing data. Another was linked to the shift in power over policy and investment decisions for public services implied by mandating the Ministry of Social Development to collect and analyse the integrated data.

Another example of the disruption that data innovation can bring concerns the role of national statistics offices. Stuart et al. (2015) argue that the data revolution is stimulating new demand for vastly improved statistical services, for which national statistical offices may lack resources and capability. Davies (2017) also highlights that the data revolution poses formidable challenges for statistical offices because big data provides far greater opportunities for quantitative analysis than any amount of statistical modelling. Moreover, Davies points out that data analytics generates an entirely new type of knowledge: data is captured first and research questions come later, when vast datasets are mined to search for patterns, trends, correlations or emergent moods. This new form of knowledge is challenging the traditional role that national statistics offices have played in providing analysis and evidence to inform the policy cycle.

These new types of knowledge are not devoid of perils and challenges. Due to the pace of the data revolution, governments can find themselves struggling to design an adequate regulatory framework to manage the complexity of the data innovation landscape. For example, privacy violation through data collection and data personalization is an area of concern for governments and the public (Bollier 2010). The question is how to maximise the benefits of data innovation for policymaking and for society at large while minimising the risk of misuse of data.

Some governments are beginning to navigate these perils and challenges, in order to take advantage of the opportunities. The New Zealand Data Futures Forum, for example, was established in 2013 to initiate a nationwide discussion of these questions and define the principles that would guide government use of data innovation. The Forum involved representatives from businesses, government, academia and members of the general public, including community groups. Through research and consultation over a two-year period, the Forum proposed four guiding principles to help New Zealand manage data innovation:

- *Value*: New Zealand should use data to drive economic and social value and create a competitive advantage for the nation.
- *Inclusion*: all members of New Zealand society should have the opportunity to benefit from data use.
- *Trust*: transparency and openness should form the foundations on which to build trust and enhance understanding about what data is held and how data is collected, stored and used.
- *Control*: individuals should have control over the use of their personal data and be able to determine the level of privacy they desire, based on improved insight into how their personal data is processed and used (New Zealand Data Futures Forum 2014b).

This chapter touches upon both the challenges and opportunities of data innovation for public policy in Indonesia. It seeks to reflect on the lessons generated by 'data for policy' pilots at the national and subnational levels implemented by Pulse Lab Jakarta, the United Nations data innovation lab established in 2012. The chapter asks: What factors enable the uptake of data innovation by policy makers? What can prevent that uptake? Is data analytics putting policy researchers and statisticians out of business? The next section turns to Indonesia and describes its rapidly expanding data ecosystem.

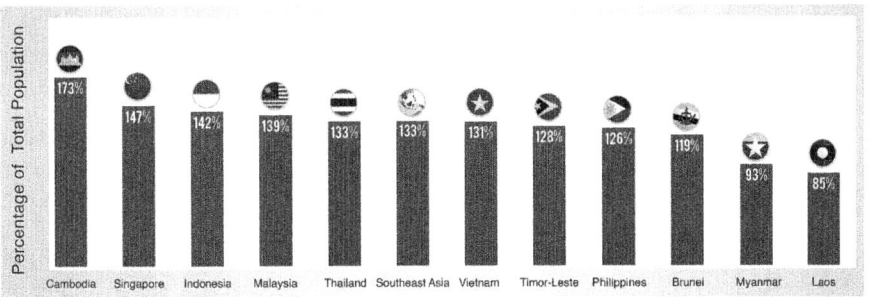

Fig. 6.2 Mobile connectivity by country as of January 2017 (Reproduced from Kemp 2017)

2 Indonesia's Data Ecosystem

Indonesia is a giant in the digital world. The number of Internet users grew from two million in 2000 to 55 million in 2012 and reached 132.7 million in 2016, with an increase of 45 million Internet users in 2016 alone (Kemp 2017). Data from Internet Live Stats show that in 2016 Indonesia was ranked at number 12 (out of 201 countries), with Internet penetration at 51% of the total population (Ibid.).

By 2013 Indonesia was already amongst the top five countries on Facebook, with 64 million users actively accessing their accounts on a monthly basis (Grazella 2013). In 2017 the number of active Facebook users was estimated at 106 million (Kemp 2017). Indonesia is the fifth largest country for Twitter use (Sadowski 2017); Jakarta posts more tweets per day than any other city in the world (Johnson 2013).

Social media and mobile technology are booming. Indonesia ranks number three in Southeast Asia in terms of mobile connectivity (Fig. 6.2). In 2016 the total number of unique mobile users was 173.6 million; by 2018 this number is expected to hit 200 million (Statista 2017). Indonesia has 371.4 million mobile phone subscriptions, representing 142% of the total population (Kemp 2017).

At present the higher estimates shown in Fig. 6.3 suggest that over half the country is online and has 106 million active social media users, representing 40% of the population (Kemp 2017).

These figures confirm the point by Das et al. (2016) that Indonesia is making progress in all four of the 'disruptive technologies' that drive the digital revolution: mobile Internet, cloud computing, Internet of Things and advanced big data analytics. Indonesia has a great and untapped potential when it comes to data innovation and data analytics, and the issue of how the country can harness the abundance of its digital data for socioeconomic development is rapidly emerging. New data sources could give policy makers near real-time feedback – by assessing public sentiment, identifying behaviour patterns and providing references for predicting the effects of policies and programmes. For example, in the case of heavy rains, the analysis of the tweets in Jakarta is used to alert emergency authorities and provide them with timely information about floods to inform emergency response as well as planning flood mitigation interventions (Floodtags 2017).

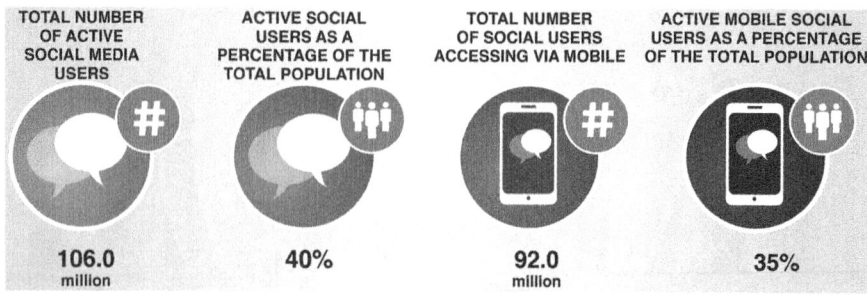

Fig. 6.3 Social media use in Indonesia as of January 2017 (Reproduced from Kemp 2017)

Data alone are not information and cannot inform decisions. It is the *analysis* of data that generates the information and evidence upon which policy makers can act. The quality of data is critical for the type of analysis that can be conducted, and therefore the quality of the evidence generated from data analytics. The Government has collected vast datasets over the years (e.g. in the areas of social welfare, health and education), which are useful for calibrating big datasets owned by the private sector, by, for example, weighting big data insights related to certain social cohorts based on government data on their prevalence in the broader population. But questions have been raised concerning the timeliness of these data, as well as their reliability, validity and interoperability. In addition, specific to Indonesia's complex institutional structure, existing data management systems are not well integrated, either within or between sectors or between national and subnational governments. The One Data Indonesia (Satu Data Indonesia) initiative being implemented by the Office of the President's Staff (Kantor Staf Presiden, KSP) and the Ministry for National Development Planning/National Development Planning Agency (Kementerian Perencanaan Pembangunan Nasional/Badan Perencanaan Pembangunan Nasional – Bappenas) is addressing these issues.

Regulatory challenges must also be overcome to maximise the opportunities for producing timely, good-quality evidence from data analytics. One issue for the Government of Indonesia is that many, if not most, of the big datasets are owned by private enterprise. Social networking organisations, telecommunications companies, online marketplaces and retailers of fast-moving consumer goods own datasets from which they can analyse economic and social trends in a more nuanced manner than that afforded by national statistics. To access these datasets, the Government must either regulate, purchase or partner – each option creates specific regulatory challenges. In addition, while one part of government may have access to a particular dataset, other applications of the data related to social, environmental or economic policy may be unexploited due to lack of coordination amongst government agencies.

Examples of applications of these new datasets to policy issues by the Government of Indonesia are beginning to emerge, such as statistical reports by the Ministry of Tourism on tourism arrivals, based on data from mobile telecommunications networks (Netralnews 2017). Similar examples are explored further in the next section.

The important point here is to highlight that these initiatives are exploratory in nature, but are generating insights into the 'social life of data' within public institutions.

In exploring the politics of data innovation in the policy cycle, it is important to return to the issues of quality, validity and integration of government statistics. These challenges, in part driven by the complexity of Indonesia's institutional arrangements, have meant that the data collected are often not used effectively across the policy cycle. Those statistics collected tend to be used for the planning and implementation stages, but not to adjust policies or respond to emerging issues. This, in turn, is connected to the fact that many existing systems do not have effective mechanisms for monitoring the impact of policy actions.

The policy cycle in Indonesia (and elsewhere) is a simplification of the reality of policymaking. The rational model involves a logical progression from defining the issue, setting priorities and analysing options to policy implementation and finally, evaluation. The reality is far more complex. Cohen et al. (1972) developed a 'garbage can model of organisational choice', which conceives of organised anarchies, characterised by problematic preferences, unclear technology and fluid participation. The model views a 'choice opportunity' as a 'garbage can' into which various kinds of problems and solutions are dumped by participants as they are generated. In such an environment, insights gleaned from data analytics sit alongside other forms of evidence, supporting or undermining competing policy agendas. Policy development processes in some Indonesian institutions more closely resemble the rational model, but others resemble the garbage can model. Either way, this overtly political space in Indonesia has resulted in some big data tools being used as political tools to advance public administration reform agendas, alongside their roles as generators of evidence. Some anecdotal evidence also suggests that big data tools have been used to respond to emerging issues, but to date no evidence is available to demonstrate that the tools are being used for policy or programme adjustment during implementation. This remains a missed opportunity.

As information systems improve, it will be possible to empower front-line staff to combine their local knowledge with evidence derived from data and to act on these insights. This will have profound implications for power relations within the state, enabling better tailoring and adaptation of policies and programmes to problems and needs. As economic competitiveness is closely linked to state effectiveness, it is imperative that the Government of Indonesia invest political and financial capital in improved knowledge production, which can then inform policy. This includes, but is not limited to, evidence from data innovation. Some progress has been made in this regard, with the centralisation of statistics production at the National Bureau of Statistics and experimentation by line ministries with big data tools. But further progress would reap rewards in policy areas ranging from agriculture and trade to social protection, health services and beyond.

The next section describes experience with some of these processes at Pulse Lab Jakarta, the data innovation lab jointly established by the Government of Indonesia and the United Nations to promote data innovation for public policy in Indonesia.

3 Pulse Lab Jakarta: Experimenting and Learning About Data Innovation for Public Policy

Pulse Lab Jakarta is part of 'Global Pulse', the flagship United Nations innovation initiative on big data and data revolution for sustainable development. The initiative was launched in 2010, driven by two important factors. The first was the decision by then-United Nations Secretary-General Ban Ki-moon to establish a 'Global Impact and Vulnerability Alert System'. This step was taken in response to member countries' request to track, in real-time, the needs of vulnerable populations in the wake of the 2008 global economic crisis and the global food price crisis that followed (United Nations Global Pulse 2015). A second driver was the recognition that big data offer opportunities to gain better understanding of changes in human well-being and obtain real-time feedback on how well policy responses or development programmes are working (United Nations Global Pulse 2017). More recently, the 2016 adoption by UN member nations of the 17 Sustainable Development Goals provided an additional imperative for the United Nations to embrace the data revolution. These goals (and their 169 targets) set an ambitious human development agenda to be reached by 2030. One of the challenges was how to track progress against these goals and their targets and indicators, a challenge that data innovation can help to address (United Nations 2017).

The vision underpinning the United Nations Global Pulse is that of a future in which big data is harnessed safely and responsibly as a public good. The objectives are to (i) promote awareness of the opportunities afforded by big data; (ii) forge public-private partnerships for data, tools and expertise; (iii) conduct joint research projects to evaluate the potential of new methodologies; (iv) build innovative tools for real-time monitoring; and (v) drive adoption of new approaches across the public sector (Ibid.).

Activities undertaken through the United Nations Global Pulse initiative are clustered under five sectors (food and agriculture, economic well-being, climate and resilience, humanitarian action and public health) and four cross-cutting themes: data privacy and data protection, gender, real-time evaluation and the Sustainable Development Goals agenda (Ibid.).

In 2012, following the annual summit of the Association of Southeast Asian Nations – where the United Nations Secretary-General and the President of Indonesia pledged their commitment to creating an innovation centre of excellence in the region – Pulse Lab Jakarta was officially opened. It was the first United Nations Global Pulse initiative office to be opened outside United Nations headquarters in New York; in 2014 a second regional office was opened in Kampala, Uganda.

3.1 Pulse Lab Jakarta

Pulse Lab Jakarta is a partnership between the United Nations, through United Nations Global Pulse, and the Government of Indonesia, through Bappenas. The overarching objective is to access and use high-quality, real-time 'big data' to inform policymaking, planning and budgeting, as well as to develop the capacity and capabilities of government agencies, including selected subnational governments, in the process. Pulse Lab Jakarta's activities are overseen by a steering committee composed of representatives of the Government of Indonesia and the United Nations in Indonesia, which provide overall guidance and strategic direction to the work of the Lab (Pulse Lab Jakarta 2016a).

The projects and prototypes developed by Pulse Lab Jakarta are guided by a two-track strategy. The first is an 'innovation driver track', where the design and implementation of research projects through the Lab provides governments across Asia and the Pacific Islands, United Nations agencies and development partners with access to data products, toolkits, platforms and expertise to strengthen and improve data-driven policy decisions. The second is an 'ecosystem catalyst track', focused on collaboration with regional governments to develop regulatory frameworks and technical standards that address data sharing and privacy protection challenges and provide public sector organisations with policy guidance and technical assistance to strengthen their capability for integrating real-time evidence from data analytics into their decisions (Pulse Lab Jakarta 2016b).

In August 2014 Pulse Lab Jakarta received funding from the Australia-Indonesia Partnership for Decentralisation to test ways to improve service delivery at the subnational level through more effective feedback loops between citizens and governments. This funding continued in 2015, when Pulse Lab Jakarta signed a partnership agreement with the Australia-Indonesia Partnership for Pro-Poor Policy: The Knowledge Sector Initiative to (1) equip government agencies with tools to generate and analyse data in real time in order to provide timely responses, engage effectively with citizens, evaluate policy effectiveness and better address the development challenges facing Indonesia; (2) demonstrate that adopting innovative IT-based methods leads to improved development outcomes, as measured by the government's own indicators; and (3) build partnerships across the technology and private sectors, civil society and government that utilise each partners' comparative advantage to raise productivity amongst the poor (*Ibid*).

The following section shows how these objectives are being pursued and the approach that Pulse Lab Jakarta has adopted to carry out its activities.

3.1.1   Pulse Lab Jakarta: Approaching Development Sensibly

At the inception of the Lab, much of its activities were supply-driven, in that the team would identify potentially useful datasets and establish proof of concepts for their application to policy issues. After publication of the results, if a partner were interested, the Lab would transform the data products into data tools and embed them within the partner's information systems.

This has evolved to a situation where the starting point is more often client demand for solutions to policy and delivery problems. Initial discussions with the partner involve an assessment of the nature of the problem(s) and the appetite for solving it together, through joint analysis, co-design and sharing of resources, as well as a discussion about the various possible solutions – some of which may not involve or require data innovation. This initial stage helps to clarify whether Pulse Lab Jakarta is best placed to address the partners' problems and whether identifying a solution falls within the Lab's areas of expertise.

After defining the problem(s), the Lab team and the partner follow an 'agile' development process, which can involve exploratory data analysis and user research to better explore the problem, its drivers and opportunities; design workshops with the partner and stakeholders; building and testing data tools based on the evidence and learning along the way; and revisiting the problem as it evolves, to re-think and revise the response.

The process, which starts from the problem(s) the partner(s) wants to solve, involves translation into real-world terms of the suggestions made by proponents of 'problem-driven iterative adaptation' (PDIA), discussed in greater depth in Chap. 8. When presenting the PDIA, Andrews et al. (2012, 2017) suggest a focus on solving local problems that are locally owned and are debated, defined and refined by local people in an ongoing process. Further, they suggest working through local conveners who mobilise all stakeholders to tackle common problems and introduce relevant changes; avoid the introduction or reproduction of 'expert' solutions considered 'best practices'; and replace predetermined linear processes involving strict monitoring and compliance systems with design and implementation through rapid cycles of planning, action and reflection. Last but not least they urge: learn throughout the process.

Over the last 4 years, Pulse Lab Jakarta has designed and implemented a number of prototypes and pilots that began as research projects to explore the use of big datasets for policy or at a client's request. For example, 'Haze Gazer' is a crisis analysis and visualisation tool that enhances disaster management responses by providing analytics of real-time data on fire/haze hotspots. A second, more client-driven, example is the work undertaken with the Indonesia Infrastructure Initiative, for which Pulse Lab Jakarta tested ways to crowdsource the monitoring of provincial road infrastructure projects in order to better target physical inspection by engineers.

The next section highlights two specific projects with explicit links between data and policymaking and the learning they provided on data for policy processes at the national and subnational levels.

3.2   National Citizen Feedback Dashboard

The first iteration of the National Citizen Feedback Dashboard was developed with the Government of Nusa Tenggara Barat Province, which through its young and progressive governor, Muhammad Zainul Majdi, already had a functioning SMS-based system for gathering citizen feedback on public services from across the province. It became clear that while the SMS-based system was gathering substantial data in the form of complaints, little analysis of this metadata was taking place. After consultations, and with the endorsement of the head of the Regional Development   Planning   Agency   (Badan   Perencanaan   Pembangunan

Daerah – Bappeda), Pulse Lab Jakarta proceeded to design and develop a citizen feedback dashboard that processed, analysed and visualised data coming from the SMS-based system, as well as data on complaints captured by public discourse on Twitter in the Nusa Tenggara Barat Province.

Based on the dashboard developed with the Nusa Tenggara Barat local government, the Pulse Lab Jakarta team worked with LAPOR!, the national citizen feedback platform, which at the time was based at the Office of the President's Staff (Kantor Staf Presiden – KSP). A national citizen feedback dashboard was developed to process, analyse and visualise data from LAPOR! and social media, notably Twitter. Both dashboards captured trends in complaints, as well as geographic complaint hotspots, which complemented the system's case-by-case administration.

KSP integrated the dashboard into the LAPOR! public website, and LAPOR! staff have confirmed that the aggregated visualisation of citizen complaints provided by the dashboard is useful for determining key issues and problems prevalent in a given area prior to a field visit. The analysis also complements reports submitted by line ministries as part of the day-to-day business of government. The tool has been used as an example of the potential of data analytics, as part of the Jokowi Administration's efforts to advance public sector reform.

The merits of such a dashboard include short-term results such as enabling decision-makers to obtain insight into public opinion and perceptions and offering a snapshot of trending topics and hotspots across Indonesia. Evidence of these short-term results is already available. In the medium term, using the dashboard enables officials to process citizens' feedback at low cost and at scale, as well as to be more responsive to citizens' needs by prioritising trending issues. Feedback from the Office of the President's Staff (Kantor Staf Presiden – KSP) indicates this to be the case. This analysis can then be complemented with triangulation and validation, using social science research methods and techniques to gain a deeper understanding of the reasons underlying citizen sentiments and needs. The long-term results could include strengthened governance, such as enhancing accountability and helping constituents understand how their feedback is processed. It is too soon to tell whether this will be the case.

This case study demonstrates the importance of political commitment to integrating data tools into public sector information systems, as well as the significance of in-house resources and capacity for managing and further developing the tool.

3.2.1 Malaria Case Rapid Reporting

In 2015 Pulse Lab Jakarta provided a small grant (approximately US$5,500) to the Malaria Centre in South Halmahera District of North Maluku Province to conduct a 2-month project on malaria case reporting (Lapor Cepat Kasus Malaria – LaCaK Malaria). This was one of Pulse Lab Jakarta's series of four data innovation mini-grants given to 'catalyse innovation in collecting, analysing and visualising data that will help the Government of Indonesia in providing more effective services to its citizens'. The funds were to be used to 'produce a workable prototype that can be scaled after testing'.

Malaria is endemic across the Maluku Islands. In South Halmahera District, the traditional system of compiling reports – by hand, from front-line health centres delivered monthly in hard copy to the district-based Malaria Centre – was considered at best inefficient and at times ineffective. The South Halmahera Malaria Centre, part of the district government, was keen to champion the target of making North Maluku Province malaria-free by 2019, in line with Ministry of Health objectives.

The Malaria Centre proposed to develop a cell phone-based malaria reporting system using an unstructured service supplementary data menu browser. Following the two-month grant period, the result was a reporting system that captures data from nine distinct fields (patient name, date of examination, test results, etc.) for malaria patients, as well as nine distinct fields on medicine stocks. Currently, 30 of 32 front-line health clinics in South Halmahera routinely report through LaCaK Malaria. The other two districts are in locations with poor cell phone coverage.

The initiative encouraged district governments to adopt regulatory measures to ensure that LaCaK Malaria is incorporated as a routine reporting mechanism. Rapid reporting and aggregation of data was facilitated by cross-checking malaria diagnoses. LaCaK Malaria also allowed South Halmahera's Malaria Centre to better monitor malaria and related malaria stocks and to promote quicker action to combat its spread.

The Malaria Centre achieved a significant result for ensuring the sustainability of LaCaK Malaria by successfully advocating for passage of a regional regulation in late 2015 to ensure that LaCaK Malaria is fully funded under the South Halmahera Malaria Centre's budget, provided from regional government funds through an annual allocation of IDR 100 million (US$ 7,500),[2] which increases the Centre's overall annual budget from IDR 400 million (US$ 30,000) to IDR 500 million (US$ 37,500). The Centre achieved this budget allocation following requests to, and sustained engagement with, both Bappeda and the district health department following the initial successful testing of the system.

LaCak Malaria has proven to be a popular and cost-effective means to improve malaria reporting and monitoring. In this instance, the local champion was the key to the success, by mobilising resources and developing capacity through trial and error (this iteration of the monitoring system was informed by learning from the Centre's previous, unsuccessful, reform efforts). Policy and technology uptake beyond the individual champions or units represents a significant challenge. Lack of interest in any initiative that does not originate from a central ministry is often cited as a barrier to uptake, as is lack of access to appropriate data sources that can feed into analytical dashboards on a regular basis.

3.3   Learning from Experimentation

Reflecting on Pulse Lab Jakarta's experience to date, Usher and Rahwidiati (2017) write: 'When Pulse Lab Jakarta started out in late 2012, we were pretty much the only big data shop in town. But 5 years later we are surrounded by a network of

---

[2] USD 1 = IDR 13,317 Google exchange rate on 24 May 2017.

policy-makers, data scientists and entrepreneurs, keen to use the affordances of the data revolution for public good'. So, what key lessons about Indonesia's data ecosystem and data innovation for policy initiatives have emerged from the work of Pulse Lab Jakarta over the last four years?

Government organisations' capability to make use of new data and data tools depends on the capacity of the organisations' staff, internal and external rules and regulations and the capacity and intent of the organisation to invest and expand those capabilities. This chapter has shown that the amount of data that the government could access is growing exponentially. In harnessing the full power of these data, however, significant challenges remain in relation to the capacity of policy makers and civil servants to develop and apply the data tools, knowledge about the kind of evidence and information that data analytics can and cannot offer and the complementarity between data analytics and other sources of evidence.

Ongoing government-led initiatives are seeking to improve access to and sharing of data. For example, the One Data Indonesia (Satu Data Indonesia)[3] initiative driven by the Office of the President's Staff (Kantor Staf Presiden – KSP) and Bappenas is testing ways to compile data from various ministries and make them available not only to government agencies but also to research organisations, think-tanks and the general public. These are promising steps, but challenges remain due to the legacy of complex rules and regulations around data governance.

Indonesia's enabling environment for the use of data in policy is evolving rapidly. Key pieces of legislation are being developed or revised to establish a more favourable environment for accessing data. Examples include laws on national development planning (Law No. 25/2004), village governance and development (Law No. 6/2014), social protection (Laws No. 40/2004 and 24/2011), population administration (Law No. 23/2006), public service (Law No. 25/2009), regional autonomy (Laws No. 32 and 33/2001) and freedom of information (Law No. 14/2008).

Big data analytics provide significant opportunities for informing policy, but alone are not sufficient to inform policy decisions. Data analytics can provide great insights on correlation, but traditional research and analysis is still necessary to understand, for example, the background and reason for trends captured through data analytics.

The data revolution is not only about big data. The analysis of *small data* can also make a difference in terms of policy. The experience from the Malaria Centre in South Halmahera shows that data innovation does not always require the most advanced technologies, sophisticated equipment or large budgets. Appropriate, and familiar, technologies can help to improve public services and introduce innovation under the leadership of local-level civil servants to address specific locally defined problems. As is often the case, leadership at the top has been shown to be a critical component for the success of data tools in Indonesia's public sector.

Regarding approaches to testing solutions for data-to-policy problems, the experience of Pulse Lab Jakarta demonstrates the power of networks. The approach adopted by Pulse Lab Jakarta was to establish strong partnerships with local players

---

[3] Available at http://data.go.id/

on data products to promote the uptake of data analytics and contribute to policy change. This network approach also helped to build relationships with government officials at the national and subnational levels, through local partners.

Policy researchers and data analysts face similar challenges in terms of seeing the results of their work being used by policy makers. Testing ways to bring more data innovation into policy requires a good understanding of the context in which policy makers and civil servants operate and the problems they face or want to solve. Political economy analysis, problem identification and prioritisation and stakeholder mapping can ensure relevance and help to reduce the risk of rushing into solutions or policy recommendations that are technically sound but politically unfeasible.

The approach adopted by Pulse Lab Jakarta – to identify problems and test data for policy solutions – took some time to consolidate. The main challenge was familiarising the stakeholders and governance partners with an approach that is not linear, is open to failure and tries to start from clear needs rather than solutions. The methods are evolving and showing that an iterative and adaptive approach to developing data-driven solutions, prioritising learning throughout, is also gaining ground in policy circles (Usher and Rahwidiati 2017).

4   Conclusions

In a 2014 article published in the *Financial Times*, entitled 'Big data: are we making a big mistake?', Tim Harford was cautious about touting the opportunities provided by big data: 'Big data do not solve the problem that has obsessed statisticians and scientists for centuries: the problem of insight, of inferring what is going on, and figuring out how we might intervene to change a system for the better'. As highlighted by the Royal Society (2017), data analytics, specifically the branch of machine learning, has issues of interpretability and validity, linked to opacity in the way machine learning systems reach conclusions, due to their inability to identify cause-effect relationships. At the end of the day, Harford quotes Professor David Hand of Imperial College London: 'Nobody wants *data*. What people want are answers'.

This chapter discussed the use of data analytics as a source of evidence for policy decisions, describing the data ecosystem in Indonesia and existing opportunities and perils for using data innovations in policymaking. Data analytics can certainly provide insights to policy makers, which they can then choose to use to inform policy decisions. Data innovation is a new source of evidence, in addition to traditional sources of insights such as research-based evidence, evaluation, administrative data and citizen knowledge (Shaxson 2016). The extent to which all these different types of evidence are demanded and used to inform policy decisions is an indicator of the strength of a country's evidence-based policy processes. The experience of Pulse Lab Jakarta demonstrates that several factors determine whether policy makers take into consideration the recommendations that emerge from data analytics. Some of these factors are technical, such as the quality of data analytics or the clarity of the policy recommendations. Other factors are political, such as the political implications of what the evidence suggests. The enabling environment of rules, regulations and capabilities that enable the production, demand and use of data analytics for policy decisions influences both the technical and political factors.

There are clear similarities in the ways that traditional forms of evidence and data analytics integrate into the policy process. In both cases, the likelihood of informing policy lies in strong analytical methods, good storytelling, a good understanding of the policy context and a clear policy problem, knowledge of the policymaking process to identify entry points and links with networks of actors who can help to synthesise or channel the evidence to policy makers (Young and Mendizabal 2009). The uptake of both research-based evidence and data analytics by policy makers is determined by similar contextual factors, such as the degree of *leadership* and *authority* to affect policy change and demand and use evidence; *acceptance* (the extent to which those who will be affected by the policy change accept the need for change and use evidence to achieve it); and *ability*, defined as the availability of time, funds, skills, regulations and the like to achieve policy change (Andrews et al. 2015).

Big data analytics, and data innovation more broadly, generate new types of evidence that complements more traditional forms of research. Case studies from Pulse Lab Jakarta suggest that to truly harness the data revolution, efforts to gain insights from new data sources should move toward exploring how these insights can be used in conjunction with existing bodies of research, instead of seeking to replace them. The insights gleaned from correlation still require validation and an analysis of causation. Big data analysis still requires a solid grounding in statistics. The added value of data analytics is that it allows a much speedier analysis of policy strategy and directions, and it can develop rapid feedback loops that allow, almost in real-time, changes to policy implementation without the need to wait for the results of the next census. While making use of the power of the data revolution may require changes in the skill set of statisticians and social science researchers (Benoit and Cukier 2015), it is the combined collaborative effort of expertise from multiple domains that will most likely yield fresh, valuable insights for policy makers.

Data innovation offers a unique opportunity to the Government of Indonesia to strengthen and expand the use of evidence to make better policy decisions on, for example, how to organise service delivery or empower citizens to have a say in policies that influence their lives. In conjunction with other types of evidence it provides, data innovation can help to better understand the problems people face and expand the options for improving solutions though policies and programmes.

References

Anderson, C. (2008). The end of theory: The data deluge makes the scientific method obsolete. *Science*. https://www.wired.com/2008/06/pb-theory/. Accessed 10 Apr 2017.

Andrews, M., Pritchett, L., & Woolcock, M. (2012). *Escaping capability traps through problem-driven iterative adaptation (PDIA)* (CGD Working Paper 299). Washington, DC: Center for Global Development. http://www.cgdev.org/content/publications/detail/1426292. Accessed 25 Mar 2017.

Andrews, M., Pritchett, L., & Woolcock, M. (2015). *Doing problem-driven work* (CID Working Paper 307). Boston: Center for International Development, Harvard University. https://bsc.cid.harvard.edu/files/bsc/files/doing_problem_driven_work_wp_307.pdf. Accessed 16 Apr 2017.

Andrews, M., Pritchett, L., & Woolcock, M. (2017). *Building state capability*. Oxford: Oxford University Press.

Benoit, K., & Cukier, K. (2015). *The challenge of big data for the social sciences. Public Lecture*. London School of Economics. http://goo.gl/Rmi56P. Accessed 12 Apr 2017.

Bollier, D. (2010). *The promise and peril of big data*. Washington, DC: The Aspen Institute. https://www.emc.com/collateral/analyst-reports/10334-ar-promise-peril-of-big-data.pdf. Accessed 19 Apr 2017.

Carr-Hill, R. (2013). Missing millions and measuring development progress. *World Development, 46*, 30–44.

Cohen, M., March, J., & Olsen, J. (1972). A garbage can model of organisational choice. *Administrative Science Quarterly, 17*(1), 1–25.

Das, K., Gryseels, M., Sudhir, P., & Tan, K. T. (2016). *Unlocking Indonesia's digital opportunity*. Jakarta: McKinsey Indonesia Office. http://www.mckinsey.com/~/media/McKinsey%20Offices/Indonesia/PDF/Unlocking-Indonesias-digital-opportunity.ashx. Accessed 20 Nov 2016.

Davies, P. (2012). The state of evidence-based policy evaluation and its role in policy formation. *National Institute Economic Review, 219*, 41–52.

Davies, W. (2017, January 19). How statistics lost their power – And why we should fear what comes next. *The Guardian*. https://www.theguardian.com/politics/2017/jan/19/crisis-of-statistics-big-data-democracy. Accessed 18 Apr 2017.

Floodtags. (2017). *Real-time flood mapping on basis of twitter and DEM*. Floodtags. http://floodtags.com.webhosting109.transurl.nl/blog/2015/10/02/twitter-used-to-crete-real-time-flood-maps. Accessed 18 Apr 2017.

Grazella, M. (2013). Facebook has 64m active Indonesian users. *The Jakarta Post*, June 18. http://www.thejakartapost.com/news/2013/06/18/facebook-has-64m-active-indonesian-users.html. Accessed 22 April 2017.

Harford, T. (2014, March 28). Big data: Are we making a big mistake? *The Financial Times*. https://www.ft.com/content/21a6e7d8-b479-11e3-a09a-00144feabdc0. Accessed 18 Apr 2017.

IEAGDRSD [Independent Expert Advisory Group on a Data Revolution for Sustainable Development]. (2014). *A world that counts: Mobilizing the data revolution for sustainable development*. New York: United Nations. http://www.undatarevolution.org/wp-content/uploads/2014/11/A-World-That-Counts.pdf. Accessed 26 Mar 2017.

Internet Live Stats. (2017). http://www.internetlivestats.com/internet-users/. Accessed 26 Apr 2017.

Johnson, P. (2013). Six Twitter statistics that you may not know. *ITWorld*. http://www.itworld.com/article/2833036/big-data/6-twitter-statistics-that-you-may-not-know.html. Accessed 22 Apr 2017.

Kemp, S. (2017). Digital in Southeast Asia in 2017: Regional overview. *We Are Social Blog*. https://wearesocial.com/blog/2017/02/digital-southeast-asia-2017. Accessed 18 Apr 2017.

Khoso, M. (2016). *How much data is produced every day?* Northeastern University Level blog. http://www.northeastern.edu/levelblog/2016/05/13/how-much-data-produced-every-day/. Accessed 4 Apr 2017.

Lips, M., & Mansell, J. (2015). *Lessons from the New Zealand Data Futures Forum: How to unlock the value of data-driven innovation and new 'evidence' in policy-making* (Working Paper 5). Jakarta: Knowledge Sector Initiative. http://www.ksi-indonesia.org/files/1447136024$1$6A28V8B$.pdf. Accessed 2 Apr 2017.

Margetts, H. (2013). The promises and threats of big data for public policy-making. *The Policy and Internet Blog October 28*. http://blogs.oii.ox.ac.uk/policy/promises-threats-big-data-for-public-policy-making/. Accessed 28 Apr 2017.

Netralnews. (2017). Indonesia's move to count on mobile positioning data lauded by UN world tourism. *Netralnews*. http://www.en.netralnews.com/news/culture/read/3093/indonesia...s.move.to.count.on.mobile.positioning.data.lauded.by.un.world.tourism. Accessed 25 Apr 2017.

New Zealand Data Futures Forum. (2014a). *New Zealand's data future*. https://www.nzdatafutures.org.nz/discussion-documents. Accessed 10 Apr 2017.

New Zealand Data Futures Forum. (2014b). *Navigating the data future: Four guiding principles*. https://www.nzdatafutures.org.nz/discussion-documents. Accessed 10 Apr 2017.

OECD [Organisation for Economic Co-operation and Development]. (2013). *Development co-operation report*. Paris: OECD. http://www.keepeek.com/Digital-Asset-Management/oecd/development/development-co-operation-report-2013/numbers-of-people-living-under-usd-1-25-per-day-1990-2010_dcr-2013-graph6-en#page1. Accessed 25 Apr 2017.

Pulse Lab Jakarta. (2016a). *Six monthly report January–June 2016*. Jakarta: United Nations.

Pulse Lab Jakarta. (2016b). *Annual report*. Jakarta: United Nations.

Royal Society. (2017). *Machine learning*. https://royalsociety.org/topics-policy/projects/machine-learning. Accessed 2 May 2017.

Sadowski, M. (2017). Social media statistics for Indonesia. *Social Memos*. http://socialmemos.com/social-media-statistics-for-indonesia. Accessed 23 Apr 2017.

Shaxson, L. (2016). *Lessons for building and managing an evidence base for policy* (Working Paper 10). Jakarta: Knowledge Sector Initiative. http://www.ksi-indonesia.org/en/news/detail/lessons-for-building-and-managing-an-evidence-base-for-policy. Accessed 5 Apr 2017.

Statista. (2017). *Number of mobile phone users in Indonesia from 2013 to 2019*. Statista. http://www.statista.com/statistics/274659/forecast-of-mobile-phone-users-in-indonesia/. Accessed 20 Apr 2017.

Stuart, E., Samman, E. Avis, W., & Berliner, T. (2015). *The data revolution: Finding the missing millions*. Report. London: Overseas Development Institute. https://www.odi.org/publications/9476-data-revolution-finding-missing-millions. Accessed 10 Apr 2017.

Timmer, J. (2008). Why the cloud cannot obscure the scientific method. *Ars Technica*, June 25. https://arstechnica.com/uncategorized/2008/06/why-the-cloud-cannot-obscure-the-scientific-method/. Accessed 12 Apr 2017.

UNESCO [United Nations Educational, Scientific and Cultural Organization]. (2010). *Education for all monitoring report: Reaching the marginalised*. Oxford: Oxford University Press.

United Nations. (2017). *Sustainable development goals*. http://www.un.org/sustainabledevelopment/sustainable-development-goals. Accessed 25 Mar 2017.

United Nations Global Pulse. (2012). *Big data for development: Challenges & opportunities*. New York: United Nations Global Pulse. http://www.unglobalpulse.org/sites/default/files/BigDataforDevelopment-UNGlobalPulseJune2012.pdf. Accessed 5 Apr 2017.

United Nations Global Pulse. (2015). *Global pulse annual report*. New York: United Nations. http://unglobalpulse.org/sites/default/files/Global%20Pulse%202015%20Annual%20Report_final%20spreads.pdf. Accessed 4 Apr 2017.

United Nations Global Pulse. (2016). *Integrating big data into the monitoring and evaluation of development programmes*. New York: United Nations Global Pulse. http://unglobalpulse.org/sites/default/files/IntegratingBigData_intoMEDP_web_UNGP.pdf. Accessed 18 Apr 2017.

United Nations Global Pulse. (2017). *United Nations global pulse*. New York: United Nations. http://www.unglobalpulse.org/about-new. Accessed 28 Mar 2017.

Usher, D., & Rahwidiati, D. (2017, March 10). Navigating Indonesia's data innovation ecosystem: A reflection. *Nesta Blogs*. http://www.nesta.org.uk/blog/navigating-indonesias-data-innova-tion-ecosystem-reflection. Accessed 12 Mar 2017.

World Bank and World Health Organization. (2014). *Global civil registration and vital statistics: Scaling up investment plan 2015–2024*. World Bank: Washington, DC.

Young, J., & Mendizabal, E. (2009). *Helping researchers become policy entrepreneurs* (Briefing Paper 53). London: Overseas Development Institute. https://www.odi.org/sites/odi.org.uk/files/odi-assets/publications-opinion-files/1730.pdf. Accessed 20 April 2017.

Part III
The Enabling Environment for Evidence-Informed Policymaking

Chapter 7
Reforming the Enabling Environment for Evidence-Informed Policymaking

Budiati Prasetiamartati, Fred Carden, and Sugiyanto

1 Introduction

This chapter starts from the premise that addressing the institutions of the knowledge sector and the rules that guide its development is key to the changes needed for a robust twenty-first-century economy. These institutions can either inhibit or foster the development of strong evidence and capacity for use in policymaking. In a study for the World Bank on how to move to high-income country status, Agenor et al. (2012) make the case that three crucial issues must be addressed: (1) access to advanced infrastructure (high-speed communications and information infrastructure), (2) enforcement of property rights and (3) labour market reform. To deliver on these issues, Indonesia needs a strong education system to build a population capable of developing an economy and creating the infrastructure for an information-based economy (to develop e-commerce). As noted by respected Indonesian economist Simanjuntak, Indonesia lags behind in both areas (Jakarta Post 2015), as was also highlighted in previous chapters.

The web of rules and regulations that surround a system can make it harder or easier to move ahead on these issues. As argued in this book and in earlier studies – such as Karetji (2010), Sherlock (2010), AusAID (2012) and Sherlock and Djani (2015) – the rules and regulations surrounding the creation and transmission of knowledge for informing policy mitigate against progress. They hamper researchers

B. Prasetiamartati (✉) · Sugiyanto
Australia-Indonesia Partnership for Pro-Poor Policy: The Knowledge Sector Initiative,
Jakarta, Indonesia
e-mail: budiati@ksi-indonesia.org; sugiyanto@ksi-indonesia.org

F. Carden
Using Evidence Inc., Ottawa, ON, Canada
e-mail: fred@usingevidence.com

© Springer Nature Singapore Pte Ltd. 2018   111
A. Pellini et al. (eds.), *Knowledge, Politics and Policymaking in Indonesia*,
https://doi.org/10.1007/978-981-13-0167-4_7

by creating conditions at universities that discourage research through a lack of both career and financial incentives and by not making funds available to researchers for undertaking the fundamental research that undergirds innovation. Moreover, rules and regulations hamper decision makers from using evidence, through strictures on how the government commissions and rewards research generation. These restrictions so limit the research that can be commissioned from Indonesian researchers that donors have become the de facto policy research unit for government. As noted by Eko Prasojo, former deputy minister of Bureaucratic Reform, 'bureaucratic reform as a collective change in various ministries and institutions as well as local governments... is declining in both orientation and motivation' (Prasojo 2016). Prasojo argues that reforming the bureaucracy is a central prerequisite to a vibrant, performance-based and well-functioning civil service that has the capacity to reform the rules and regulations that govern economic and social development.

This chapter focuses on two challenges to the enabling environment where recent progress has been made, creating significant changes: regulations governing the procurement of research and funding channels for research. The first is very much a government issue, regulating how and where research can be procured by government departments and agencies, and requirements around its implementation (Jackson et al. 2017). The regulations hamper the government's flexibility in procuring research from Indonesian research centres, many of which are in the non-profit sector. It also discourages other researchers due to issues related to financing and short time frames. As a consequence, a large proportion of policy research is funded (hence managed) by international agencies, each of which has its own agenda and priorities. The second issue discussed in this chapter, funding for research, suffers from two challenges. One is the serious underfunding of research, as outlined in Chap. 2; the other is lack of appropriate mechanisms to support transparent, competitive multi-year research grants (Brodjonegoro and Greene 2012).

The chapter adopts the 'development entrepreneurship' approach articulated by Faustino and Booth (2014). The four distinctive features of development entrepreneurship touched upon here in relation to reforms are:

- *Goal*: Selection of reform objectives that are technically sound, politically feasible and can be sustained over the long term by local institutions.
- *Process*: Explain how the programme worked flexibly and politically, which should demonstrate responsiveness to opportunities, adaptation to changing conditions and the power to adjust resources to address these opportunities and conditions.
- *People*: Identify partners in reform; partners should have the capacity to undertake the work, relationships to support the changes sought, knowledge of the socio-political systems at play and a willingness to take risks.
- '*Intrapreneurship*': Describing the role of external support. The team and approach should be able to identify and build on external supporters to meet its goals.

The chapter concludes with a final reflection on the use of the development entrepreneurship framework and suggestions about regulatory changes that may be still be required to continue the reform of Indonesia's enabling environment for the knowledge sector.

2 Two Key Challenges in the Enabling Environment

During the design of the Australia-Indonesia Partnership for Pro-Poor Policy: The Knowledge Sector Initiative (KSI) in 2011 and 2012, diagnostic studies were undertaken to identify a range of issues that inhibit the production of research evidence and its use in policymaking at both the national and local levels.[1] This included exploration of the enabling environment, where policies, rules and regulations govern how the supply and demand sides interact and how research systems operate (Guggenheim 2012). At this early stage, these issues were only broadly defined as rigid and restrictive procurement regulations, the structure and administrative procedures of the civil service, limited government funding for policy research and the roles and functions of knowledge intermediaries in the national research system (Guggenheim 2012; AusAID 2012).

Early in its implementation, KSI supplemented this review of barriers with a focus on gaps in the institutions of the knowledge sector, notably the lack of a strong institution to play a policy advisory role with government (e.g. a robust academy of science), as well as the weak research culture in Indonesian universities (Carden 2016; Nugroho et al. 2016).

Limited government funding for research was discussed in detail in Chap. 2. In summary, Indonesia spends less than 0.2% of its GDP on research – at least ten times lower than other countries in the region. Within this modest budget, there are more than 17 different research granting schemes for universities managed by the Ministry of Research, Technology and Higher Education (Kementerian Riset, Teknologi dan Pendidikan Tinggi – KemRistekDikti)[2] each with its own requirements and eligibility criteria. Not all academic staff are eligible to apply for these grants; they depend on the Ministry's classification of their university research capacity. Due to limits on funding, fewer than half the academic research proposals are funded (see Chap. 2). Indonesia has no state budget allocation for research grants to non-governmental research institutions.

Particularly important in relation to state-funded research is that current Indonesian fiscal law and regulation discourages multi-year research programmes. Although annual renewals are permitted, the inherent uncertainty discourages researchers from planning multi-year initiatives. Finally, research funding from state budgets follows rigid reporting and budgeting guidelines and involves cumber-

---

[1] See http://www.ksi-indonesia.org/index.php/publications/2015/08/10/14/diagnostic-studies-on-the-knowledge-sector.html.

[2] The chapter uses the Bahasa Indonesia acronym KemRistekDikti to refer to the Ministry of Research, Technology and Higher Education (Kementerian Riset, Teknologi dan Pendidikan Tinggi).

some bureaucratic procedures (McCarthy and Ibrahim 2010; Brodjonegoro and Greene 2012).

In addition to limited investment in research, government procurement regulations make it difficult to source research externally. The provision of goods and services to government, including research, is ruled by procurement regulations. Procurement regulations are open to multiple interpretations, and high-level officials continue to insist that nothing in the regulations prevents government from engaging with universities and non-government policy research institutes (Guggenheim 2012). In practice, however, for universities to engage with government, they need to create a commercial entity; they cannot engage directly as a university. This added layer of bureaucracy discourages institutional research, leaving research projects in the domain of universities that are subject to different regulations and can be engaged through 'self-managed' (swakelola) contracts (Sherlock and Djani 2015). In practice, government generally uses 'self-managed' contracts to engage with individual experts from universities and non-government policy research institutes, which is easier than contracting with the universities' private sector entities. This more casual approach to commissioning research consultancies limits the potential for providing the government with high-quality research and policy analysis, as it does not draw on the broader resources of the university and, given time restraints, does not permit depth in the research. From the perspective of universities and non-governmental policy research institutes, this practice builds personal connections rather than building sustainable universities and research centres.

Finally, as noted in the introduction to this chapter, when government departments and agencies want to commission serious research, these financial and regulatory impediments often lead them to seek assistance from the international donor community. This outsourcing of policy research negatively affects the government's ability to manage its own research agenda, because the research commissioned must also align with the agenda of the external agency. Further, the research is likely to be conducted largely by the agency's staff or its own national researchers, drawing on the Indonesian research community only for secondary support. This further undermines the development of strong Indonesian research capacity.

3 Understand Problems and Develop Solutions

Despite this somewhat daunting picture, the KSI team, drawing from the development entrepreneurship framework, has been able to identify two key problems in Indonesia's enabling environment for evidence-informed policy. This section explains how the programme arrived at these two reforms and facilitated local leadership to develop solutions.

3.1 Goal: Selection of Reform Objectives

Working politically requires the identification of reforms that are both technically sound and politically feasible. Technical soundness is judged in terms of sustainable impact on development processes, using the three criteria of impact, scale and sustainability. Faustino and Booth (2014) define *impact* as the likelihood that the reform will change the incentives and behaviour of organisations and individuals, thus improving outcomes. *Scale* refers to the likelihood the reform will have effects going well beyond the project, while *sustainability* refers to the likelihood the reform will continue beyond the life of the intervention; that is that it will be institutionalised as part of the everyday practice of the government bureaucracy or locked in through market dynamics.

The idea of an Indonesian Science Fund[3] emerged from the thinking and experience of Satryo Brodjonegoro, an Indonesian professor who spent many years considering why it was that even elite Indonesian universities didn't have the same research culture that he found in the United States and Japan. He found many causes; in particular, Indonesian professors are paid extremely poorly, forcing them to divert time that should be dedicated to scholarly pursuits to activities such as consulting; and government funding available for university research was limited to short-term practical applications, making it hard for Indonesians interested in basic research to secure funding for their projects (Emont and Pellini 2017).

This question motivated Brodjonegoro, then vice-president of the Indonesian Academy of Sciences (Akademi Ilmu Pengetahuan Indonesia – AIPI)[4] to collaborate with Michael Greene from the United States National Academy of Sciences to write a white paper on 'Creating an Indonesian Science Fund' (2012). The white paper was published by AIPI, with support from the World Bank and the Australian Government.

In mid-2014 the Australian aid agency (then AusAID) and the KSI team met with AIPI officials. The president of the Academy, Sangkot Marzuki, brought up the white paper written in 2012 in the discussion. The paper describes the lack of independent funding for scientific research and the bureaucratic complexities associated with existing research grants. It outlines a way forward in the form of a proposal for a grants scheme to fund basic scientific research. AIPI's vision of revitalising its role in developing scientific excellence and establishing an independent Indonesian Science Fund was strongly aligned with KSI's aim of strengthening Indonesia's enabling environment for research, including resolution of the problem of limited investment in research. AIPI understood that if the science fund was to be sustainable, it needed both political and financial support.

---

[3] The Indonesia Science Fund in Bahasa Indonesia is called Dana Ilmu Pengetahuan Indonesia (DIPI). The chapter uses the English language wording.

[4] The chapter uses the Bahasa Indonesia acronym AIPI to refer to the Indonesian Academy of Sciences (Akademi Ilmu Pengetahuan Indonesia).

The Knowledge Sector Initiative, as a programme, required authorisation to proceed on such an initiative, especially given its political nature. The Programme Steering and Technical Committee is co-chaired by the Ministry for National Development Planning/National Development Planning Agency (Kementerian Perencanaan Pembangunan Nasional/Badan Perencanaan Pembangunan Nasional – Bappenas) and the Australian Department of Foreign Affairs and Trade. Former Minister of Bappenas, Armida Alisjahbana, was a strong advocate for AIPI and, as KSI's main government counterpart, actively encouraged the programme's support for the Academy and the science fund proposal. This green light made it possible for the KSI team to develop a programme of support with AIPI.

At the same time, KSI was exploring other constraints in the enabling environment that had been identified in the programme's design document. In mid-2014, the programme commissioned an update of the 2010 diagnostic study on regulatory obstacles to evidence-informed policymaking. The study found that despite some reforms, procurement regulations remained largely unchanged vis-à-vis the production of policy research (Sherlock and Djani 2015).

In consultation with KSI-supported policy research institutes, and recognising the serious limitations these regulations placed on the institutes, KSI agreed that it might be politically feasible to address this issue. Defining the reform objective began with strengthening the evidence base and scanning for possible political allies in the government. In mid-2015, a political opportunity arose when Bappenas, KSI's government partner, informed the KSI team that the National Goods/Services Public Procurement Agency (Lembaga Kebijakan Pengadaan Barang Jasa Pemerintah – LKPP)[5] – which falls under Bappenas' jurisdiction – was in the process of drafting revisions to procurement regulations. KSI acted on this opportunity, and together with its policy research partners discussed a plan to engage with the LKPP.

Both of the reforms discussed here met the requirement of being technically sound (Faustino and Booth 2014), because they directly relate to the impact, scale and sustainability of the enabling environment for a healthy knowledge sector. Revisions to procurement legislation affect government procurement practices and will become part of the everyday practice of government bureaucracy. Establishment of the Indonesian Science Fund would change the way research funding is awarded, basing it on a competitive and merit-based selection process, open to any type of research entity in Indonesia.

One criterion for good development entrepreneurship that was not raised by Faustino and Booth (Ibid.) is the role of evidence as a critical tool for raising awareness and focusing the attention of policymakers and potential coalitions.

---

[5] The chapter uses the acronym LKPP to refer to the National Goods/Services Public Procurement Agency (Lembaga Kebijakan Pengadaan Barang Jasa Pemerintah).

3.2   Process: How the Programme Worked Flexibly and Politically

The KSI programme team explored the context of these two reforms to find the most effective entry points. This section describes both the role of external actors and events and how KSI's team contributed to the change process. The interventions are successful because all necessary players were involved. Ongoing coordination and exchange, both formal and informal, made a difference to the contributions of each actor.

3.2.1   Funding for Research[6]

The Indonesian Academy of Sciences had a vision for an independent science fund that did not fall under the country's bureaucratic umbrella. The Act of Parliament that established the Academy (Government of Indonesia 1990) permits it to operate both within and outside the parameters of government, so bringing the Fund under that same umbrella would give it the necessary flexibility. The Academy also committed to a second point: that the bulk of the funding for the Indonesian Science Fund should be Indonesian. Although foreign aid programmes offered support, AIPI wanted to ensure that the initial funding was Indonesian. Using its network and influence, the Academy turned into the Ministry of Finance, which supported establishment of the fund. In December 2014, the Academy organised an event during which the Minister of Finance stated his support for an Indonesian Science Fund, in the presence of the Ambassador of the United States, representatives from the Embassy of Australia and Bappenas officials.

Following this initial success, the AIPI Silver Jubilee celebrations in May 2015 provided an opportunity to generate further support. At this high-level event – attended by the ministers of Finance and National Development Planning, members of the Academy and international donors – the Indonesian Academy of Sciences formally announced the establishment of the Indonesian Science Fund. The event was widely reported by national media and generated significant interest among Indonesian researchers and scientists (Emont and Pellini 2017).

Following the achievement of this milestone, the Ministry of Finance's Education Endowment Fund (Lembaga Pengelola Dana Pendidikan – LPDP) was the first government body to commit funds for the science fund. The Ministry signed a memorandum of understanding with the Academy in August 2015 for the establishment of the Indonesian Science Fund.

The Jubilee announcement raised public expectations. However, at that time the Indonesian Science Fund still had no legal basis, no established sources of funding and no presidential approval. Although AIPI housed prominent and well-connected Indonesian scientists, they could not swiftly advance the fund through the remaining

---

[6] This section draws on Emont and Pellini (2017).

hoops of Indonesia's bureaucracy. It was clear that the Academy needed a dedicated, full-time individual to see the project through. In August 2015, KSI supported AIPI to hire a consultant with strong academic and government networks to fill the post of national coordinator and work closely with the Academy to guide the embryonic Science Fund through the maze of bureaucratic approvals. A team of legal advisors was also recruited by KSI to provide legal analysis for the Fund's establishment and work closely with the coordinator. The first attempt to hire a legal team was not successful, as the team did not have the ability to translate the Academy's vision into a suitable legal analysis (Prasetiamartati 2016). For the second attempt, the consultant hired to coordinate the establishment of the Fund acted as an intermediary between the Academy's vision and the legal analysis prepared by the team of legal advisers, with good results.

During this time, the United States National Academy of Sciences continued its long-standing support to the Academy, through support from the United States Agency for International Development (USAID). The United States National Academy of Sciences had contributed to a number of capacity building and research efforts with AIPI, such as support for a consensus report on maternal and child mortality (NRC and AIPI 2013), as well as support to young researchers to join the Indonesian-American Kavli Frontiers of Science Symposium (AIPI 2014, 2017) – a symposium that brings young researchers together to explore the frontiers of science in a range of fields. USAID and KSI also supported AIPI and its 'Young Academy' to propose a long-term research agenda for the nation (AIPI 2016). President Barack Obama's former science envoy to Indonesia, Bruce Alberts (2009 to 2011), who is also a distinguished scientist and former president of the United States National Academy of Sciences, maintained a long-term relationship and advisory role with AIPI. Taken together, these collaborative initiatives contributed to the formal and informal relationships needed for the Fund's success.

The coming together of external and internal players resulted in the formal establishment of the Indonesian Science Fund. The coordinator had met with members of the Academy's executive committee and other AIPI members to urge them to support the Fund. In October 2015, the Academy's General Assembly voted in favour of amending the bylaws and constitution to support the Indonesian Science Fund. The coordinator also lobbied his networks close to President Joko Widodo to gain his support. These efforts paid off when, during his first state visit to the United States in October 2015, the President announced the Indonesian Science Fund as part of Indonesia's commitment to the US-Indonesian scientific cooperation. In concerted efforts, the president and vice president of the Academy, its secretary general, the coordinator and legal team then began the lengthy bureaucratic process of legally establishing the Fund, drafting documents and meeting with officials at the ministries of Finance, State Apparatus and Bureaucratic Reform and Ministry of Research, Technology and Higher Education (KemRistekdikti), to obtain approval and signatures. These efforts culminated in the signing of a presidential decree in February 2016, which formally established the Indonesian Science Fund.

3.2.2 Reforms in the Procurement of Research[7]

Following an updated diagnostic study that signalled no significant change in the procurement regulations that inhibit institutional engagement between non-profit organisations and government (Sherlock and Djani 2015), the KSI programme team tried different approaches to identify champions and key actors who shared this concern. The programme was aware that policy change requires individual Indonesian champions and actors as well as coalitions. Finding these champions was achieved through interactions with KSI's core partners from policy research institutes, as well as using KSI events to interact with potential champions. For example, the team organised a knowledge-sharing event to promote the findings of the diagnostic study.

At least four junctures contributed to the reform process; that these took place during a short time frame was important to building momentum.

First The programme team learned from Bappenas in mid-2015 that LKPP had begun to revise the presidential regulation on procurement. It was important to act quickly if unique research-related needs were to be inserted into the process. This news was followed by a meeting of the KSI team, a representative from one of its policy research partner organisations, the Indonesian Forum for Budget Transparency (Sekretariat Nasional Forum Indonesia Untuk Transparansi Anggaran – SEKNAS FITRA), with a deputy director of LKPP in early July 2015. The meeting discussed the particular obstacles faced by government actors in procuring policy research. During the meeting, the deputy director confirmed that the Agency was revising the regulations and acknowledged that the current regulations did not effectively address procurement of research. He welcomed the programme's input.

Second KemRistekDikti was created in October 2014, when the President Joko Widodo's new administration merged the Ministry of Research and Technology with the Directorate General of Higher Education. Two key champions of the reform process were appointed to serve in this new structure and promoted the issue of procurement for research. Starting in August 2015, KSI began to engage with two individuals at the new Ministry, and in the months to follow, they played a lead role in reforming procurement regulations. One had been an academic and thus had a keen understanding of the issues at stake.

Third Two of KSI's policy research partner organisations (Article 33 and SEKNAS FITRA) were engaged from early on in the process. Both organisations cited procurement regulations as a key factor inhibiting them from bringing research evidence to bear on policymaking, as well as having a negative impact on their financial sustainability.

---

[7] This section draws on Jackson et al. (2017)

Fourth The interests of another partner organisation (AKATIGA, a research and advocacy organisation focused on marginalised groups) went beyond research. One of AKATIGA's senior researchers saw an opportunity to expand NGOs' access to public funding by amending the procurement regulations on self-managed (swakelola) contracts to allow these organisations to bid for any government contract, for example, contracts to provide services for vulnerable groups. In pursuing this agenda, the researcher was able to draw on his personal connection to the director of LKPP. At a meeting in early November 2015, the director responded positively to this idea. AKATIGA provided LKPP with a policy brief outlining its recommendations and continued to engage with the Agency over the following months.

These four junctures supported the reform process. More broadly, in the last decade, some government agencies have become more open to seeking input from civil society organisations, in part due to recognition of these organisations' expertise. These factors meant that high-level officials at KemRistekDikti and other government agencies were more disposed to collaborating with the KSI programme and its policy research partners, a situation on which the programme was able to capitalise.

Knowing that policy research institutes, LKPP, Bappenas and KemRistekDikti all supported a change in research procurement legislation, KSI facilitated interactions among key actors and brought in relevant expertise. To help develop recommendations to improve the regulations, in July 2015 KSI engaged a procurement specialist from Transparency International Indonesia who had previously worked with LKPP. His analysis of the country's procurement regulations identified a number of areas where changes could be made to accommodate procurement of research. This analysis was then presented to a number of KSI's research partners as well as to KemRistekDikti. Following these discussions, a policy brief highlighting the importance of open competition, fairness, consistency, transparency and streamlined processes for multi-year funding for research projects was submitted to LKPP.

Also in mid-2015, the KSI team established a working group around the broad theme of research and higher education. It was made up of representatives from the programme's research partners, AIPI and KemRistekDikti. A subgroup was tasked to work specifically on procurement and develop a strategy for change. The subgroup's first meeting in October 2015 included representatives from Bappenas and five KSI research partners: Article 33, SEKNAS FITRA, AKATIGA, Institute for Social Research and Advocacy (Lembaga Studi dan Advokasi Masyarakat – ELSAM) and the Indonesian Centre for Law and Policy Studies (Pusat Studi Hukum dan Kebijakan Indonesia, PSHK). During the meeting, KSI facilitated a discussion using the Overseas Development Institute's 'RAPID Outcome Mapping Approach' to define policy change objectives and the 'Alignment Influence and Interest Matrix' (Hearn 2014) to map key stakeholders. This process helped to identify a number of important actors who had not yet been engaged. The discussion also produced a change strategy and action plan for the next 18 months.

One of the action plans was to convene all relevant stakeholders and research partners to discuss what had been achieved to date and determine the next steps for improving the environment for research. Facilitated by KSI in late December 2015,

KemRistekDikti hosted an intergovernmental and multi-stakeholder meeting, attended by high-level representatives from LKPP, KemRistekDikti, Bappenas, the University Rectors' Forum, the Ministry of Finance and the Audit Board. Participants agreed that the revised regulations needed to accommodate procurement of research over multiple years. They suggested that a new section be included in the regulations.

Changes in the context and bringing key actors together aligned to support the reform process. In January 2016 KemRistekDikti held a number of meetings with the LKPP and the Ministry of Finance to follow up on these discussions. As a result, in addition to the revised procurement regulations, it was agreed that a new Ministry of Finance decree to streamline financial reporting requirements for research projects was needed. Implementing regulations would be issued by LKPP and guidelines on quality assurance by KemRistekDikti. To support the development of these documents, KSI engaged a research administration specialist from Diponegoro University and a legal drafter from the Indonesian Centre for Law and Policy Studies (Pusat Studi Hukum dan Kebijakan Indonesia – PSHK). The Ministry of Finance decree on output-based research was issued in June 2016, followed by implementing guidelines on quality assurance processes for research outputs issued by KemRistekDikti.

During the course of a series of workshops facilitated by KSI, staff from LKPP and KemRistekDikti worked together with research partners from the Indonesian Centre for Law and Policy Studies (Pusat Studi Hukum dan Kebijakan Indonesia – PSHK) and AKATIGA to draft the new section of the procurement regulation covering research. The team also drafted two implementing regulations on procurement of research services and on self-managed (*swakelola*) contracts, to be issued by KemRistekDikti and LKPP, respectively.

Following the workshops, KSI continued to engage with LKPP and the Ministry to refine the draft. The Agency confirmed that the draft includes articles on procurement of multi-year research, as well as provisions allowing NGOs to bid on a wide range of government contracts. The draft of the revised procurement regulation was discussed at a Cabinet meeting in late December 2016, chaired by the President, and has since gone through a series of inter-ministerial meetings led by the Coordinating Ministry of Economic Affairs, before its submission to the Cabinet Secretariat for endorsement by the President. The procurement regulation was endorsed by President Joko Widodo on 15 March 2018.

3.3   People: Partners in Reform

The third distinguishing feature of development entrepreneurship is the people and organisations that play a role in the process. Faustino and Booth (2014) defined development entrepreneurs as leaders who commit to making social organisations work for the greater good by creating the circumstances that lead to the adoption of better institutions.

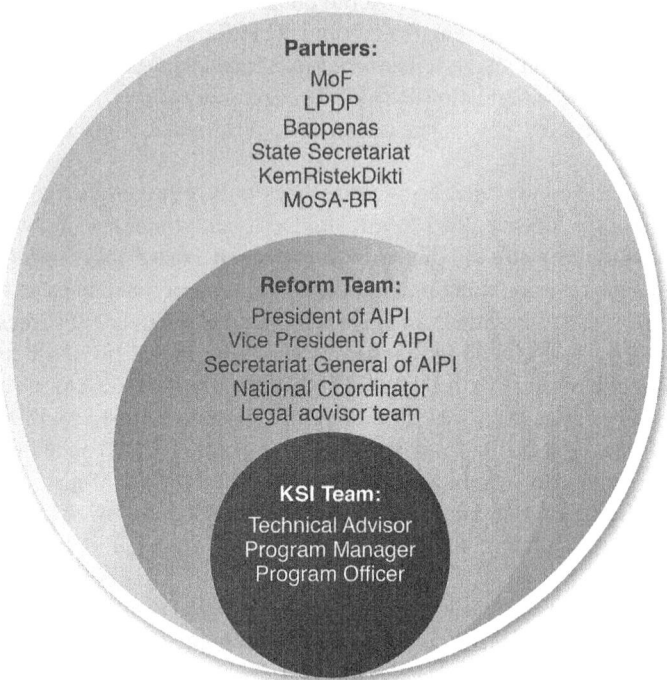

Fig. 7.1 Layers of reform actors in the research funding reform. (Adapted from Denney 2016)

3.3.1 Partners in Research Funding Reform

Leadership by key actors at AIPI determined the overall strategy and tactics for promoting the Indonesian Science Fund and defined the stakeholders that needed to be engaged in the Fund's establishment. KSI played a supporting and facilitation role, providing financing and technical expertise to help AIPI to build the legal foundation for the Fund. A critical factor allowing the Academy to bring the Indonesian Science Fund to fruition was the identification of sustainable sources of funding. Throughout the process, the Academy engaged with potential funders, including the Ministry of Finance Education Endowment Fund (Lembaga Pengelola Dana Pendidikan – LPDP) and USAID – with which the Academy had been collaborating for many years – to secure financial commitments and support.

Denney (2016) describes the layers of reform actors, as depicted in Fig. 7.1:

- *KSI team*: Technical advisor, programme manager, programme officer
- *Reform team*: President and vice president of AIPI, secretary general of AIPI, national coordinator, a legal advisory team
- *Partners*: Ministry of Finance (MoF), the Ministry of Finance Education Endowment Fund (Lembaga Pengelola Dana Pendidikan – LPDP), Bappenas,

the State Secretariat, KemRistekDikti, and Ministry of State Apparatus and Bureaucratic Reform (MoSA-BR in the figure)

Faustino and Booth (2014) suggest a need to map the different layers of actors involved in an intervention. In the case of the Indonesian Science Fund, the layers could be defined as follows. At the foundation were KSI's technical advisor and programme manager, who coordinated actors within the KSI team and liaised with the reform team. The programme manager identified technical and political gaps within the reform team and worked with KSI's programme officer to mobilise a national coordinator and legal advisory team to join the AIPI reform team. The KSI programme played an integral role in enhancing the ability of key actors to bring about reform. Its programme staff maintained momentum through regular coordination and meetings with the reform team.

The reform team was comprised of the senior leadership of the Academy, along with the coordinator and the legal advisory team. The national coordinator relied on political skills and networking, using personal and professional contacts to ensure that the technical analysis was seen by the appropriate people. The legal advisor provided technical analysis of legal issues. AIPI's president and vice president also used their personal and professional networks to bring the technical analysis to the right people. Administrative support for penetrating the government bureaucracy was provided by AIPI staff.

3.3.2 Partners in Procurement Reform

The procurement issue was addressed jointly by KSI's partner organisations, making use of the earlier diagnostic study (Sherlock and Djani 2015). The KSI programme team and partners then built a reform team consisting of a procurement specialist, a legal specialist and a research specialist. These specialists provided technical analysis, as well as utilising their personal and professional networks to ensure that it was seen by appropriate stakeholders. The reform team came from different institutions, but they communicated frequently, talking and listening in equal measure. Their interactions at formal meetings or discussions were facilitated by the KSI team, which led to iterative learning, coordination of effort and brokering of relationships.

The layers of reform actors shown in Fig. 7.2 included:

- *KSI Team*: Technical advisor, programme manager, programme officers
- *Reform team*: Procurement specialist, the Indonesian Centre for Law and Policy Studies (Pusat Studi Hukum dan Kebijakan Indonesia, PSHK) legal specialist, research specialist, KemRistekDikti, National Goods/Services Public Procurement Agency (Lembaga Kebijakan Pengadaan Barang Jasa Pemerintah – LKPP), AKATIGA
- *Partners*: Bappenas, SEKNAS FITRA, ELSAM, Coordinating Ministry for Human Development and Cultural Affairs (Kementerian Koordinator Bidang Pembangunan Manusia dan Kebudayaan – PMK), the Office of the President's

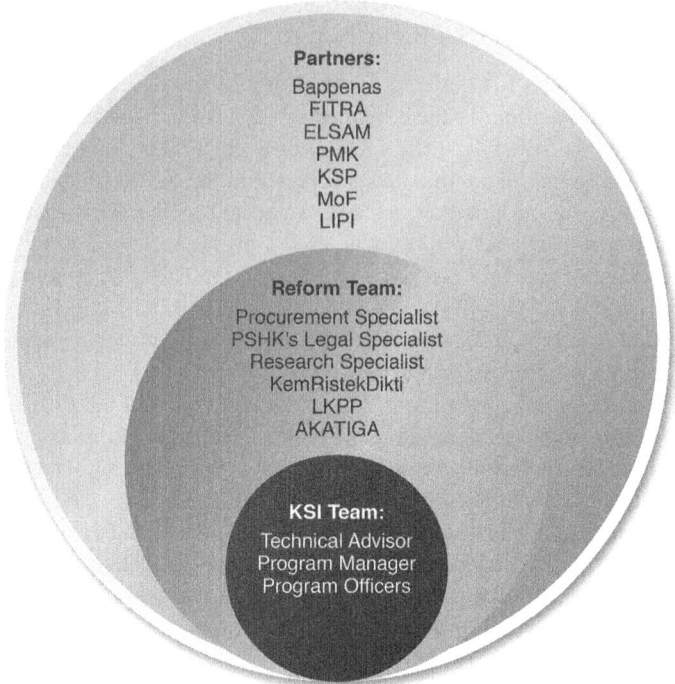

Fig. 7.2 Layers of reform actors in the research procurement reform. (Adapted from Denney 2016)

Staff (Kantor Staf Presiden – KSP), Ministry of Finance (MoF), Indonesian Institute of Sciences (Lembaga Ilmu Pengetahuan Indonesia – LIPI)

The loose coalition of reform-minded senior bureaucrats and policymakers, non-governmental policy research institutes and individuals with technical expertise hired by KSI was a critical factor in moving the procurement reform forward. KSI played an active role in brokering relationships between key stakeholders, particularly in the initial phase of the reform. In addition, KSI played an important role by providing technical expertise on the issue of procurement to key government stakeholders. KSI staff identified the main actors who needed to be engaged and brought them together. Through a series of meetings and discussions, KSI worked with these stakeholders to build consensus around the problem and develop a strategy for addressing it. This approach facilitated the creation of new links between the research partners and relevant government agencies, as well as among government agencies.

Leadership by key individuals was also critical to the procurement reform. The deputy director of LKPP (later its director) provided authority for the reform, although it was like-minded mid-level agency staff who attended the working meetings in which the issues were discussed and the regulations drafted. The two senior

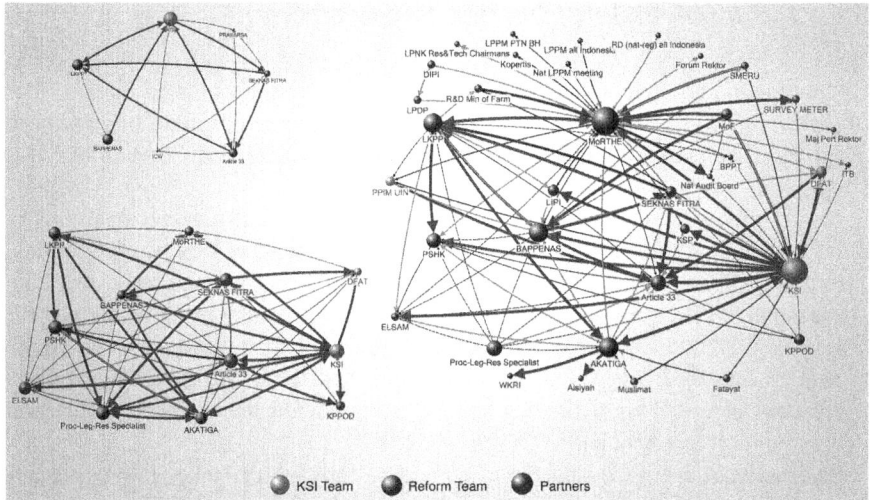

Fig. 7.3 Social network analysis in the procurement reform (Authors)

officials from KemRistekDikti took on a much more active leadership role, utilising their own political networks and understanding of bureaucratic systems and processes to bring in stakeholders from other government agencies whose support was necessary for the reform to succeed.

The evolution of relationships and networks around procurement regulation can be illustrated using a social network analysis (Fig. 7.3). The node represents the organisation; the size of the node refers to the organisation's level of importance (centrality) within the network. The line between two nodes represents levels of interaction; the thicker the line the more intensive and routine the communication. The graph shows the evolution of interactions (i.e. the network) from June 2015 to December 2016, demonstrating that the reform team increasingly performed its role of facilitation.

The graph shows a significant shift of role played by KemRistekDikti, marked by increasingly bigger node in three stages. Although negligible in the first stage, it increased during the second stage and then became the most influential actor on the last stage. The Ministry has authority to develop research policy. Moreover, KSI's partner organisations have shown effective pathways for bringing their capital into the network. This capital was then transferred into strategic action to achieve outputs, increasing the number of partners brought in by the reform team.

These teams shared the three building blocks of trust summarised by Heathfield (2016). They had trust in each other and the expertise needed to maintain the reform and perceived their actions and direction as mutually reinforcing rather than self-serving.

3.4   Intrapreneurship: External Supporters

'Intrapreneurs' are people who start new businesses or lines of work *within their organisations* to add value. Development intrapreneurs demonstrate the ability to adapt and change a development programme to increase its usefulness, rather than simply following a clearly defined path.

As described earlier, the process of policy change requires iterative 'learning by doing'. KSI is able to work this way because of the support from its Programme Steering and Technical Committee, co-chaired by Bappenas and the Australian Department of Foreign Affairs and Trade. Both KSI shareholders approved the programme's work plan and reports. With their support, KSI staff could facilitate the reform process and engage closely with key stakeholders. In addition, they engaged as stakeholders, working with other stakeholders to define the problem and break it down into its component parts.

In the case of the Indonesian Science Fund, as early as 2014 a key Bappenas staff member told the KSI team that success in seeing through the establishment of the Indonesian Science Fund would be the programme's 'legacy'. While this intervention was not in KSI's original work plan, Bappenas endorsed the programme's support to AIPI for establishment of the new Fund. Without this green light, it would have not been possible for KSI to continue its support (Prasetiamartati 2016; Emont and Pellini 2017).

In addition to the development intrapreneurship of Bappenas and the Australian Department of Foreign Affairs and Trade, the Indonesian Science Fund exists due to support from the USAID, as well as the Newton Fund and British Council, with whom AIPI partners. These international development agencies also exercised intrapreneurship by providing critical support for establishing the Fund and its early operations.

In September 2015, the Indonesian Academy of Sciences and the national coordinator of the Fund met in Washington, D.C., with the National Academy of Science, National Science Foundation, National Institutes of Health, Smithsonian Institution, State Department and USAID. The meetings revealed a commitment by those institutions to support the establishment of the Indonesian Science Fund. In January 2016, a delegation from AIPI and the Indonesian Science Fund visited the Royal Society in the United Kingdom and learned about research funding systems and areas of scientific excellence (Emont and Pellini 2017). This expansion of the Fund's contacts and relationships was another factor permitting its successful establishment and will serve the Fund well in years to come.

4 Conclusions

This chapter tells the story of how the KSI team put the concepts of working flexibly and politically into practice. It provides practical illustrations from which other practitioners seeking to work in these ways can draw. The emphasis on drawing together staff and networks with strong political relationships, and the ability to leverage these relationships to influence reform, offers insight into how programmes might work politically.

This chapter follows the framework of development entrepreneurship built by Faustino and Booth (2014). However, one criterion not raised in their study is the role of evidence as a critical tool both for raising awareness and gaining the attention of policymakers and for developing potential coalitions. In the case of the Indonesian Science Fund, considerable space for change existed from the outset. The evidence presented in Brodjonegoro and Greene's 2012 paper, together with the professional reputations and deep understanding of the issues of key individuals within the leadership of the Indonesian Academy of Sciences, lent credibility to the problem and the proposed solution. It also provided the authority to begin the reform process. In the case of procurement reform, a policy brief highlighting the importance of open competition, fairness, consistency and transparency and streamlined processes for multi-year funding of research projects was discussed thoroughly with reform actors and sent to LKPP (Jackson et al. 2017).

The changes to procurement regulations, however, do not address the financial and human resource costs of bidding, complex bureaucratic procedures, slow disbursement of funds and an aversion to what are perceived to be corrupt procurement practices that make many research organisations reluctant to bid on government contracts (Sherlock 2010). These challenges need ongoing efforts and suggest the need for behavioural change, which will take many years. But the revised regulation does open doors for non-profit organisations to provide knowledge services to the government. It also opened the door to broad consultations on deficiencies in procurement that could be built on to address the remaining challenges.

As noted in Jackson et al. (2017) the policy reforms described in this chapter represent initial steps toward improving the enabling environment for evidence-informed policymaking. However, for the reforms to be successful in improving the way policy research is commissioned and used, policymakers' attitudes and behaviour on seeking and procuring research will also need to change. Universities and policy research institutes will also need to be willing to engage with government agencies and participate actively in government procurement processes. As the Knowledge Sector Initiative moves into its second phase, as of mid-2017, it will continue to monitor this and other reforms in the enabling environment to evaluate whether the interventions are having the expected impact.

References

Agenor, P. R., Canuto, O., & Jelenic, M. (2012). *Avoiding middle income growth traps* (World Bank. Poverty Reduction and Economic Management Series. Number 98). The World Bank.

AIPI [Indonesian Academy of Sciences]. (2014). *Indonesian-American Kavli Frontiers of Science symposia 2011–2013*. Jakarta: AIPI.

AIPI [Indonesian Academy of Sciences]. (2016). In https://aipi.or.id/index.php?pg=detilpublikasi &pid=58&type=2. Accessed 9 June 2017 (Ed.), *SAINS45: Indonesian science agenda -towards a century of independence*. Jakarta: AIPI.

AIPI [Indonesian Academy of Sciences]. (2017). *Indonesian Academy of Sciences annual report 2016*. Jakarta: AIPI. https://aipi.or.id/index.php?pg=isidata&jurnal=65. Accessed 9 June 2017.

AusAID [Australian Agency for International Development]. (2012). *Australia-Indonesia partnership for pro-poor policy: The knowledge sector initiative, design document*. http://dfat.gov.au/about-us/publications/Documents/indo-ks-design.pdf. Accessed 11 Mar 2014.

Brodjonegoro, S. S., & Greene, M. P. (2012). *Creating an Indonesian science fund*. Jakarta: AIPI and World Bank. https://aipi.or.id/index.php?pg=detilpublikasi&pid=19&type=3. Accessed 9 June 2017.

Carden, F. (2016). *Reflections on academies and science advice* (Working Paper 13). Jakarta: Knowledge Sector Initiative. http://www.ksi-indonesia.org/en/news/detail/reflections-on-academies-and-science-advice. Accessed 24 June 2017.

Denney, L. (2016). *Reforming solid waste management in Phnom Penh* (The Asia Foundation and the Overseas Development Institute. Working Politically in Practice Series. Case Study No. 8). London: Overseas Development Institute. http://asiafoundation.org/wp-content/uploads/2016/06/Working-Politically-and-Flexibly-to-Reform-Solid-Waste-Management-in-Phnom-Penh.pdf. Accessed 19 Apr 2017.

Emont, J. & Pellini, A. (2017). *Investing in knowledge: The establishment of the Indonesian science fund* (Working Paper 20). Jakarta: Knowledge Sector Initiative. http://www.ksi-indonesia.org/en/news/detail/investing-in-knowledge-the-establishment-of-the-indonesian-science-fund. Accessed 20 June 2017.

Faustino, J. & Booth, D. (2014). *Development entrepreneurship: how donors and leaders can foster institutional change* (Working Politically in Practice Series – Case Study No. 2). London: Overseas Development Institute and San Francisco: The Asia Foundation.http://asiafoundation.org/wp-content/uploads/2014/12/Development-Entrepeneurship-How-Donors-and-Leaders-Can-Foster-Institutional-Change.pdf. Accessed 19 Apr 2017.

Government of Indonesia. (1990). *Law 8/1990 on the Indonesian Academy of Sciences*. http://www.hukumonline.com/pusatdata/detail/19965/node/671/undangundang-nomor-8-tahun-1990. Accessed 17 Apr 2018.

Guggenheim, S. (2012). Indonesia's quiet springtime: Knowledge, policy and reform. In A. Reid (Ed.), *Indonesia rising. The repositioning of Asia's third giant* (pp. 141–169). Institute of Southeast Asian Studies: Singapore.

Hearn, S. (2014). *Outcome mapping practitioner guide: Alignment, interest, influence matrix*. London: Overseas Development Institute. http://www.outcomemapping.ca/nuggets/alignment-interest-influence-matrix. Accessed 12 Mar 2017.

Heathfield, S. M. (2016, August 26). Trust rules: The most important secret about trust. about. com. http://humanresources.about.com/od/workrelationships/a/trust_rules.htm. Accessed 9 June 2017.

Jackson, E., Prasetiamartati, B., Sadikin, M. C., Sugiyanto, and Pellini, P. (2017). *Commissioning knowledge for policy reforms in the procurement of research in Indonesia* (Working Paper 23). Jakarta: Knowledge Sector Initiative. http://www.ksi-indonesia.org/file_upload/Commissioning-Knowledge-for-Policy-Reforms-in-the-14Jun2017160257.pdf. Accessed 24 June 2017.

Jakarta Post. (2015, December 16). *RI should focus on e-economy study: Djisman*. http://www.the-jakartapost.com/news/2015/12/16/ri-should-focus-e-economy-study-djisman.html. Accessed 9 June 2017.

Karetji, P.C. (2010). *Overview of the Indonesian knowledge sector*. Jakarta: AusAID. Available at http://dfat.gov.au/about-us/publications/Documents/indo-ks8-overview.pdf. Accessed 5 June 2017.

McCarthy, J. & Ibrahim, R. (2010). *Review of social science capacity building support to Indonesia's knowledge sector*. Jakarta: AusAID. http://dfat.gov.au/about-us/publications/Documents/indo-ks9-socialscience.pdf. Accessed 5 June 2017.

National Research Council & AIPI. (2013). *Reducing maternal and neonatal mortality*. Washington DC: National Academies Press. https://aipi.or.id/index.php?pg=isidata&jurnal=24. Accessed 9 June 2017.

Nugroho, Y., Prasetiamartati, B., Ruhanawati S. (2016). *Addressing Barriers to University Research* (Working Paper No. 8). Knowledge Sector Initiative. http://www.ksi-indonesia.org/en/news/detail/addressing-barriers-to-university-research. Accessed 9 June 2017.

Prasetiamartati, B. (2016). *End of intervention report: Capacity development for AIPI and the establishment of the Indonesia science fund* (Internal report). Jakarta: Knowledge Sector Initiative.

Prasojo, E. (2016, January 7). *One Year On: The turning point of bureaucracy reform*. http://eko-prasojo.com/2016/01/07/one-year-on-the-turning-point-of-bureaucracy-reform/. Accessed 16 Jan 2016.

Sherlock, S. (2010). *Knowledge for policy: Regulatory obstacles to the growth of a knowledge market in Indonesia*. Jakarta: AusAid. https://dfat.gov.au/about-us/publications/Documents/indo-ks13-knowledge-to-govt.pdf. Accessed 9 June 2017.

Sherlock, S. & Djani, L. (2015). *Update on constraints in the enabling environment to the provision of knowledge in the executive and legislative government* (KSI diagnostic study). Jakarta: Knowledge Sector Initiative. http://www.ksi-indonesia.org/en/news/detail/update-on-constraints-in-the-enabling-environment-to-the-provision-of-knowledge-in-executive-and-legislative-government. Accessed 9 June 2017.

Chapter 8
Doing Development Differently at Scale

Arnaldo Pellini, Petrarca C. Karetji, and Ade Soekadis

1 Introduction

Development is a process of change and transformation that involves finding new and better ways to solve such problems as providing more and better education, reforming social security or piloting a universal minimum wage. The list is long. Change can emerge from within a society and political system or be the result of external political influence. Whatever the origin of the change, with change comes unpredictability (Pellini 2007). Jane Jacobs (2000) in her book, *The Nature of Economies*, highlights this unpredictability, describing development as an open-ended process, a qualitative change that 'can't be usefully thought of as a line, or even a collection of open-ended lines. Development operates as a web of interdependent co-developments' (19).

Since the 1950s academicians, researchers, politicians, civil society leaders, bureaucrats, civil servants, philanthropists, experts, administrators and others have grappled with the unpredictability and complexity of change processes in development. The search for answers to development problems has resulted in a constant process of change in social and economic theories, as well as in the ways that devel-

A. Pellini (✉)
Overseas Development Institute, London, UK
e-mail: a.pellini@odi.org.uk

P. C. Karetji
Australia-Indonesia Partnership for Pro-Poor Policy: The Knowledge Sector Initiative,
Research Triangle Institute International, Jakarta, Indonesia
e-mail: pkaretji@ksi-indonesia.org

A. Soekadis
CARE Indonesia, Jakarta, Indonesia
e-mail: ade_soekadis@careind.or.id

© Springer Nature Singapore Pte Ltd. 2018
A. Pellini et al. (eds.), *Knowledge, Politics and Policymaking in Indonesia*,
https://doi.org/10.1007/978-981-13-0167-4_8

opment programmes are designed, funded and implemented. In the 1950s, economic modernisation theory suggested that higher rates of economic growth could be achieved through linear stages of development (Rostow 1960). In the 1960s the emphasis shifted to the need to provide education and health services and strengthen human capital (Schultz 1962; Singer 1964). In the mid-1960s, Albert Hirschman was one of the first intellectuals to reflect on the nature of development programmes, describing them as 'a long voyage of discovery on the most varied domains, from technology to politics' (1967, 35). The late 1970s and 1980s brought a renewed emphasis on neo-liberal economic theory and the emergence of structural adjustment programmes, under the so-called Washington Consensus (Arndt 1987; Adelman 2000; Addison 2005). During this decade Dennis Rondinelli challenged development orthodoxy, reflecting on how governments and development organisations around the world designed and implemented programmes and projects. He concluded that while the complexity and uncertainty of development activities were growing, the methods used to plan and manage development activities were not adapting to the growing complexity and uncertainty (Rondinelli 1989). The 1990s and 2000s brought a focus on *sustainable* development and the recognition that development has multiple social, cultural and political dimensions and that in essence 'development' means that individuals have the freedom to make life choices (Sen 1988, 1999). This led to the emergence of a *post-development era* discourse, which acknowledged that 'there is not a proven formula for growth that can be rolled out in country after country like some kind of development franchise' (Wheelan 2002, 207). Development involves searching for solutions to problems that local stakeholders and communities see as their own, without relying on blueprints from overseas or cultural and moral guidance from donor agencies (Parfitt 2002; Escobar 2011).

The point of this excursus into 50 years of development theory is to show that the evolution of development theories has shifted in parallel to that of ideas on how to operationalise and implement development interventions. The previous chapters of this book describe problems, solutions and opportunities in the Indonesian knowledge sector on evidence-informed policymaking from the viewpoint of a relatively large development initiative, such as the Australia–Indonesia Partnership for Pro-Poor Policy: The Knowledge Sector Initiative (KSI 2017). This chapter focuses on the Australia-Indonesia Partnership for Pro-Poor Policy: The Knowledge Sector Initiative (KSI) itself and reflects on the principles and mechanisms required to manage a large programme seeking solutions to problems in the Indonesian knowledge sector. In particular, the authors reflect on the applicability of emerging ideas that fall into the category of 'doing development differently' (DDD).

2 Doing Development Differently: One Way to Find Solutions to the Wicked Hard Problems of Development

Albert Hirschman, during the 1960s, and Dennis Rondinelli, in the 1980s, were rather isolated in their critique of how development programmes were being designed and implemented. More recently, however, their work has contributed to revamping the debate over whether development interventions work and, if not, what ought to change. This has led to the emergence of a discourse and literature known as 'doing development differently' (Andrews et al. 2012, 2017).[1] This literature draws on multiple analyses of development interventions in the area of governance and building state capacity and makes the case for a different approach and tools to development interventions that practitioners, civil servants and researchers can adopt to design, fund and implement development programmes seeking to address the so-called wicked hard problems.[2] These are problems that Andrews et al. (2015) define as being simultaneously 'logistically complex, politically contentious, without known solutions and containing numerous opportunities for professional discretion' (126).

Over the past two decades, Andrews et al. (2012) argue, the idea of transplanting solutions and models from modern economies has permeated too many − if not most − governance programmes, which has led many of them to fail to deliver on their stated objectives and outcomes: strengthening the capability of state systems. The Quality of Government Institute at Sweden's University of Gothenburg[3] assessed countries' improvements in capability and service provision from 1984 to 2008 and showed that of the 87 countries they track, 62 have achieved no progress in state capability (see Pritchett 2013). Even among the 25 that show improvement, the typical country may take over 200 years to reach the level of state capability of Portugal in 1985 (Ibid.).

Government interventions fail because they attempt to (1) introduce and reproduce expert solutions considered 'best practices', (2) develop predetermined linear processes, (3) impose strict monitoring and compliance systems, (4) evaluate progress too late in the process, and (5) assume that implementation and reaching goals largely happen by edict, with support at the top (Andrews et al. 2012). In other words, development interventions fail because they tend to focus on what institutions and organisations in the recipient countries should *look like* rather than on *what they actually do* and the problems they face (Pritchett 2013).

A number of communities of practice have emerged over the last few years to discuss and debate the insights and suggestions emerging from DDD thinking and analysis. Algoso and Hudson (2016) identified nine different communities of practice involving practitioners, policymakers, researchers and activists.[4] While these

---

[1] Other terms have emerged during the last few years, e.g. 'Thinking and Working Politically' and 'Problem-Driven Iterative Adaptation'. We cluster them under the doing development differently umbrella of ideas.

[2] See Grindle (2004), Briggs (2008), Ramalingam and Jones (2008), Rodrik (2008), Adler et al. (2009), Booth (2011), Pritchett et al. (2013), Ramalingam (2015), and Green (2016).

[3] See http://qog.pol.gu.se/.

[4] *Doing Development Differently* is a community of researchers and practitioners convened by the Overseas Development Institute and Harvard Kennedy School. Its manifesto calls for development to focus on locally defined problems, tackled through iteration, learning and adaptation (http://doingdevelopmentdifferently.com/).

Thinking and Working Politically is a semi-regular convening of representatives from various donor agencies, think tanks and international NGOs that discusses the use of politically aware approaches to aid and development work (https://twpcommunity.org/).

communities and initiatives may differ in the emphasis they assign to specific DDD elements or actors, what they have in common is their critique of pre-planned, linear, solution-based approaches to development.

Communities of practices are contributing to the growing body of evidence derived from programmes that are trying to apply and operationalise DDD principles. The key suggestions, drawn from a number of contributions (Fabella et al. 2011; Booth and Unsworth 2014[5]; DDD Manifesto 2014; Faustino and Booth 2014; Williamson 2015; Green 2016; Andrews et al. 2017), are summarised below:

- Focus on solving problems that are owned, debated and defined by local people and stakeholders.
- Engage a broad set of actors to ensure that reforms are viable, legitimate and relevant. In other words, identify and test interventions that are *technically sound* and, importantly, *politically feasible.*

Global Delivery Initiative (GDI) is a cross-donor collaboration led by the World Bank to deepen the know-how for effective operational delivery of aid and development (http://www.worldbank.org/reference/GDI/).

Global Partnership for Social Accountability (GPSA) was established by the World Bank in 2012 and funds and convenes civil society organisations and governments to discuss social accountability initiatives (http://www.thegpsa.org/).

Making All Voices Count (MAVC) is a 5-year programme that started in 2013, funded by multiple development partners (i.e. UK Department for International Development, USAID, Swedish International Development Agency and the Omidyar Network) to find, fund and learn from innovations that support accountable governance (http://www.makingallvoicescount.org/).

Transparency and Accountability Initiatives is a community of practice composed of transparency and accountability practitioners from many countries (http://www.transparency-initiative.org/workstream/impact-learning).

Analysis-Driven Agile Programming Techniques (ADAPT) is a collaboration between Mercy Corps and the International Rescue Committee to identify, develop and spread the use of adaptive management approaches in complex aid and development projects (https://www.rescue.org/adaptcasestudies).

Smart Rules is an internal initiative that started in 2014 at the UK Department for International Development, which acknowledges that complex interventions require a different approach to programme management that can adapt to and influence local contexts and support evidence-based decision-making   (https://www.gov.uk/government/publications/dfid-smart-rules-better-programme-delivery).

Collaborating, Learning and Adapting (CLA) is the USAID framework and internal change effort for incorporating collaboration, learning and adaptation at its missions and among implementing partners (https://usaidlearninglab.org/faq/collaborating-learning-and-adapting-cla).

[5] Booth and Unsworth (2014) looked at seven programmes implemented between 2000 and 2014 in different parts of the world to identify positive lessons for adopting an iterative and adaptive approach to programme implementation: the Western Odisha Rural Livelihoods Programme in India (WORLP); the Rural Livelihoods Programme; Land Titling in the Philippines and the Tax and Health Reform Programme in the Philippines by The Asia Foundation; the Disarmament, Demobilisation and Reintegration in DRC Peace Direct in North Kivu led by the Centre Résolution Conflits (CRC); the European Union Forest Law Enforcement, Governance and Trade (FLEGT) Action Plan; the Pyoe Pin programme in Myanmar; and the Enabling State Programme in Nepal.

- Work through local conveners who have the authority and credibility to mobilise all those with a stake in the process to tackle common problems and introduce relevant change.
- Develop a good knowledge of the political economy of the space in which a development programme operates to be able to design pilots and experiments, pursuing activities that look promising and dropping others.
- Programme teams have to be politically informed, with an in-depth understanding of what has happened previously in a particular sector, including the evolution of formal and informal relationships and linkages among actors.
- Development interventions that address 'wicked hard problems' need to be able to invest considerable time and resources into brokering relationships and discovering common interests around problems with local partners.
- Project management needs to avoid following linear paths and instead allow for considerable *muddling through* and experimentation around defined and agreed goals.
- Do not wait for statutory evaluations to learn. Blend design and implementation through rapid cycles of planning, action and reflection to discuss and share lessons and design new solutions.
- Development partners' staff need to continuously update their knowledge of the political economy dynamics of the country and/or sector in which they invest.
- Programme funders provide resources, ideas and suggestions but must also be willing to take a back seat, avoiding dominating the agenda (i.e. what to do) or the process (i.e. how to do it).
- Programme funders can support this adaptive process by not setting spending targets but rather allowing funding requirements to emerge.

The authors of this chapter agree and embrace these principles and suggestions; however, as individuals working in large development programmes that tackle some of the wicked hard problems of governance and state capability, they ask whether and how these principles can be applied when operating at scale. For example, the first phase of the KSI programme (2013–2017) managed a yearly budget of approximately AUD 12–14 million (c. US$9.1–10.6 million) and operated in the vast landscape that is the Indonesian knowledge sector. Can a programme of this size be adaptive, flexible and iterative as DDD proponents suggest?

3 The Challenges for Doing Development Differently at Scale

KSI is a joint programme between the governments of Indonesia and Australia that supports the Indonesian government to address its key development challenges through more effective public policies that make better use of research, analysis and evidence (KSI 2017). KSI operates at scale at two levels: (1) the landscape, or context, in which the programme operates – the Indonesian knowledge sector – discussed in previous chapters, and (2) the size of the programme in terms of budget, team and operations, which is the focus of this section. In particular, it explores four major challenges for a programme that is learning to apply DDD principles at scale: (1) a challenge to programme operations and administrative systems, (2) a challenge related to the capacity required within the programme team, (3) a challenge for monitoring and learning, and (4) a challenge of replication and learning to be a DDD programme. The authors' reflections are based on the experience of implementing the programme over the last 4 years and the results that emerged from the international workshop 'Doing Development Differently: A Workshop on Thinking and Working Politically and Problem-Driven Iterative Adaptation' co-organised by KSI, KOMPAK (Kolaborasi Masyarakat dan Pelayanan untuk Kesejahteraan) and the World Bank, held in Jakarta in March 2017.[6]

A programme such as KSI – which explicitly attempts an integrated approach to solving problems in the demand, use, production and intermediation and enabling environment for evidence-informed policymaking in a country – has never been tried before. The first phase of the programme, from May 2013 to June 2017, received a budget of AUD 60.5 million (c. US$45.8 million).[7] The programme team at the time consisted of 45 full-time staff and numerous consultants. The second phase of the programme began in July 2017 and will run through mid-2022, with a budget of up to AUD 60 million (c. US$45.4 million). The KSI programme reports and is accountable to Bappenas, which co-chairs the programme's technical secretariat and steering committee, along with the Australian Department of Foreign Affairs and Trade, which is the sole funder of the programme.[8]

During its first phase, the programme worked with a wide range of ministries and government agencies, including the Ministry of Research, Technology and Higher Education (Kementerian Riset, Teknologi dan Pendidikan Tinggi, KemRistekDikti); the Office of the President's Staff (Kantor Staf Presiden, KSP); the National Institute of Public Administration (Lembaga Administrasi Negara, LAN); the National Goods/Services Public Procurement Agency (Lembaga Kebijakan Pengadaan Barang Jasa Pemerintah, LKPP); the Ministry of Finance and the Ministry of State Administrative and Bureaucratic Reform (Kementerian Pendayagunaan Aparatur Negara dan Reformasi Birokrasi); the National Civil Service Agency (Badan

---

[6] See http://www.dddworkshop2017.org.

[7] The original value of the first phase of the program was AUD 100 million (c US$75.7 million). This was amended in 2015, following adjustments to Australia's aid program. The pilot programme to inform the design of KSI – implemented by The Asia Foundation – commenced in March 2010 and included core funding and technical, advocacy and organisational capacity-building support for eight Indonesian policy research organisations over a period of 18 months. The Australian Department of Foreign Affairs and Trade (then Australian Agency for International Development or AusAID) also commissioned a range of diagnostic studies on the state of Indonesia's knowledge sector. These are available at http://www.ksi-indonesia.org/en/news/detail/diagnostic-studies-on-the-knowledge-sector.

[8] Within Bappenas, the programme is managed under the Deputy Minister for Economic Affairs and within the Australian Agency for International Development by the Minister Counsellor for Governance and Human Development.

Kepegawaian Negara, BKN); the Ministry of Villages, Development of Disadvantaged Regions and Transmigration (Kementerian Desa, Daerah Tertinggal dan Transmigrasi); and the Coordinating Ministry for Human Development and Cultural Affairs (Kementerian Koordinator Bidang Pembangunan Manusia dan Kebudayaan). In addition to these government counterparts and partners, KSI engaged in partnerships with 16 prominent Indonesian policy research institutes and think tanks (see Chap. 2).[9]

Due to its experimental nature and the political nature of the wicked hard problems that affect Indonesia's knowledge sector, KSI was uniquely positioned to adopt a DDD approach. However, during the first phase of the programme, it became clear that a large-sized programme faces specific challenges to do so.

3.1 The Challenge for Programme Operations

Large-scale development programmes require a large operations system, that is, the processes and teams responsible for financial management, bookkeeping, procuring goods and services and managing grants to programme partners and overall administration (payrolls, office rental, etc.) In a large programme like KSI, there is a tension between being adaptive and flexible in terms of the design, planning and implementation of activities and the need to follow the administrative requirements spelled out in a standard operating procedure manual signed by both the government counterpart and the funder. Finding solutions to thorny problems, as suggested by the proponents of PDIA, involves analysis and identification of subproblems as well as planning and implementing a number of parallel activities (i.e. experiments, pilots, prototypes, etc.) to test some solutions, as depicted by the orange lines in Fig. 8.1. Activities that do not seem to work are then dropped, while those showing progress are continued.

This way of working poses a challenge related to administrative and financial procedures for programme operations, which usually follow a linear logic based on plans and budgets that describe predictable activities and outputs over a 12-month period. Moreover, these yearly plans and budgets are submitted for approval to a steering committee chaired by the government counterpart and the programme funder. Sign-off by the steering committee means that the programme is committed to deliver specific activities to government and non-government partners for the fol-

---

[9] The 16 policy research partners were AKATIGA, Article 33, CSIS, ELSAM, Institute for Research and Empowerment (IRE), Komite Pemantauan Pelaksanaan Otonomi Daerah (KPPOD), Pusat Kebijakan dan Manajemen Kesehatan Universitas Gadjah Mada (PKMK UGM), Pusat Penelitian HIV/AIDS Universitas Atma Jaya (PPH Atma Jaya), Pusat Pengkajian Islam dan Masyarakat Universitas Islam Negeri (PPIM UIN), Pusat Studi Hukum dan Kebijakan (PSHK), Pusat Studi Agama dan Demokrasi Universitas Paramadina (PUSAD Paramadina), Pusat Kajian Politik Universitas Indonesia (Puskapol UI), Sajogyo Institute (SAINS), Seknas FITRA, SMERU Research Institute and SurveyMETER. Short profiles of the 16 partners can be found at http://www.ksi-indonesia.org/files/1444374225$1$BTXGW$.pdf.

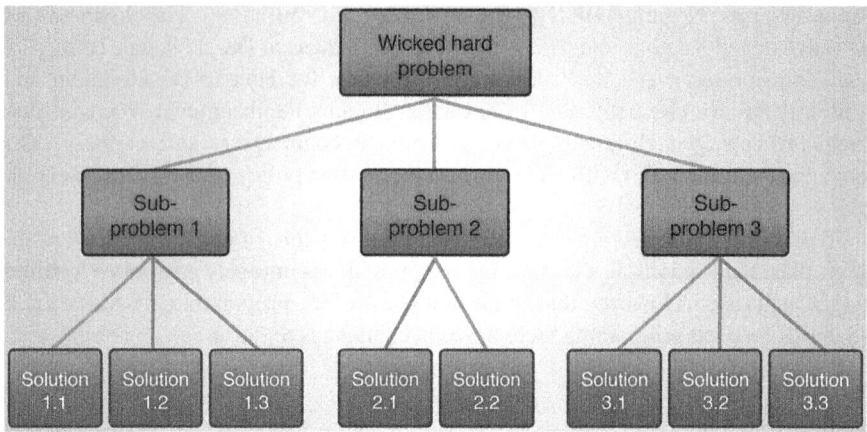

Fig. 8.1 From identifying problems to testing solutions (authors)

lowing 12 months. Because of the need to present a clear and coherent annual plan and budget to the steering committee, these do not usually include parallel pilot activities to solve a particular problem. Changing plans during the year is not simple, as it requires approval from the programme's technical secretariat and steering committee. This rigidity is compounded by the fact that a large programme such as KSI usually plans to utilise 100% of the annual budget allocated by the funder. As a result, the programme team is under considerable pressure over the course of the 12 months to spend the allocated budget, since it is usually not possible to shift unspent funds to the following financial year. An interesting dynamic of large-scale programmes is that the larger the budget, the greater the perceived risks of not being able to deliver on programme objectives and outcomes, and thus the more systems in place to control the use of funds and, simultaneously, the greater the pressure to spend down the budget.

Not all of the problems identified by the KSI programme and its partners are wicked hard or require doing development differently. Problems of capacity to carry out and communicate policy research can be solved with simple and straightforward training and mentoring support. However, the problems of capability in demand and use of evidence (see Chap. 5) or in the enabling environment (see Chap. 7) can benefit from the flexibility and adaptability suggested by the DDD approach. It is possible to do so if all the systems in a programme (planning, implementation and operations) support this way of working. If, on the other hand, the implementation and operations teams follow different principles and logic, the opportunity cost inherent in multiple, small-scale experiments running in parallel, with uncertain outcomes, becomes too high, and the only choice is to fall back to a set number of activities and pilots.

The KSI programme experienced these challenges and tried to find ways to enable a more flexible and adaptive approach to the implementation of programme activities. For example, funding for the 16 policy research organisations and think tanks that partner with KSI was not based on detailed annual activity plans, deliverables and budgets. The approach was to require the research partners to prepare overarching plans to address problems they wanted to solve in their organisations and to broadly define the cost categories for doing so. Some policy research partners decided to fund new research activities; others used the funding to create new roles in the organisation and hire new staff, while others sent staff to conferences and workshops to present research results. The advantage of this flexible grant-making arrangement was that changes in specific activities by the policy research partners did not require contract modifications but simply a communication and discussion with the KSI programme and operations teams, thus saving time and costs.

Pilots with government partners on the demand and use of evidence have not enjoyed the same flexibility and tend to be planned over a 12-month cycle. Due to regulations governing bilateral programmes, government partners cannot receive grants and funding in the same way as non-government partners. This means that the programme officers who design and develop the plans with government partners are also directly involved in the implementation of activities, making it difficult to manage and oversee a number of parallel pilots. This, in addition to pressure for spending the allocated budget, means that priority is placed on implementing and delivering outputs, rather than taking the time to assess whether or not solutions show sign of traction. Moreover, a pilot with a government partner cannot always be stopped quickly if the effort is not showing results, as this can imply a political cost for the programme.

Large-scale development programmes, which, like KSI, would benefit from adopting DDD, need to find ways to extend the flexible approaches and adaptive implementation to the ways in which operations teams function. This requires changes in the way plans and budget are developed and signed-off by the programme's governing bodies. Among possible solutions are:

- Plan activities for 6 months instead of 12 months.
- Enable a partial budget allocation in the annual plan, which would leave funding available for new pilots and emerging solutions the following year.
- Decentralise implementation decisions within the team, allowing the team leader and senior management team to spend more time on building relationships with key stakeholders rather than administrative tasks.
- Invest in strengthening the capacity and understanding of the whole team (programme and operations) in adaptive management and flexible budgeting, and revise standard operating procedures accordingly.
- Invest time and resources to continuously communicate with the funder and government partners about how flexible planning and budgeting can help reduce the opportunity costs of adjusting fixed plans.

Some interesting initiatives and emerging lessons can be cited in this area. For example, work by The Asia Foundation in the Philippines, in conjunction with the Coalition for Change programme (Faustino and Booth 2014), has shown that six simple management tools can be sufficient to manage the sharing of information and accountability reporting between the implementing team and the funder, which in this case was the Australian Agency for International Development.[10] The USAID Learning Lab[11] and Collaborating, Learning and Adapting Framework[12] are another example of a development partner taking concrete action to find ways to include more collaboration, learning and adaptation in the programmes it designs and funds, in order to ensure that programmes are grounded in a strong evidence base and remain relevant throughout implementation.

A number of programmes implemented by Oxfam showed that 'implementing evolutionary approaches, such as setting up multiple pilots, can improve the design of programmes in contexts where processes for achieving outcomes are not clear' (Schlingheider et al. 2017, 27).

However, much needs to be learned and tested to strengthen the capability of programme operations to support and adopt DDD principles when it would be effective and useful to do so. KSI is learning how to do that and can therefore continue to build on interesting lessons as it enters its second phase of implementation.

3.2   The Challenge of Skills on the Programme Team

Applying DDD principles requires a programme team with the experience and capacity to do so. From the point of view of senior management, it means either finding individuals with experience in adaptive management of programmes or investing the necessary financial resources and time to build the skills and knowledge of the existing team. Both options present some challenges. Since DDD principles are part of an emerging discourse, only a small number of programmes worldwide are currently experimenting with this approach. It is not yet a mainstream approach, thus it is not easy to find people with the requisite skills and understanding. The second option involves capacity building. The staffing of large-scale programmes occurs relatively quickly during the inception phase (i.e. the first 6 to 10 months). It has to happen quickly because from day one, a large programme is under pressure to use the available budget and needs to move quickly into planning and implementation of activities. This limits the resources and time available for training staff on DDD. Moreover, the funder may also expect that a programme that claims to adopt DDD is able to hire the staff needed to do so and may thus prohibit the use of the programme budget for staff training. But what are the skills needed?

---

[10] The six management tools described in Section 7 of the paper by Faustino and Booth (2014) are '1) a table to describe the political economy analysis of the interventions called technically sound, politically possible reform; 2) a theory of change; 3) a table to describe the link between project intervention and outcomes; 4) a timeline table to record significant events, key milestones or progress markers achieved and relevance, setbacks and other major changes; 5) a table to describe the team of development entrepreneurs; 6) a mapping of coalition attitudes toward reforms and influence' (29–30).

[11] See https://usaidlearninglab.org.

[12] See https://usaidlearninglab.org/faq/collaborating-learning-and-adapting-cla.

KSI has learned that a résumé showing 10–12 years of experience with donor-funded programmes is not sufficient for building a team able to apply DDD principles. It may even be the wrong skills and type of experience. Team members need to have strong facilitation and moderation skills. They also need to have analytical skills to understand a particular political and economic context. These skills are usually acquired only after years of engagement in policy advocacy and coalition building and limited to individuals with the leadership, confidence and creativity to undertake activities with uncertain outcomes. The challenge for large-scale development programmes is not just to find and hire these individuals but also how to give them the space required to maximise the skills and experience they bring to the team. This is a problem because, in reality, staff in large programmes tend to devote a considerable amount of time to administrative tasks (development of terms of references, budgets, monitoring of spending, hiring of consultants, accountability reporting, etc.). In addition, funders of large programmes often want to see smaller and leaner teams implementing highly political programmes, which in a sense goes against the principles of investing sufficient time in building a large network of relationships with partners. The latter approach not only allows better understanding of the underlying problems that partners want to solve but also leads to better understanding of how to choose and decide which solutions to test and which not to test.

3.3 The Challenge with Monitoring and Learning

Doing development differently requires programme teams to invest considerable time and effort in actively monitoring and learning from programmes. Feedback and reflections during meetings are critical to gaining better understanding of the problems, choosing possible solutions and deciding which pilots to stop and which to continue or expand. This cannot be done by a dedicated monitoring and learning team or unit in isolation but rather requires all team members to see learning (and the sharing of learning) as part of their job description.

Three sets of challenges exist in relation to monitoring and learning in large development programmes. First, due to the need to quickly establish a programme team during the inception phase and get on with planning activities and allocating budgets, monitoring and learning units tend to consist of experts with considerable experience in meeting donor accountability reporting requirements. But the job description of programme team members may not include learning responsibilities. Monitoring, evaluation and learning teams tend to be separated from the work of the programme teams and from day-to-day interaction with partners, and their leaders may not sit on the senior management team. As a result, monitoring, evaluation and learning teams develop their own plans for monitoring activities, which may exclude the programme team and external partners (Pellini and Shaxson 2017). The second challenge is related to one of the key early deliverables of the monitoring, evaluation and learning teams: the monitoring, evaluation and learning framework. This often triggers a milestone payment from the funder and demands a great deal of detail, resulting in complicated fretworks and systems (Ibid.).[13] A third challenge is that adaptive programmes – especially in the field of social change and policy innovation – may implement several pilots at the same time. This is challenging for the monitoring and learning team, especially if its work is not closely linked with that of the programme team. The rich compilation of very specific case studies and stories of change may also be seen by the funder and government counterparts as being too specific and not answering well the *so what?* question. At the same time, too much aggregation and synthesis carry the risk that the information becomes too generalised – and again not useful for funders and government counterparts (Ibid.)

Possible solutions to these challenges involve a commitment by senior programme management to invest resources in developing different learning capacities within teams and making sure that monitoring and learning are seen as a key part of the job description by every team member. To strengthen a learning culture, it is possible to create incentives for contributing to learning by rewarding writing and publications, creating space for open discussion about what works and what does not and generating evidence that being involved in monitoring and learning actually helps to improve day-to-day work with partners. The senior management of the programme has to put in place a strategy to ensure collaboration between the monitoring and learning and programme teams by creating space for reflection and sharing that has a clear purpose, such as informing programme staff about decisions, validating evidence of progress or involving the monitoring and learning team in the design of prototypes. All this requires a flexible environment that provides authentic delegation of authority and decision-making within teams.

Monitoring and learning systems have to be fit for purpose. There is no need to over-engineer them. It can be useful to apply the same principles suggested by the DDD approach: start small, test a few simple tools, and ask questions that help you learn. Work with the funder and government counterpart to agree on a DDD approach to monitoring and learning, and define the tools and processes that work for the programme, the funder and the counterpart. Finally, invest in team capacities and capabilities that really help to inform an adaptive approach.

3.4   The Challenge of Replication

Every development programme is under pressure to replicate and scale up successful approaches and solutions. But what does replication and scaling up means for a programme adopting DDD principles? Doesn't scaling up and replication go against the principles of finding and testing technically sound and politically feasible solutions to locally defined problems? A traditional interpretation of replication and scaling up by development partners works for problems that require the same

---

[13] A closely linked issue here is that an upfront plan with predetermined indicators is more in tune with a 'logframe' mindset than with a more adaptive 'theory of change'. The former makes adaptation more difficult, as it may result in less flexibility to design new pilots as opportunities emerge.

technical solutions over and over again, for example, building schools, health centres or roads in rural areas. It is, however, inadequate for solving wicked hard problems as defined in this chapter (Sect. 2). Owen Barder (2014) noted that for programmes addressing wicked hard problems, the idea of 'scaling up' is more elusive than it may appear. He refers to Lant Pritchett's work on problem-driven iterative adaptation, which notes that the aim should not be to build successful organisations but rather to create instances of success from which effective, locally owned organisations can emerge. The problem for funders and development programmes is that replicating such instances is not possible, because the nature of the problem is always specific to a particular context and circumstances. Instead of replication and scaling up, programmes that seek to adopt the DDD approach should replicate the use of the principles they try to embrace, learning to become DDD programmes by replicating and scaling up the art of 'muddling through' to find solutions to wicked hard problems – not the solution itself (Lindblom 1959).

4 Conclusions

The KSI programme is learning about doing development differently. The increasing understanding of the knowledge sector landscape acquired during the first phase of the programme is contributing to changes in approach to addressing the problems that programme partners want to solve in the knowledge sector. As the programme entered its second phase in July 2017, it is worth noting some key differences with phase one, which represent a sign of being more explicit about adopting some DDD principles:

1. During the first phase, KSI provided grants to 16 local policy research institutes and focused on building individual organisations' capacity. In the second phase, the programme will prioritise efforts to solve common problems affecting the research partners and mobilise their collective capacity to do so.
2. Much effort during in the first phase of the programme went into establishing relationships of trust with a broad range of stakeholders across national ministries, civil society and private sector. During the second phase, the team will try to leverage these relationships to address problems in the knowledge sector that matter to a wider range of actors.
3. The first phase of the programme focused on national-level problems related to the demand for and use of evidence in Indonesia's development planning process. During phase two, the programme will pilot and test some problem-driven interventions at the subnational level to start building a foundation for engagement with local government and other subnational knowledge sector actors.
4. During the first phase of the programme, the team was at times overwhelmed by the scale of the country's knowledge sector. The number of problems and actors made it difficult to decide where to start. During phase two the programme will continue to apply a problem-driven approach but will do so by seeking more

specific entry points – looking at Indonesia's policy cycle and the problems of accessing and using evidence during the agenda-setting stage, planning and budgeting through to implementation and monitoring and evaluation of public policies and programmes.

As KSI enters its second 5-year phase, it has become clear that the programme is doing more than addressing problems in the Indonesian *knowledge sector*; instead KSI is part of the evolution of Indonesia's *knowledge system*. This is an important distinction because it influences the way the programme plans, implements and monitors its activities and operations and makes a DDD approach even more relevant. Defining the knowledge sector as a *sector* can lead to a traditional approach to implementation that aims to find scalable solutions across the sector. It can lead to a technocratic approach focused more on technical solutions than on their political feasibility. To see the knowledge sector as a *system* means to accept that individuals, organisations and institutions do not operate in a vacuum. Each is in a process of evolution, shaped by an external environment that includes other institutions, which are themselves evolving.

It is not possible to solve problems that organisations face within a system if the authorising and enabling environments are not in place to do so (Adler et al. 2009). The programme team, government partners and funder need to agree on what that enabling environment is. It starts by accepting, as Jane Jacobs (2000) put it, that development and social change is an open-ended process that operates as a web of interdependent co-developments and not along linear paths. It continues by hiring the right skills, putting in place management and operational systems that decentralise decision-making and allowing continuous adaptation and learning from successes and failures. In the words of the ancient Chinese sage Lao-Tsu, it means to 'let reality be reality': accept complexity, embrace failure, treasure learning and experience. Acceptance does not mean resignation or fatalism. It means, to paraphrase Burkeman (2016), ceasing to pretend that policy change and social change aren't as complex, complicated, uncertain and political as they actually are.

References

Addison, T. (2005). *Development policy. An introduction for students* (Discussion Paper No. 9). Helsinki: World Institute for Development Economics Research.

Adelman, I. (2000). The role of government in economic development. In F. Tarp (Ed.), *Foreign aid and development. Lessons learnt and directions for the future* (pp. 48–79). London: Routledge.

Adler, D., Sage, C., & Woolcock, M. (2009). *Interim institutions and the development process: Opening spaces for reform in Cambodia and Indonesia* (Working Paper No. 86). Brooks World Poverty Institute, University of Manchester. https://doi.org/10.2139/ssrn.1421808. Accessed 12 Mar 2017.

Algoso, D. and Hudson, A. (2016). *Where have we got to on adaptive learning, thinking and working politically, doing development differently etc.? Getting beyond the People's Front of Judea.* From Poverty to Power Blog, http://oxfamblogs.org/fp2p/where-have-we-got-to-on-adaptive-learning-thinking-and-working-politically-doing-development-differently-etc-getting-beyond-the-peoples-front-of-judea/. Accessed 19 Mar 2017.

Andrews, M., Pritchett, L., Woolcock, M. (2012). *Escaping capability traps through problem-driven iterative adaptation (PDIA)* (Working Paper 299). Washington, DC: Center for Global Development. http://www.cgdev.org/content/publications/detail/1426292. Accessed 21 Mah 2017.

Andrews, M., Pritchett, L., & Woolcock, M. (2015). Building capability by delivering results: Putting Problem-Driven Iterative Adaptation (PDIA) principles into practice. In A. Whaites, E. Gonzales, S. Fyson, & G. Teskey (Eds.), *A governance practitioner's notebook: Alternative ideas and approaches* (pp. 123–133). Paris: OECD-DAC Network on Governance.

Andrews, M., Pritchett, L., & Woolcock, M. (2017). *Building state capability*. Oxford: Oxford University Press.

Arndt, H. W. (1987). Economic development. In *History of an idea*. Chicago: The University of Chicago Press.

Barder, O. (2014). *Evidence and scale*. Notes for remarks to the CIFF Board dinner, 16th May 2014. http://cf.owen.org/wp-content/uploads/2014-05-16-CIFF-Board-Dinner-Evidence-and-scale-as-delivered2.pdf. Accessed 18 Mar 2017.

Booth, D. & Unsworth, S. (2014). *Politically smart, locally led development* (Discussion Paper). London: Overseas Development Institute. https://www.odi.org/sites/odi.org.uk/files/odi-assets/publications-opinion-files/9158.pdf. Accessed 28 Mar 2017.

Booth, D. (2011). *Aid effectiveness: Bringing country ownership (and politics) back in* (Working Paper 336). London: Overseas Development Institute.

Briggs, X. (2008). *Democracy as problem-solving: Civic capacity in communities across the globe*. Cambridge, MA: MIT Press.

Burkeman, O. (2016, April 8 How to love your daily commute. *The Guardian*. https://www.the-guardian.com/lifeandstyle/2016/apr/08/how-to-love-your-daily-commute-oliver-burkeman. Accessed 25 Mar 2017.

Escobar, A. (2011). *Encountering development: The making and unmaking of the third world*. Princeton: Princeton University Press.

Fabella, R. V., Faustino, J., Mirandilla-Santos, M. G., Ciatiang, P., & Paras, R. (2011). *Built on dreams, grounded on reality: Economic policy reform in the Philippines*. Manila: The Asian Foundation.

Faustino, J. & Booth, D. (2014). *Development entrepreneurship: how donors and leaders can foster institutional change* (Working Politically in Practice Series – Case Study No. 2). London: Overseas Development Institute and San Francisco: The Asia Foundation.

Green, D. (2016). *How change happens*. Oxford: Oxford University Press.

Grindle, M. (2004). Good enough governance: Poverty reduction and reform in developing countries. *Governance: An International Journal of Policy, Administration and Institutions, 17*, 525–548.

Hirschman, A. O. (1967). *Development projects observed*. Washington, DC: Brookings Institution Press.

Jacobs, J. (2000). *The nature of economies*. New York: Random House.

KSI. [Australia-Indonesia Partnership for Pro-Poor Policy: The Knowledge Sector Initiative]. (2017). *About KSI*. http://www.ksi-indonesia.org/en/pages/knowledge-sector-initiative. Accessed 18 Mar 2017.

Lindblom, C. E. (1959). The science of muddling through. *Public Administration Review, 19*(2), 79–88.

Parfitt, T. W. (2002). *The end of development? Modernity, post-modernity and development*. London: Pluto Press.

Pellini, A. (2007). Decentralisation policy in Cambodia. *Exploring community participation in the education sector* (Acta Universitatis Tamperensis 1235). Tampere: University of Tampere.

Pellini, A. & Shaxson, L. (2017). *Doing development differently means doing monitoring, evaluation & learning differently too*. BetterEvaluation.org. https://goo.gl/4ocNgy. Accessed 10 May 2017.

Pritchett, L. (2013). *Folk and the formula. Fact and fiction in development.* Helsinki: World Institute for Development Economics Research.

Pritchett, L., Samji, S., Hammer, J. (2013). *It's all about MeE: Learning in development projects through monitoring ("M"), experiential learning ("e") and impact evaluation ("E")* (Working Paper 322). Washington, DC:. Center for Global Development. https://www.cgdev.org/publication/its-all-about-mee-using-structured-experiential-learning-e-crawl-design-space. Accessed 23 Mar 2017.

Ramalingam, B. (2015). *Aid on the edge of chaos. Rethinking international cooperation in a complex world.* Oxford: Oxford University Press.

Ramalingam, B., and Jones, H. (2008). *Exploring the science of complexity: Ideas and implications for development and humanitarian efforts* (Working Paper 285). London: Overseas Development Institute.

Rodrik, D. (2008). Second-best institutions. *American Economic Review: Papers and Proceedings, 98*(2), 100–104.

Rondinelli, D. A. (1989). *Development projects as policy experiments: An adaptive approach to development administration.* London: Routledge.

Rostow, W. W. (1960). *The stages of economic growth: A non-communist manifesto.* Cambridge: Cambridge University Press.

Schlingheider, A., Pellfolk, E., Maneo, G., Desai, H. (2017). *Managing to adapt. Analysing adaptive management for planning, monitoring, evaluation, and learning.* London: London School of Economics and Political Science.

Schultz, W. T. (1962). Investment in human capital. In E. S. Phelps (Ed.), *The goal of economic growth* (pp. 106–120). New York: W.W. Norton & Company Inc..

Sen, A. (1988). The concept of development. In H. Chenery & T. N. Srinivasan (Eds.), *Handbook of development economics* (Vol. I, pp. 9–26). Amsterdam: North Holland.

Sen, A. (1999). *Development as freedom.* Oxford: Oxford University Press.

Singer, H. W. (1964). Education and economic development. In H. W. Singer (Ed.), *International development: Growth and change.* New York: McGraw-Hill.

Wheelan, C. (2002). Naked economics. In *Undressing the dismal science.* New York: W.W. Norton & Company.

Williamson, T. (2015). *Change in challenging contexts* (How does it happen? Research report). London: Overseas Development Institute. https://www.odi.org/sites/odi.org.uk/files/odi-assets/publications-opinion-files/9829.pdf. Accessed 28 Mar 2017.

Chapter 9
Conclusion

Arnaldo Pellini, Budiati Prasetiamartati, Kharisma Priyo Nugroho, Elisabeth Jackson, and Fred Carden

1 Introduction

These are not easy times to argue, as do the authors of this book, for an evidence-informed approach to policymaking. Changes in politics, policymaking and the way citizens see and perceive the policymaking process seem to conspire against it.

One of the most prominent campaign claims made during the United Kingdom's Brexit referendum (23 June 2016) was that the United Kingdom is sending GBP 350 million (c. US$450 million)[1] a week to the European Union and that these funds should instead be spent on the British National Health Service. The claim relied on the maximum possible calculation of the costs of the United Kingdom's European Union membership, disregarding both the rebate that the country receives and direct

---

[1] 1 GBP = 1.26 US$. Google 8 July 2017

A. Pellini (✉)
Overseas Development Institute, London, UK
e-mail: a.pellini@odi.org.uk

B. Prasetiamartati · E. Jackson
Australia-Indonesia Partnership for Pro-Poor Policy: The Knowledge Sector Initiative, Jakarta, Indonesia
e-mail: budiati@ksi-indonesia.org; eljackson@ksi-indonesia.org

K. P. Nugroho
Indonesian Alliance for Policy Research (ARK Indonesia), Jakarta, Indonesia

Winrock International, Bangkok, Thailand

F. Carden
Using Evidence Inc., Ottawa, ON, Canada
e-mail: fred@usingevidence.com

© Springer Nature Singapore Pte Ltd. 2018
A. Pellini et al. (eds.), *Knowledge, Politics and Policymaking in Indonesia*,
https://doi.org/10.1007/978-981-13-0167-4_9

European Union spending in the United Kingdom.[2] This fact caught people's attention only after the results were presented (Rose 2017).

A second recent example is President Donald Trump's decision to make good on his campaign pledge to abandon the October 2016 Paris Agreement on climate change. So far of the 197 countries that signed the agreement, 150 countries have ratified it. President Trump's decision ignores a huge amount of scientific evidence about the human contributions to climate change and places the United States alongside Nicaragua and Syria as the only countries that are not part of this landmark accord.

Chapter 6 demonstrated that digital information technologies are providing unique opportunities to add new, timely and less costly analysis and evidence to the toolkits that policymakers can use to inform their decisions. At the same time, technology is also changing politics and the way elections are won or lost and by whom. *The Guardian* newspaper has been investigating how some data analytic companies, by collecting and analysing information on British and American voters from social network platforms and datasets, have managed to identify 'persuadable' voters on a massive scale and target them with individualised political messages and evidence (Cadwallader 2017).

Widespread accessibility to digital and social media is contributing to the rise of 'fake news', that is, 'wholly or mostly fabricated stories in the style of news reports usually posted online and often shared virally which cater separately to both those on the left and the right' (Rose 2017, 2). Politics seems to have contributed to this phenomenon, possibly because of the strong ideological split between political perspectives on right and left (Ibid.).

Twenty years have passed since Tony Blair was elected as Prime Minister of the United Kingdom. His emphasis was on generating and using more and better-quality evidence to modernise the government and improve the way policy decisions were made. Today a similar belief in the need to use evidence in policymaking appears to be lacking. For Rose (2017), we live in a time of bitter divisions between different groups of citizens and 'politicians are routinely placed at or towards the bottom of indices of trust' (Rose 2017, 1). Political philosopher Michael Sandel believes that this mistrust between citizens and politicians has its roots in the increasing marginalisation of large parts of society as a result of globalisation (Sandel 2017). Many believe the political system is broken and cannot be trusted. The policymaking process is perceived as technocratic and removed from people's lives and problems. Data, figures and analysis presented by the system cannot be trusted and are either 'fake' or manipulated.

---

[2]Bennet and Kirkup (2017) report that in 2015, the United Kingdom full membership fee to the European Union was GBP17.8 billion. This amount is reduced to GBP 12.9 billion by the instant rebate the United Kingdom receives and to ca. GBP 6 billion due to the amount spent by or through the European Union in the United Kingdom. This corresponds to ca. GBP 115 million per week.

These are not easy times for arguing in favour of evidence-informed policymaking. But is the situation so dire? Andrew Anthony (2017), in a recent interview with scientist Shaughnessy Naughton,[3] notes that scientific evidence can be used to justify a bad policy decision. However, it is important to question everything and remember that experts are needed to question facts, derive new facts and help to accept facts.

The underlying assumption of this book is that high-quality, timely evidence can help to make policy decisions that can solve the problems people face. No perfect evidence-informed policymaking system exists anywhere in the world. Due to the political nature of policymaking, an evidence-informed approach is something that can be achieved through incremental reforms and changes in the way evidence is produced, demanded and used. The editors of this book argue that a strong knowledge sector and the consistent and systematic use of evidence in policymaking contributes to the social, political and economic evolution and development of a country, equipping it to meet the challenges of the Fourth Industrial Revolution playing out in the twenty-first century (Schwab 2016).

Therefore, it is important to argue for an evidence-informed approach to policymaking. The alternative – opinion-based policymaking based on ideologically driven evidence – should be avoided. Good evidence matters for policy more than ever, and there is room for optimism. Brexit, fake news, and ideology versus climate change science are not, after all, global phenomena. They are alarming symptoms in some Western countries, but are not global trends.

Louise Ball (2017) has collected some examples from middle-income countries that are investing in processes and systems to demand and introduce more evidence into policymaking. In South Africa two initiatives are particularly significant. In 2012, the Department of Environmental Affairs published a plan to ensure that all its policies are based on robust evidence (Department of Environmental Affairs 2012). The Department for Planning, Monitoring and Evaluation, established in 2009 within the presidency, has a mandate to facilitate, influence and support effective planning, monitoring and evaluation of government programmes. It also engages in building a culture of evidence use through capacity development and training for senior ministry officials (Cassidy and Tsui 2017a). The Government of Colombia is another example of building a culture of demand and use of evidence within government. The Government Monitoring and Evaluation Unit (Sistema Nacional de Evaluación de Gestión y Resultados – SINERGIA)[4] has been instrumental in holding government to account for over two decades and is currently engaging in generating and using evidence to drive the National Development Plan to achieve the Sustainable Development Goals (Cassidy and Tsui 2017b). The Malaysian Government's Performance Management and Delivery Unit (Unit

---

[3] Shaughnessy Naughton is the founder of science activist group 314 Action, which seeks to promote science, technology, engineering and maths education and helps scientists become politicians. The name refers to the first three digits of the mathematical ratio pi, a scientific imprint that occurs everywhere in life (Anthony 2017).

[4] See https://sinergia.dnp.gov.co/Paginas/inicio.aspx.

Pengurusan Prestasi Dan Pelaksanaan - PEMANDU)[5] is the largest delivery unit in the world. Its mandate is to implement and monitor the National Transformation Programme, which consists of a set of high-level governmental priorities to transform the economy and society, in addition to making data publicly available and having a strong emphasis on public communications to increase government accountability to citizens (Cassidy and Tsui 2017c).

Indonesia, which is at the centre of this this volume, is among these countries (and governments) that are investing in their development processes by strengthening the capability the country's policymaking systems and testing ways to make better use of evidence to inform policy decisions and support and sustain the development of effective public policies (see Chap. 1). In this concluding chapter, the editors summarise the key findings and share some thoughts about what lies ahead for Indonesia's knowledge sector.

2   Summary of Findings

The intent of this book was to examine and describe the evolution of the Indonesian knowledge sector and the use of knowledge and evidence to inform policy decisions.[6] Among the questions that the authors wanted to investigate were: How well equipped is Indonesia to face the challenges posed by the Fourth Industrial Revolution? Is the country developing the intellectual capital required to transform knowledge into public policies that support and sustain equitable growth? Are universities and think tanks producing research and evidence that is relevant to the needs of policymakers or is post-truth politics on the rise? How do policymakers make use of evidence to inform policy decisions? In what ways are new information and communication technologies changing the way evidence informs policymaking in Indonesia? What rules and regulations are in place to support the production of policy research and its use in policymaking? (See Chap. 1.)

To raise these questions and provide responses, the authors drew on the analytical framework developed by Karetji (2010) who describes the Indonesia's evolution from a recent past of low accountability, top-down decision-making with very limited demand for evidence to inform policy to today's semi-decentralised governance environment. In the new environment, accountabilities are still towards the centre or local patrons, but the demand for evidence to inform public policy by the national and local governments is evolving and increasing. The future scenario is one of solid democratic rules, with accountability mainly to citizens and with government organisations that proactively invest in funding and procuring evidence to inform policy decisions. Each chapter applies this evolutionary analytical framework to a

---

[5] See https://www.pemandu.gov.my.

[6] The Indonesian knowledge sector was defined in Chap. 1 as 'the institutional landscape of government, private sector, and civil society organizations that provide research and analysis to support the development of public policy' (AusAID 2012).

specific aspect of Indonesia's knowledge sector: the role of universities; the role of policy research institutes in informing policymaking; the function of knowledge intermediaries within government organisations; how government organisations demand and utilise evidence; the changes that the data revolution and data analytics are bringing to evidence-informed policymaking; and the rules and regulations that can support and enable an evidence-informed approach to policymaking. Last but not least, the book offers reflections on designing and implementing a flexible and adaptive development programme in the knowledge sector 8.[7]

The concluding section of each chapter presents specific findings linked to the topic of the chapter; below the editors draw some high-level key findings.

2.1   Leadership at the Top Alone Is Not Sufficient for Developing a Culture That Values the Use of Evidence in Policymaking

Chapter 1 points out that the *idea* of a 'knowledge sector' is a construct. The Indonesian knowledge sector isn't a *sector* in a traditional sense like, for example, the education sector or the health sector. There isn't a single ministry in Indonesia that focuses on ensuring the development and strengthening of evidence use in policymaking. The knowledge sector cuts across all sectors, as policy decisions are made in all economic and social sectors.

The findings from Chap. 2 about stronger involvement of policy research institutes in policymaking, Chap. 3 on the establishment of the policy analyst role, Chap. 5 on the evolving demand for evidence from government organisations and Chap. 7 on significant reforms in the regulatory environment of the knowledge sector seem to confirm Karetji's analysis about the evolving demand and use of evidence in policymaking, as well as the implementation of reforms to help strengthen and sustain this trend.

These are positive signs, but they need to be balanced against the evidence that research organisations – such as universities, research and development units within government and policy research organisations – struggle to produce quality research when compared to similar organisations in other middle-income countries. The quality of research and evidence and the availability of evidence are aspects of the problem in the knowledge sector. Improving the quality of evidence and the communication of research findings needs to be complemented by a strong and consistent demand for evidence from policymaking and policy-implementing organisations. A clear role for knowledge intermediates within and outside of government is also required, along with a set of rules and regulations that create the incentives required

---

[7]As mentioned in Chap. 1, as editors and authors, we derived insights, experiences and evidences from the experience acquired through the implementation of the Australia-Indonesia Partnership for Pro-Poor Policy: The Knowledge Sector Initiative, a donor-funded programme which was launched in 2013 which aims to strengthen the demand and use of evidence in policymaking in Indonesia.

to continue the development of a culture of demand and use of evidence within the bureaucracy and throughout the policy cycle.

Given that the knowledge sector is cross-cutting, a strong culture of demand and use of evidence requires, across the bureaucracy, the recognition that high-quality and timely evidence matters for policymaking and that strengthening demand and use is ultimately as much about strengthening the quality of the processes through which evidence is sourced, appraised, interpreted and used as it is about the quality of the evidence itself (see Chap. 5).

Leadership is key to achieving this recognition and attitude. However, drawing in particular from the insights in Chap. 8, the authors stress that it is not realistic to expect this leadership to exist at the very top of the political systems (i.e. the presidency) and that it will somehow trickle down within the bureaucracy. This type of unrealistic assumption about the role of champions in public policy reforms, as mentioned by Andrews et al. (2012), is one of the reasons why so many governance and public policy development programmes and reforms have actually failed. Leadership, intent and commitment from the top are certainly necessary, but success in shaping a new culture of demand and use of evidence requires acceptance (and leadership) at different levels of the bureaucracy, by civil servants and others responsible for implementing the many changes required to translate a policymaking culture that *values* evidence into a policymaking system that *demands and uses* evidence to inform policy decisions. In other words, without acceptance by civil servants within the bureaucracy, leadership (even from the very top) alone cannot change behaviours and attitudes towards the use of evidence in policymaking.

2.2 A Strong Knowledge Sector Requires Strong Foundations

A strong culture that favours the use of evidence for policymaking is not only the result of strong leadership and acceptance throughout the bureaucracy but also of strong foundations in research capability, which in turn is linked to a strong education system. Human capital, which is the result of investment and reform in education and higher education, is the foundation upon which a sustainable, evidence-informed policymaking culture and system can be built.

The authors of Chap. 2 stressed that Indonesian academics, in terms of publication and international visibility, are struggling to compete with their colleagues in Southeast Asia and East Asia. Moreover, and more worryingly, according to the international comparison by the Organisation for Economic Co-operation and Development (OECD) Programme for International Student Assessment for 2015, Indonesia's 15-year-old students struggle to understand core school subjects such as science, reading and mathematics.[8] Indonesian schools, despite large budget alloca-

---

[8]The Programme for International Students Assessment results, comparing the education outcomes of high school students (15 years of age) in a number of countries, ranked Indonesia 62nd out of 72 economies assessed (See http://www.oecd.org/pisa/) (OECD 2016).

tions to primary and lower secondary education, cannot yet compete with those of other middle-income economies.

The point is that there is a link between the quality of education (and higher education) and the strength of a culture within the bureaucracy that demands and uses evidence. Strengthening the use of evidence in policymaking requires the identification of specific problems in the systems, tools, capability and attitudes within the knowledge sector. It also requires that solutions to these problems are not only technically sound but also politically feasible. At the same time, it is important to recognise that without also addressing problems in the education system and thus strengthening of human capital, the knowledge sector will always remain weak. This weakness will have an influence on all areas of the knowledge sector. A strong education system not only prepares future generations of researchers but also future generations of public servants and bureaucrats.

The need to address problems in the education sector is made even more urgent by the data revolution. The authors of Chap. 6 note that big data is profoundly changing the way we approach social science (Benoit and Cukier 2015) and the evolution of evidence-informed policymaking trends over the next 10–20 years. If over the next 10 years Indonesia's education system acquires the capability to produce the research and analytical capacity and skills required today, it will still be 10 years behind, particularly in the areas of data analytics and innovation. After all, as noted by Benoit and Cukier (Ibid.), 10 years from now, social science researchers will need to know and work with coding, or else their knowledge and skills may well be outdated.

2.3   The Knowledge Sector is an Evidence Ecosystem

Chapter 1 defines the Indonesian knowledge sector as a *sector* in which government, private sector and civil society organisations provide research and analysis to support the development of public policy (AusAID 2012). This definition is used explicitly and implicitly throughout all chapters. Only in Chap. 8, when discussing the principles of doing development differently applied to a large development programme, have the authors used the term *knowledge system*.

This is a subtle but significant difference. The term *sector*, particularly when applied to actors, systems and processes related to evidence-informed policymaking, is reminiscent of a linear approach to the design and implementation of policy reforms and programmes to tackling persistent problems. This approach has often resulted in technocratic interventions that are solution-driven and measured by inadequate behavioural indicators. Utilising the *sector* definition of Indonesia's knowledge sector carries the risk that the design of programmes and reforms by the Indonesian government and development partners will reflect traditional bureaucratic structures and accountabilities. Traditional sectors such as health and education have a ministry in charge of designing and implementing policies and managing the policy cycle for specific reforms. However, this is not the case for the knowledge sector which, as mentioned above and in Chap. 1, is horizontal in nature with no one ministry or department responsible. The complexity, the politics and the diversity of actors and types of evidence in the knowledge sector are more reminiscent of a *system* or, to borrow a term from big data, an *evidence ecosystem*.

Why is it important to see the knowledge sector as an *evidence ecosystem*?

First, to see the knowledge sector as an *evidence ecosystem* means to accept that the actors in the system are linked in a complex web of interlinked relationships whereby they not only want to produce and use evidence but also want to influence each other. This web cuts across policy areas and policy sectors. It is wider than any individual sector.

Second, it is because changes in capability within the *evidence ecosystem* are evolutionary, rather than linear and based on the principles of engineering, which are so common in development programmes (Green 2017). The evolution of a system, as noted by Jacobs (2000), involves a process that constantly produces increasing diversity and co-development relationships. As it evolves, it generates greater complexity. Importantly, the evolution of such a system is governed by uncertainty, rather than the certainty and linearity of results-based programmes.

Donella Meadows (2009) defines a system as 'an interconnected set of elements that is coherently organised in a way that achieves something' (11). In brief, a system consists of *elements*, *interconnections* and a *purpose*. The *elements* are the easiest parts to see, because they are visible and tangible. In the knowledge system, elements include, for example, universities, policy research institutes, policy analysis units, ministries, local governments, civil servants, researchers and data scientists. *Interconnections* are the relationships that hold these elements together. It is more difficult to understand these interconnections and why elements are linked as they are. Interconnections often reflect information flows. The government, for example, needs information about the economy, social problems, education and health to decide on policies and fund programmes. The *purpose* is the hardest part of a system to spot, as it may not be articulated orally or in writing. The purpose must be deduced from behaviour, rather than rhetoric or stated goals, for example, a commitment to use more research-based evidence in policymaking followed by the establishment of new funding mechanisms for think tanks and policy research organisations (see Chap. 7).

Changes in a system require mapping and understanding all three aspects of the system. Government interventions and development programmes often focus on changes to the *elements* (e.g. new research organisations, trained civil servants, etc.) – which usually have the least impact on the system but are easier to measure and report on. Some interventions venture further, looking at ways to change or influence *interconnections* in the system (e.g. forums between researchers and policymakers, coalitions among advocacy organisations and knowledge producers, etc.). This can have a positive impact on the system but may not last. Very few interventions venture so far as to try to influence or change the system's *purpose*, which is the level capable of instituting the most profound changes to the system.

Duncan Green (2016) posits that trying to change a system requires that the implementing team, government counterparts, programme partners and funders are comfortable with the fact that change is a slow and steady process that may not fit the set timeframe often imposed on development programmes. Time is required to learn about the system and identify the spaces where change is happening or the conditions for change are in place. Rushing quickly into planning and delivery of outputs is not productive. The ideas that emerge from this approach are like bets; they may or may not work.[9] Activities and plans need to be flexible and should be stopped if the conditions for change are no longer in place. System change demands being alert to changes in elements, interconnections or purposes by being an active member of several networks and coalitions. It also calls for acknowledgement that luck plays an important role in success and that, as Albert Hirschman once said, solutions may be found by accident. Practitioners should undertake multiple parallel experiments and be prepared to learn and discuss openly why pilots and experiments may have failed. They should explore and broker partnerships with local and international actors to learn about alternative solutions. Finally, they should be curious and look for positive deviances, that is, for individuals or organisations that have managed to solve similar problems.

All this, Green admits, poses an overwhelming challenge to traditional linear planning approaches and established ways of working in development and reform programmes, which prefer simple and neat narratives that in reality are only possible in hindsight (Gladwell 2010; Green 2016).

3 Final Thoughts

Klaus Schwab (2016) argues that the world has entered the early stages of the Fourth Industrial Revolution. To be part of this new industrial revolution and to benefit from it in terms of equitable economic growth, better services and technology that contribute to improve people's livelihood will require Indonesia to invest in and develop a strong knowledge system/evidence ecosystem. This investment has two dimensions. The first is to create the enabling environment in which knowledge producers, actors who demand and use evidence, and knowledge intermediaries have the resources and spaces for the generation and critical sharing of knowledge and evidence. The second is to continue to develop a culture and positive attitude towards the value of high-quality and timely evidence for informing policy decision and the overall strategic direction of the country. This requires investments in human capital through building strong capabilities and foundations through investments to strengthen the education system and universities.

As Indonesia enters the Fourth Industrial Revolution, the complexity and range of public policy issues faced by the country are increasing and require well-trained

---

[9] See the interview with Jaime Faustino of the Asia Foundation in the Philippines at https://youtu.be/TYBdeljpMz0 (ODI 2014).

policy professionals (Friedberg and Hildebrand 2017). Such professionals should be able to understand and navigate the politics of policymaking as well as knowing how different types of evidence can help inform policy decisions throughout the policy cycle. This new industrial revolution is accompanied by a data revolution, creating enormous opportunities for governments and policymakers to strengthen knowledge systems and better understand policy problems, progress, responses and solutions.

Introducing more and better evidence into policy decisions is one of the opportunities that can be nurtured as Indonesia seeks ways to maximise the benefits of the data revolution and the Fourth Industrial Revolution. To do so requires an optimistic and progressive view of the future. It requires what Adelman (2013), describing the influence that the Italian intellectual Eugenio Colorni had on Albert Hirschman, defines as the 'benefit of the doubt'. For Colorni, doubt was creative because it opened the door for alternative ways of seeing the world and freedom from ideological constraints, all of which could lead to new political strategies. Doubt also meant accepting the limits of individual knowledge, liberating actors from the belief that one must know everything before taking action.

Writing this book has helped the authors to better understand the elements and interconnections of the Indonesian knowledge system. It has also raised questions about how well we understand the purpose of the knowledge system and its subsystems. The process has provided some answers but also raised questions (i.e. doubt). This is not a failure but rather part of the discovery to which it is hoped that this book will contribute.

References

Adelman, J. (2013). *Worldly philosopher: The Odyssey of Albert O. Hirschman*. Princeton: Princeton University Press.

Andrews, M., Pritchett, L., & Woolcock, M. (2012). *Escaping capability traps through problem-driven iterative adaptation (PDIA)* (Working Paper 299). Washington, DC: Center for Global Development. http://www.cgdev.org/content/publications/detail/1426292. Accessed 21 Mar 2017.

Anthony, A. (2017, March 18). The climate change battle dividing Trump's America. *The Guardian*. https://www.theguardian.com/science/2017/mar/18/the-scientists-taking-the-fight-to-trump-climate-change-epa. Accessed 25 Apr 2017.

AusAID [Government of Australia. Australian Agency for International Development]. (2012). *Australia-Indonesia Partnership for Pro-Poor Policy: The Knowledge Sector Initiative: Design document*. Jakarta. http://dfat.gov.au/about-us/publications/Documents/indo-ks-design.pdf. Accessed 18 May 2014.

Ball, L. (2017). *Developing and emerging countries buck the 'post-truth' trend, ODI opinion*. London: Overseas Development Institute. https://www.odi.org/comment/10512-developing-and-emerging-countries-buck-post-truth-trend. Accessed 3 June 2017.

Bennet, A., & Kirkup, J. (2017, March 10). How much money does Britain currently pay the EU?. *The Telegraph*. http://www.telegraph.co.uk/news/0/how-much-do-we-spend-on-the-eu-and-what-else-could-it-pay-for/. Accessed 10 June 2017.

Benoit, K., & Cukier, K. (2015). *The challenge of big data for the social sciences*. Public Lecture, London School of Economics. http://goo.gl/Rmi56P. Accessed 12 Apr 2017.

Cadwallader, C. (2017, May 19). Did big data tips it for Brexit? *The Guardian Weekly* (pp. 26–30).

Cassidy, C., & Tsui, J. (2017a). *Global evidence policy unit in South Africa: The Department for Planning, Monitoring and Evaluation (DPME)*. Jakarta: Knowledge Sector Initiative. http://www.ksi-indonesia.org/en/news/detail/evidence-policy-unit-in-south-africa-the-department-for-planning-monitoring-and-evaluation-dpme-. Accessed 15. June 2017.

Cassidy, C., & Tsui, J. (2017b) *Global evidence policy units Colombia: SINERGIA*. Jakarta: Knowledge Sector Initiative. http://www.ksi-indonesia.org/en/news/detail/evidence-policy-unit-in-colombia-sinergia. Accessed 15 June 2017.

Cassidy, C., & Tsui, J. (2017c). *Global evidence policy units Malaysia: PEMANDU*. Jakarta: Knowledge Sector Initiative. http://www.ksi-indonesia.org/file_upload/Global-Evidence-Policy-Unit-in-Malaysia-PEMANDU-14Jun2017162907.pdf. Accessed 15 June 2017.

Department of Environmental Affairs. (2012). *Environment sector research, development and evidence framework: An approach to enhance science-policy interface and evidence-based policymaking*. Pretoria: Department of Environmental Affairs of the Republic of South Africa. https://www.environment.gov.za/sites/default/files/docs/environmental_research_framework.pdf Accessed 4 June 2017.

Friedberg, E., & Hilderbrand, M. E. (Eds.). (2017). *Observing policy-making in Indonesia*. Singapore: Springer.

Gladwell, M. (2010). *What the dog saw: And other adventures*. London: Penguin.

AusAID [Australian Agency for International Development]. (2012). *Australia-Indonesia Partnership for Pro-Poor Policy: The Knowledge Sector Initiative, Design document*. http://dfat.gov.au/about-us/publications/Documents/indo-ks-design.pdf. Accessed 11 Mar 2014.

Green, D. (2017). *How change happens*. Oxford: Oxford University Press.

Jacobs, J. (2000). *The nature of economies*. New York: Random House.

Karetji, P. C. (2010). *Overview of the Indonesian knowledge sector*. Jakarta: AusAID. Available at http://dfat.gov.au/about-us/publications/Documents/indo-ks8-overview.pdf. Accessed on 21 May 2017.

Meadows, D. H. (2009). *Thinking in systems. A primer*. London: Earthscan.

OECD [Organisation for Economic Co-operation and Development]. (2016). *PISA 2015 Results in Focus*. https://www.oecd.org/pisa/pisa-2015-results-in-focus.pdf. Accessed 5 June 2017.

ODI [Overseas Development Institute]. (2014). *Jaime Faustino on development entrepreneurship*. https://www.youtube.com/watch?v=TYBdeljpMz0. Accessed 10 June 2017.

Rose, J. (2017). Brexit trump, and post-truth politics. *Public Integrity: American Society for Public Administration, 19*, 555. https://doi.org/10.1080/10999922.2017.1285540.

Sandel, M. (2017). *In conversation with Michael Sandel: Capitalism, democracy, and the public good* (London School of Economics Public Lecture podcasts). London: London School of Economics and Political Sciences. http://www.lse.ac.uk/website-archive/newsAndMedia/videoAndAudio/channels/publicLecturesAndEvents/player.aspx?id=3770. Accessed 27 May 2017.

Schwab, K. (2016). *The fourth industrial revolution*. Geneva: World Economic Forum.

Printed by Printforce, the Netherlands